DATE DUE	

Chicago Public Library

Form 178 rev. 11-00

SICK!

*Diseases and
Disorders,
Injuries and
Infections*

SICK!

*Diseases and
Disorders,
Injuries and
Infections*

volume

3

I to **P**

**David Newton,
Donna Olendorf,
Christine Jeryan,
Karen Boyden,
Editors**

AN IMPRINT OF THE GALE GROUP

DETROIT · SAN FRANCISCO · LONDON
BOSTON · WOODBRIDGE, CT

Sick!
Diseases and Disorders, Injuries and Infections
David Newton, Donna Olendorf, Christine Jeryan, Karen Boyden, Editors

STAFF

Christine Slovey, *U•X•L Editor*
Carol DeKane Nagel, *U•X•L Managing Editor*
Meggin Condino, *Senior Analyst, New Product Development*
Thomas L. Romig, *U•X•L Publisher*

Shalice Shah-Caldwell, *Permissions Specialist (Pictures)*

Rita Wimberley, *Senior Buyer*
Evi Seoud, *Assistant Production Manager*
Dorothy Maki, *Manufacturing Manager*
Mary Beth Trimper, *Production Director*

Robert Duncan, *Imaging Specialist*
Michelle Di Mercurio, *Senior Art Director*

GGS Information Services, Inc., *Typesetting*
Michelle Cadoree, *Indexer*
Cover illustration by Kevin Ewing Illustrations.

Library of Congress Cataloging-in-Publication Data

Sick! diseases and disorders, injuries and infections/ David E. Newton...[et al.].
   p. cm.
Includes bibliographical references and indexes.
Summary: Presents articles describing the causes and symptoms, diagnosis, treatment (both traditional and alternative), prognosis, and prevention of various diseases, disorders, injuries, and infections.
   ISBN 0-7876-3922-2 (set)
   1. Diseases—Encyclopedias, Juvenile. [1. Health—Encyclopedias. 2.Diseases—Encyclopedias.] I.Newton, David E.
R130.5 .S53 1999
616'.003–dc21
                                                      99-044739

ISBN 0-7876-3922-2 (set)
ISBN 0-7876-3923-0 (vol. 1)
ISBN 0-7876-3924-9 (vol. 2)
ISBN 0-7876-3925-7 (vol. 3)
ISBN 0-7876-3926-5 (vol. 4)

Printed in United States of America
10 9 8 7 6 5 4 3

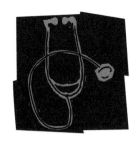

Contents

VOLUME 2: D–H

VOLUME 3: I–P

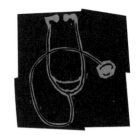

Reader's Guide

Sick! Diseases and Disorders, Injuries and Infections presents the latest information on 140 wide-ranging illnesses, disorders, and injuries. Included are entries on familiar medical problems readers might encounter in daily life, such as acne, asthma, chickenpox, cancer, and learning disorders. Some rare and fascinating illnesses are covered as well, such as smallpox, hantaviruses, and Creutzfeld Jakob disease (also known as mad cow disease).

Entries are arranged alphabetically across the four-volume set and generally range from three to eight pages in length. Each entry provides the details students need for reports and other health-related assignments under the following standard subheads: definition, description, causes, symptoms, diagnosis, treatment, prognosis, and prevention.

A "Words to Know" box included at the beginning of each entry provides definitions of words and terms used in that entry. Sidebars highlight interesting facts and individuals associated with the medical condition discussed. At the end of each entry, under the heading "For More Information," appears a list of sources for further information about the disease. The set has approximately 240 black-and-white photos. More than 80 images appear in color in an insert in each volume.

Each volume of *Sick!* begins with a comprehensive glossary collected from all the "Words to Know" boxes in the entries and a selection of research and activity ideas. Each volume ends with a general bibliography section listing comprehensive sources for studying medical conditions and a cumulative index providing access to all major terms and topics covered throughout *Sick!*

Related Reference Sources

Sick! is only one component of the three-part U•X•L Complete Health Resource. Other titles in this library include:

- *Body by Design:* This two-volume set presents the anatomy (structure) and physiology (function) of the human body in twelve chapters spread over two volumes. Each chapter is devoted to one of the eleven organ systems that make up the body. The last chapter focuses on the special senses, which allow humans to connect with the real world. Sidebar boxes present historical discoveries, recent medical advances, short biographies of scientists, and other interesting facts. More than 100 photos, many of them in color, illustrate the text.
- *Healthy Living:* This three-volume set examines fitness, nutrition, and other lifestyle issues across fifteen subject chapters. Topics covered include hygiene, mental health, preventive care, alternative medicine, and careers in health care. Sidebar boxes within entries provide information on related issues, while over 150 black-and-white illustrations help illuminate the text.

Acknowledgments

A note of appreciation is extended to U•X•L's Complete Health Resource advisors, who provided invaluable suggestions when this work was in its formative stages:

Carole Branson
Seminar Science Teacher
Wilson Middle School
San Diego, California

Bonnie L. Raasch
Media Specialist
Vernon Middle School
Marion, Iowa

Doris J. Ranke
Science Teacher
West Bloomfield High School
West Bloomfield, Michigan

Comments and Suggestions

We welcome your comments on *Sick! Diseases and Disorders, Injuries and Infections.* Please write: Editors, *Sick!,* U•X•L, 27500 Drake Rd., Farmington Hills, Michigan 48331–3535; call toll free: 1–800–877–4253; fax: 248–414–5043; or send e-mail via http://www.galegroup.com.

Please Read: Important Information

Sick! Diseases and Disorders, Injuries and Infections is a medical reference product designed to inform and educate readers about medical conditions. U•X•L believes this product to be comprehensive, but not necessarily definitive. While U•X•L has made substantial efforts to provide information that is accurate and up to date, U•X•L makes no representations or warranties of any kind, including without limitation, warranties of merchantability or fitness for a particular purpose, nor does it guarantee the accuracy, comprehensiveness, or timeliness of the information contained in this product.

Readers should be aware that the universe of medical knowledge is constantly growing and changing, and that differences of medical opinion exist among authorities. They are also advised to seek professional diagnosis and treatment for any medical condition, and to discuss information obtained from this book with their health care provider.

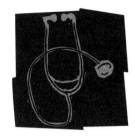

Words to Know

Diseases that are featured as main entries in *Sick!* are not covered in Words to Know.

A

Abortive: Describes an action that cuts something short or stops it.

Abscess: A pocket of infection within tissue.

Accommodation: The ability of the lens of the eye to change its shape in order to focus light waves from distant or near objects.

Acetylsalicylic acid: The chemical name for the primary compound from which aspirin is made. Shorthand terms for acetylsalicylic acid include acetylsalicylate, salicylic acid, and salicylate.

Acute: A disorder that comes on suddenly and usually does not last very long.

Acute retroviral syndrome: A group of symptoms resembling mononucleosis that are the first sign of HIV infection in 50 to 70 percent of all patients and in 45 to 90 percent of women.

Adenoid: A mass of lymph tissue located near the pharynx.

Adenoviruses: A group of viruses that usually cause infections of the lungs and ears.

African endemic Kaposi's sarcoma: A form of Kaposi's sarcoma that affects boys and men, has symptoms like those of classic Kaposi's sarcoma, and can spread rapidly and cause death.

Agoraphobia: A fear of open spaces.

AIDS dementia complex: A type of brain dysfunction caused by HIV infection that causes confusion, difficulty thinking, and loss of muscular coordination.

AIDS-related Kaposi's sarcoma: A form of Kaposi's sarcoma that occurs primarily in gay and bisexual men; it is much more dangerous than classic Kaposi's sarcoma.

Allergen: A substance that provokes an allergic response.

Allergic reaction: A series of events initiated by the immune system against substances that are normally harmless to the body.

Alveoli: Small air sacs at the ends of bronchioles through which oxygen passes from the lungs into blood.

Amalgam: A mixture of mercury, silver, and other metals used to make fillings for dental cavities.

Amenorrhea: Absence of menstrual periods.

Amnesia: Loss of memory sometimes caused by a brain injury, such as a concussion.

Amniocentesis: A medical procedure in which a sample of the fluid surrounding the fetus in a woman's womb is withdrawn and examined.

Amputation: A surgical procedure in which an arm, leg, hand, or foot is removed.

Anaphylaxis: An increased sensitivity to an allergen causing dilation (expansion) of blood vessels and tightening of muscles. Anaphylaxis can result in sharp drops in blood pressure, difficulty in breathing, and death if left untreated.

Androgen: A male sex hormone found in both males and females.

Anemia: A medical condition caused by a reduced number of red blood cells and characterized by general weakness, pale skin color, irregular heartbeat, shortness of breath, and fatigue.

Aneurysm: A weak spot in a blood vessel that may break open and lead to a stroke.

Angiography: A method for studying the structure of blood vessels by inserting a catheter into a vein or artery, injecting a dye in the blood vessel, and taking X-ray photographs of the structure.

Anti-androgen: A drug that slows down the production of androgens.

Antibiotic: A substance derived from bacteria or other organisms that fights the growth of other bacteria or organisms.

Antibody: Specific protein produced by the immune system to destroy specific invading organisms.

Anticoagulant: Describes a substance that prevents the blood from clotting.

Anticonvulsant medication: A drug used to prevent convulsions or seizures that is sometimes also effective in the treatment of bipolar disorder.

Antidepressant: A drug used to prevent or relieve depression.

Antigen: Any substance that stimulates the body to produce antibodies.

Antioxidant: A substance that prevents oxidation from taking place. Oxidation is a chemical reaction that can create heat, pain, and inflammation in the body.

Anxiety: Feeling troubled, uneasy, or worried.

Anxiety disorder: An experience of prolonged, excessive worry about the circumstances of one's life.

Aplastic: Having incomplete or faulty development.

Apnea: A temporary pause in one's breathing pattern. Sleep apnea consists of repeated episodes of temporary pauses in breathing during sleep.

Appendectomy: Surgical removal of the appendix.

Appendix: The worm-shaped pouch near the beginning of the large intestine.

Appetite suppressant: Drugs that decrease feelings of hunger and control appetite.

Aqueous humor: A watery fluid that fills the inside of the eyeball, providing nourishment to the eye and maintaining internal pressure in the eyeball.

Arteries: Blood vessels that carry blood from the heart to organs and tissues of the body.

Arteriosclerosis: Hardening of the arteries that can be caused by a variety of factors. Atherosclerosis is just one form of arteriosclerosis, but the two terms are often used interchangeably.

Artery: A blood vessel that carries blood from the heart to other parts of the body.

Arthrography: An imaging technique in which a dye is injected into a joint to make X-ray pictures of the inside of the joint easier to study.

Asperger syndrome: A type of autism that involves no problems with language.

Aspiration: Inhalation of food or saliva.

Astigmatism: A condition in which light from a single point fails to focus on a single point of the retina. The condition causes the patient to see a blurred image.

Ataxia: A condition in which balance and coordination are impaired.

Athetonia: A condition marked by slow, twisting, involuntary muscle movements.

Atopy: A condition in which people are more likely to develop allergic reactions, often because of the inflammation and airway narrowing typical of asthma.

Atrium: (plural: atria) One of the two upper chambers of the heart.

Audiometer: An instrument for testing a person's hearing.

Auditory nerve: A bunch of nerve fibers that carries sound from the inner ear to the brain.

Auditory canal: A tube that leads from the outside of the ear to the tympanic membrane.

Auricle: The external structure of the ear.

Autoimmunity: A condition in which the body's immune system produces antibodies in response to its own tissues or blood components instead of foreign particles or microorganisms.

Autonomic responses: Bodily responses that occur automatically, without the need for a person to think about it.

Autopsy: A medical examination of a dead body.

B

Bacillus Calmette-Guérin (BCG): A vaccine made from a weakened mycobacterium that infects cattle. It is used to protect humans against pulmonary tuberculosis and its complications.

Barium enema: A procedure in which a white liquid is injected into a patient's rectum in order to coat the lining of the colon so that X-ray photographs of the colon can be taken.

Becker muscular dystrophy (BMD): A type of muscular dystrophy that affects older boys and men and usually follows a milder course than Duchenne muscular dystrophy (DMD).

Benign: A growth that does not spread to other parts of the body, making recovery likely with treatment. Often used to describe noncancerous growths.

Binge: To consume large amounts of food without control in a short period of time.

Biofeedback: A technique in which a person learns to consciously control the body's response to a stimulus. Biofeedback enables a person to gain some control over involuntary body functions.

Biopsy: A procedure in which a small sample of tissue is removed and then studied under a microscope.

Blind spot: An area on the retina that is unable to respond to light rays.

Blood-brain barrier: A network of blood vessels between the neck and the brain that prevents many chemicals from passing into the brain.

Bone marrow: Soft, spongy material found in the center of bones from which blood cells are produced.

Bone marrow biopsy: A procedure by which a sample of bone marrow is removed and studied under a microscope.

Bone marrow transplantation: A process by which marrow is removed from the bones of a healthy donor and transferred to the bones of a person with some kind of blood disorder.

Bortadella pertussis: The bacterium that causes whooping cough.

Brain stem: A mass of nervous tissue that connects the forebrain and the cerebrum to the spinal cord.

Bronchi: Two large tubes that branch off the trachea and lead to the lungs; each tube is called a bronchus when referred to singularly. Also called bronchial tubes.

Bronchial tubes: Another name for bronchi. The major airways that lead to the lungs.

Bronchioles: Smaller extensions of the bronchi.

Bronchodilator: A substance that causes muscles in the respiratory system to relax, making breathing easier.

Bronchoscope: A device consisting of a long thin tube with a light and camera on the end for looking into a patient's airways and lungs.

BSA: Refers to "body surface area," a unit used in the treatment of burns to express the amount of the total body surface area covered by the burn.

C

C. botulinum: A very deadly bacteria that causes a disease known as botulism.

Calcium: An essential mineral with many important functions in the body, one of which is in the formation of bone.

Campylobacter jejuni (C. jejuni): A bacteria that is the leading cause of bacterial diarrhea in the United States. It occurs in healthy cattle, chickens, birds, and flies.

Carcinogen: Any substance capable of causing cancer.

Cardiovascular: A term that refers to the heart and blood system.

Carditis: Inflammation of the heart.

Caries: The medical term for tooth decay.

Carpal tunnel: A passageway in the wrist, created by bones and ligaments, through which the median nerve passes.

Carrier: A person whose body contains the organisms that cause a disease but who does not show symptoms of that disease.

Cartilage: Tough, elastic tissue that covers and protects the ends of bones.

Cataplexy: A sudden loss of muscular control that may cause a person to collapse.

Catatonic behavior: Behavior characterized by muscular tightness or rigidity and lack of response to the environment.

Catheter: A thin tube inserted into the patient's body, often into a vein or artery, to allow fluids to be sent into or taken out of the body.

Cavity: In dentistry, a hole or weak spot in tooth enamel caused by decay.

CD4: A type of protein molecule in human blood that is present on the surface of 65 percent of immune cells. The HIV virus infects cells that have CD4 surface proteins, and as a result, depletes the number of T cells, B cells, natural killer cells, and monocytes in the patient's blood. Most of the damage to an AIDS patient's immune system is done by the virus's destruction of CD4 lymphocytes.

Central nervous system: A system of nerve cells in the brain and the spinal cord.

Cephalosporin: A specific type of antibiotic used to treat many types of infections.

Cerebral thrombosis: Blockage of a blood vessel in the brain by a blood clot that formed in the brain itself.

Cerebral edema: Swelling of the brain caused by an accumulation of fluid.

Cerebral embolism: Blockage of a blood vessel in the brain by a blood clot that originally formed elsewhere in the body and then traveled to the brain.

Cerebrospinal fluid (CSF): Fluid made in chambers of the brain that flows over the surface of the brain and the spinal cord. CSF provides nutrients to cells of the nervous system and provides a cushion for the structures of the nervous system. It is often used to diagnose infections of the central nervous system (the brain and spinal cord).

Cerumen: Earwax.

Cervical traction: The process of using a mechanism to create a steady pull on the neck in order to keep it in the correct position while it heals.

CFTR: An abbreviation for cystic fibrosis transmembrane conductance regulator, a chemical that controls the amount of water in mucus.

Chelation therapy: Treatment with chemicals that bind to a poisonous metal and help the body quickly eliminate it.

Chemotherapy: A method of treating cancer using certain chemicals that can kill cancer cells.

Child abuse: Intentional harm done to infants and children, usually by parents or care givers.

Chlamydia: A family of microorganisms that causes several types of sexually transmitted diseases in humans.

Chloroquine: An antimalarial drug first used in the 1940s as a substitute for quinine, and still widely used in Africa because of its relatively low cost.

Cholesterol: A waxy substance produced by the body and used in a variety of ways.

Chorea: Involuntary movements that may cause the arms or legs to jerk about uncontrollably.

Chromosome: A structure located inside the nucleus (center) of a cell that carries genetic information.

Chronic: Recurring frequently or lasting a long time.

Cilia: Fine, hair-like projections that line the trachea and bronchi. Cilia wave back and forth, carrying mucus through the airways and clearing the airways of foreign materials.

Circadian rhythm: Any body pattern that follows a twenty-four-hour cycle, such as waking and sleeping.

Circumcision: The procedure in which the foreskin is removed from the penis.

Cirrhosis: A liver disorder caused by scarring of liver tissue.

Classic Kaposi's sarcoma: A form of Kaposi's sarcoma that usually affects older men of Mediterranean or eastern European background.

Clostridium tetani: The bacterium that causes tetanus.

Clonic phase: The stage of a grand mal seizure in which muscles alternately contract and relax.

Clotting factor: One of the chemicals necessary for blood clotting.

Cobb angle: A measure of the curvature of the spine, determined from measurements made on X-ray photographs.

Cognitive-behavioral therapy: A form of psychological counseling in which patients are helped to understand the nature of their disorder and reshape their environment to help them function better.

Colonoscopy: A procedure in which a long, thin tube is inserted through a patient's rectum into the colon to permit examination of the inner walls of the colon.

Colostomy: An opening created surgically that runs from the colon to the outside of the body to provide an alternative route for the evacuation of body wastes.

Comedo: A hard plug composed of sebum and dead skin cells that develops in the pores of the skin. The mildest form of acne.

Comedolytic: Drugs that break up comedos and open clogged pores.

Compulsion: A very strong urge to do or say something that usually cannot be resisted and is repeated again and again.

Computed tomography (CT) scan: A technique in which X-ray photographs of a particular part of the body are taken from different angles. The pictures are then fed into a computer that creates a single composite image of the internal (inside) part of the body. CT scans provide an important tool in the diagnosis of brain and spinal disorders, cancer, and other conditions.

Computerized axial tomography (CAT) scan: Another name for a computed tomography (CT) scan.

Condom: A thin sheath (covering) worn over the penis during sexual activity to prevent pregnancy and the spread of sexually transmitted diseases.

Conduct disorder: A behavioral and emotional disorder of childhood and adolescence. Children with a conduct disorder act inappropriately, infringe on the rights of others, and violate social rules.

Conductive hearing loss: Hearing loss that occurs in the external or middle ear.

Cone cells: Special cells in the retina responsible for color vision.

Congenital disorder: A medical condition that is present at birth.

Contact dermatitis: Inflammation of the skin caused by exposure to an allergen.

Contracture: A permanent shortening and tightening of a muscle or tendon causing a deformity.

Contrast hydrotherapy: A procedure in which a series of hot- and cold-water applications is applied to an injured area.

Contusion: A bruise.

Cornea: The transparent outer coating on the front of the eyeball.

Coronary: Referring to the heart.

Coronavirus: A type of virus that can cause the common cold.

Coxsackie virus: A virus that causes a disease known as herpangina.

Crabs: A slang term for pubic lice.

Crib death: Another name for sudden infant death syndrome.

Cryosurgery: The use of liquid nitrogen for the purpose of removing diseased tissue.

Cyanosis: A condition that develops when the body does not get enough oxygen, causing the skin to turn blue.

D

Debridement: The surgical removal of dead skin.

Decompression stops: Stops divers should make when returning to the surface to let the nitrogen in their blood dissolve safely out of their bodies. Charts developed by the U.S. Navy and other groups list the number of stops and the time to be spent at each stop.

Delusion: A fixed, false belief that is resistant to reason or factual disproof.

Dementia: Impaired intellectual function that interferes with normal social and work activities.

Densitometry: A technique for measuring the density of bone by taking photographs with low-energy X rays from a variety of angles around the bone.

Dentin: The middle layer of a tooth.

Dependence: A state in which a person requires a steady amount of a particular drug in order to avoid experiencing the symptoms of withdrawal.

Depot dosage: A form of medication that can be stored in the patient's body for several days or weeks.

Depression: A psychological condition with feelings of sadness, sleep disturbance, fatigue, and inability to concentrate.

Detoxification: The phase of treatment during which a patient gives up a substance and harmful chemicals are removed from his or her system.

Diaphragm: As a form of birth control, a thin rubber cap inserted into the vagina.

Diastolic blood pressure: Blood pressure exerted by the heart when it is resting between beats.

Digital rectal examination: A medical procedure in which a doctor inserts a lubricated gloved finger into the rectum to look for abnormal structures.

Dimercaprol (BAL): A chemical agent used in chelation therapy.

Diopter: The unit of measure used for the refractive (light bending) power of a lens.

Diplegia: Paralysis of the arm and leg on one side of the body.

Disease reservoir: A population of animals in which a virus lives without causing serious illness among the animals.

Distal muscular dystrophy (DD): A form of muscular dystrophy that usually begins in middle age or later, causing weakness in the muscles of the feet and hands.

Dominant gene: A form of a gene that predominates over a second form of the same gene.

Dopamine: A neurotransmitter that helps send signals that control movement.

DSM-IV: The *Diagnostic and Statistical Manual of Mental Disorders,* Fourth Edition, the standard reference book used for diagnosing and treating mental disorders.

Duchenne muscular dystrophy (DMD): The most severe form of muscular dystrophy, usually affecting young boys, beginning in the legs, and resulting in progressive muscle weakness.

Duodenum: The upper part of the small intestine, joined to the lower part of the stomach.

Dyslexia: Difficulty in reading, spelling, and/or writing words.

Dysthymic disorder: An ongoing, chronic depression that lasts two or more years.

Dystonia: Loss of the ability to control detailed muscle movement.

E

Echocardiogram: A test that uses sound waves to produce an image of the structure of the heart.

ECT: Electroconvulsive shock therapy, a method for using electric shocks to treat patients with mental disorders, such as bipolar disorder.

Edetate calcium disodium (EDTA calcium): A chemical agent used in chelation therapy.

Electrocardiogram: A test that measures the electrical activity of the heart to determine whether it is functioning normally.

Electroencephalogram (EEG): A test used to measure electrical activity of the brain to see if the brain is functioning normally.

Electrolytes: Salts and minerals present in the body that produce electrically charged particles (ions) in body fluids. Electrolytes control the fluid balance in the body and are important in muscle contraction, energy generation, and almost all major biochemical reactions in the body.

Electromagnetic radiation (ER): Radiation that travels as waves at the speed of light.

Electromyography: A test used to measure how well a nerve is functioning.

Enamel: The hard, outermost layer of a tooth.

Encephalopathy: A brain disorder characterized by loss of memory and other mental problems.

Endemic: The widespread occurrence of a disease over a given area that lasts for an extended period of time.

Endoscope: An instrument consisting of a long, narrow tube that can be inserted down a patient's throat to study the health of a patient's digestive system.

Enema: The injection of liquid into the intestine through the anus. This procedure is used either to induce a bowel movement or to coat the lining of the colon so that X-ray photographs can be taken of the colon.

Enzymes: Chemicals present in all cells that make possible the biological reactions needed to keep a cell alive.

Epidemic: An outbreak of a disease that spreads over a wide area in a relatively short period of time.

Epidermis: The outer layer of skin.

Epithelium: The layer of cells covering the body's outer and inner surfaces.

Epstein-Barr virus (EBV): A virus that causes mononucleosis and other diseases.

***Escherichia coli* (*E. coli*):** A bacteria that commonly causes food poisoning, most often from food products derived from cows, especially ground beef.

Estrogen: A female hormone with many functions in the body, one of which is to keep bones strong.

Eustachian tube: A passageway that connects the middle ear with the back of the throat.

Evoked potential test (EPT): A test that measures the brain's electrical response to certain kinds of stimulation, such as light in the eyes, sound in the ears, or touch on the skin.

Extrapulmonary: Outside of the lungs.

F

Facioscapulohumeral muscular dystrophy (FSH): A form of muscular dystrophy that begins in late childhood to early adulthood; affects both men and women; and causes weakness in the muscles of the face, shoulders, and upper arms.

Fecal occult blood test: A laboratory test designed to find blood in feces.

Fibrin: A thick material formed over an injured section of a blood vessel by the process of blood clotting.

Fibromyalgia: Pain, tenderness, and stiffness in muscles.

Fistula: An abnormal tubelike passage in tissue.

Flashback: A sudden memory of an event that occurred months or years earlier.

Fluoride: A chemical compound that is effective in preventing tooth decay.

Fragile X syndrome: A genetic condition involving the X chromosome that results in mental, physical, and sensory problems.

Frequency: The rate at which a wave vibrates in space.

Frostbite: A medical condition in which some part of the body has become frozen.

Fungus: A large group of organisms that includes mold, mildew, rust fungi, yeast, and mushrooms, some of which may cause disease in humans and other animals.

G

Ganglioside: A fatty substance found in brain and nerve cells.

Gangrene: Death and decay of body tissue.

Gastrointestinal system: The digestive system, consisting of the stomach and intestines.

Gel electrophoresis: A laboratory test that separates different types of molecules from each other.

Gene: A chemical unit found in all cells that carries information telling cells what functions they are to perform.

General autoimmune disorder: An autoimmune disorder that involves a number of tissues throughout the body.

Genetic disorder: A medical problem caused by one or more defective genes.

Genital: Having to do with the organs of the reproductive system.

Gingiva: The outer layer of the gums.

Ginkgo: An herb obtained from the ginkgo tree, thought by some alternative practitioners to be helpful in treating patients with Alzheimer's disease.

Glucose: A type of sugar present in the blood and in cells that is used by cells to make energy.

Gonorrhea: A sexually transmitted disease caused by the *Gonococcus* bacterium that affects the mucous membranes, particularly in the urinary tract and genital area. It can make urination painful and cause puslike discharges through the urinary tract.

Grand mal: An alternate term used for tonic-clonic epilepsy.

Granules: Small packets of reactive chemicals stored within cells.

Gray (Gy): A unit used to measure damage done to tissue by ionizing radiation.

H

Hairy leukoplakia of the tongue: A white area of diseased tissue on the tongue that may be flat or slightly raised. It is caused by the Epstein-Barr virus and is an important diagnostic sign of AIDS.

Hallucination: A perception of objects (or sounds) that have no reality. Seeing or hearing something that does not actually exist.

Helicobacter pylori: A bacterium that lives in mucous membranes and is responsible for the development of ulcers.

Hemiplegia: Paralysis of one side of the body.

Hemodialysis: A mechanical method for cleansing blood outside the body.

Hemoglobin: A molecule found in blood that gives blood its red color. Hemoglobin is responsible for transporting oxygen through the blood stream.

Hemorrhage: Heavy or uncontrollable bleeding.

Herpes virus: A group of viruses that cause many different infections in the human body, including cold sores and infections of the genital area.

Histamine: A chemical released by mast cells that activates pain receptors and causes cells to leak fluids.

Hormone replacement therapy (HRT): A method of treating osteoporosis by giving supplementary doses of estrogen and/or other female hormones.

Hormone therapy: Treatment of cancer by slowing down the production of certain hormones.

Hormones: Chemicals that occur naturally in the body and control certain body functions.

Human immunodeficiency virus (HIV): A transmissible virus that causes AIDS in humans. Two forms of HIV are now recognized: HIV-1, which causes most cases of AIDS in Europe, North and South America, and most parts of Africa; and HIV-2, which is chiefly found in West African patients. HIV-2, discovered in 1986, appears to be less virulent than HIV-1 and may also have a longer latency period.

Human papilloma virus (HPV): A family of viruses that cause hand, foot, flat, and genital warts.

Hydrocephalus: An abnormal accumulation of cerebrospinal fluid (CSF) in the brain.

Hyperbaric chamber: A sealed compartment used to treat decompression sickness, in which air pressure is first increased and then gradually decreased.

Hyperopia: Farsightedness. A condition in which vision is better for distant objects than for near ones.

Hypersomnia: The need to sleep excessively; a symptom of dysthymic and major depressive disorder.

Hyperthermia: The general name for any form of heat disorder.

Hyperventilation: Deep, heavy breathing.

Hypotonia: A condition in which muscles lack strength.

I

Iatrogenic: Caused by a medical procedure.

Iatrogenic Kaposi's sarcoma: A form of Kaposi's sarcoma that develops in people who have had organ transplants and are taking immunosuppressant drugs.

Ideal weight: Weight corresponding to the appropriate, healthy rate for individuals of a specific height, gender, and age.

Idiopathic epilepsy: A form of epilepsy for which no cause is known.

Immune system: A system of organs, tissues, cells, and chemicals that work together to fight off foreign invaders, such as bacteria and viruses.

Immunization: The process of injecting a material into a person's body that protects that person from catching a particular infectious disease.

Immunodeficient: A condition in which the body's immune response is damaged, weakened, or is not functioning properly.

Immunotherapy: Treatment of cancer by stimulating the body's immune system.

Incubation period: The time it takes for symptoms of a disease to appear after a person has been infected.

Infestation: A situation in which large numbers of organisms come together in a single area.

Inflammation: The body's response to tissue damage that includes heat, swelling, redness, and pain.

Inflammatory bowel disease: A group of disorders that affect the gastrointestinal (digestive) system.

Insomnia: Difficulty in falling asleep or in remaining asleep.

Insulin: A hormone (type of protein) produced by the pancreas that makes it possible for cells to use glucose in the production of energy.

Intestinal perforation: A hole in the lining of the intestine that allows partially digested foods to leak into the abdominal cavity.

Intracerebral hemorrhage: Bleeding that occurs within the brain.

Intraocular pressure (IOP): The pressure exerted by aqueous humor (clear liquid) inside the eyeball.

Ionizing radiation (IR): Any form of radiation that can break apart atoms and molecules and cause damage to materials.

J

Jaundice: A yellowing of the skin, often caused by a disorder of the liver.

Jet lag: A temporary disruption of the body's sleep/wake rhythm caused by high-speed air travel through different time zones.

Joint: A structure that holds two or more bones together.

K

Karyotype: The specific chromosomal makeup of a particular organism.

Ketoacidosis: A condition that results from the build-up of toxic chemicals known as ketones in the blood.

Koplik's spots: Tiny white spots on a reddish bump found inside of the mouth that are a characteristic marker for measles.

L

Lactobacillus acidophilus: A bacterium found in yogurt that changes the balance of bacteria in the intestine in a beneficial way.

Laparoscopy: A procedure in which a tube with a small light and viewing device is inserted through a small incision near the navel, allowing a surgeon to look directly into the patient's abdomen.

Laparotomy: A surgical procedure that allows a surgeon to view the inside of the abdominal cavity.

Larva: An immature form of an organism.

Larynx: The part of the airway between the pharynx and trachea, often called the voice box.

Laser: A device for producing very intense beams of light of a single color. Used in surgery to cut and/or dissolve tissues.

Latency: A period during which a disease-causing organism is inactive but not dead.

Lens: In the eye, a transparent, elastic, curved structure that helps focus light on the retina.

Lesion: Any change in the structure or appearance of a part of the body as the result of an injury or infection.

Ligament: Tough, fiber-like tissue that holds bones together at joints.

Limb-girdle muscular dystrophy (LGMD): A form of muscular dystrophy that begins in late childhood to early adulthood, affects both men and women, and causes weakness in the muscles around the hips and shoulders.

Lumbar puncture: A procedure in which a thin needle is inserted into the space between vertebrae in the spine and a sample of cerebrospinal fluid is withdrawn for study under a microscope.

Lumpectomy: A procedure in which a cancerous lump is removed from the breast.

Lymph nodes: Small round or oval bodies within the immune system. Lymph nodes provide materials that fight disease and help remove bacteria and other foreign material from the body.

Lymphocyte: A type of white blood cell that is important in the formation of antibodies and that can be measured to monitor the health of AIDS patients.

Lymphoma: A cancerous tumor in the lymphatic system that is associated with a poor prognosis in AIDS patients.

M

Macrophage: A large white blood cell, found primarily in the bloodstream and connective tissue, that helps the body fight off infections by ingesting the disease-causing organism. HIV can infect and kill macrophages.

Magnetic resonance imaging (MRI): A procedure that uses electromagnets and radio waves to produce images of a patient's internal tissue and organs. These images are not blocked by bones, and can be useful in diagnosing brain and spinal disorders and other diseases.

Malignant: Describes a tumor that can spread to other parts of the body and that poses a serious threat to a person's life.

Malnutrition: A condition in which a person is not eating enough of the right kinds of foods.

Mammogram: An X-ray photograph of the breast.

Mandible: The scientific term for the lower jaw.

Mania: A mental condition in which a person feels unusually excited, irritated, or happy.

Mantoux test: Another name for the purified protein derivative (PPD) test, which is used to determine whether a person has been infected with the tuberculosis bacterium.

Mast cells: A type of immune system cell that is found in the lining of the nasal passages and eyelids. It displays a type of antibody called immunoglobulin type E (IgE) on its cell surface and participates in the allergic response by releasing histamine from intracellular granules.

Mastectomy: Surgical removal of a breast.

Meconium ileus: A condition that appears in newborn babies with cystic fibrosis, in which the baby's first bowel movement is abnormally dark, thick, and sticky.

Median nerve: A nerve that runs through the wrist and into the hand, providing feeling and movement to the hand, thumb, and fingers.

Melanocyte: A specialized skin cell that produces melanin, a dark pigment (color) found in skin.

Melatonin: A hormone thought to control the body's natural sleep rhythms.

Meninges: The three-layer membranous covering of the brain and spinal cord.

Menopause: The end of menstruation.

Menstruation: The discharge of menses (a bloody fluid) from the uterus of women who are not pregnant that occurs approximately every four weeks from puberty to menopause.

Metabolism: A series of chemical reactions by which cells convert glucose to energy.

Metastasis: The process by which cancer cells travel from one area of the body to another.

Methadone: A chemical given to heroin addicts to help them overcome their addiction.

Miliary tuberculosis: A form of tuberculosis in which the bacillus spreads throughout the body producing many thousands of tubercular lesions.

Miscarriage: When a human fetus is expelled from the mother before it can survive outside of the womb.

MMR vaccine: A vaccine that contains separate vaccines against three diseases: measles, mumps, and rubella.

Monocyte: A large white blood cell that is formed in the bone marrow and spleen. About 4 percent of the white blood cells in normal adults are monocytes.

Mosaic: Medically, a condition in which an individual cell may contain more than one type of chromosomal composition, with forty-six chromosomes in one cell, for example, and forty-seven chromosomes in another cell, which causes relatively mild symptoms of Down's syndrome.

Motor function: A body function controlled by muscles.

Motor neuron: A nerve cell that controls a muscle.

Mucolytic: Any type of medication that breaks up mucus and makes it flow more easily.

Mucus: A mixture of water, salts, sugars, and proteins, which has the job of cleansing, lubricating, and protecting passageways in the body.

Myalgia: Muscle pain.

Myalgic encephalomyelitis: An inflammation of the brain and spinal cord.

Myelin: A layer of tissue that surrounds nerves and acts as an insulator.

Myelograph: A test in which a dye is injected into the spinal column to allow examination of the spine with X rays or a computed tomography (CT) scan.

Myocardial infarction: The technical term for heart attack.

Myopia: Nearsightedness. A condition in which far away objects appear fuzzy because light from a distance doesn't focus properly on the retina.

Myotonic dystrophy: A form of muscular dystrophy that affects both men and women and causes generalized weakness in the face, feet, and hands.

N

Narcolepsy: A sleep disorder characterized by sudden sleep attacks during the day and often accompanied by other symptoms, such as cataplexy, temporary paralysis, and hallucinations.

Narcotic: A drug that relieves pain and induces sleep.

Natural killer cells: Cells in the immune system that help fight off infections.

Necrosis: Abnormal death of body tissues.

Nervous tic: An involuntary action, continually repeated, such as the twitching of a muscle or repeated blinking.

Neural tube: A structure that forms very early in the life of a fetus and eventually develops into the central nervous system of the body.

Neurasthenia: Nervous exhaustion.

Neurofibrillary tangle: Twisted masses of peptides (fragments of protein fibers) that develop inside brain cells of people with Alzheimer's disease.

Neuron: A nerve cell.

Neurotransmitter: A chemical found in the brain that carries electrical signals from one nerve cell to another nerve cell.

Nitrogen: A tasteless, odorless gas that makes up four-fifths of Earth's atmosphere.

Nits: The eggs produced by head or pubic lice.

Nonsteroidal anti-inflammatory drugs (NSAIDs): A group of drugs, including aspirin, ibuprofen, and acetaminophen, used to treat pain and fever.

Nucleoside analogues: A medication that interferes when HIV tries reproduce by making copies of itself inside cells.

O

Obsession: A troubling thought that occurs again and again and causes severe distress in a person.

Oculopharyngeal muscular dystrophy (OPMD): A form of muscular dystrophy that affects adults of both sexes and causes weakness in the muscles of the eyes and throat.

Opiate blockers: Drugs that interfere with the action of natural opiates, substances that cause sleepiness and numbness.

Opportunistic infection: An infection by organisms that usually don't cause infection in people whose immune systems are working normally.

Optic nerve: A nerve at the back of the eyeball that carries messages from the retina to the brain.

Organ specific disorder: An autoimmune disorder in which only one type of organ is affected.

Ossicles: Tiny bones located within the middle ear responsible for transmitting sound vibrations from the outer ear to the inner ear.

Osteoarthritis: A type of arthritis that weakens the joint cartilage. It is most common among the elderly.

Otosclerosis: A disorder in which the bones of the middle ear become joined to each other.

P

Pancreas: A gland located behind the stomach that produces insulin.

Paralysis: The inability to move one's muscles.

Paranoia: Excessive or irrational suspicion or distrust of others.

Penicillin: A specific type of antibiotic used to treat many types of infections.

Peptic ulcer: A general name referring to ulcers in any part of the digestive system.

Pericardium: The membrane surrounding the heart.

Peristalsis: Periodic waves of muscular contractions that move food through the digestive system.

Peritonitis: Inflammation of the membranes that line the abdominal wall.

Persistent generalized lymphadenopathy (PGL): A condition in which HIV continues to produce chronic painless swellings in the lymph nodes during the latency period.

Petit mal: An alternative term for absence epilepsy.

Pharynx: The part of the throat that lies between the mouth and the larynx, or voice box. It connects the nose and mouth with the upper part of the digestive system.

Phenylketonuria (PKU): A genetic disorder in which a person's body is unable to break down the amino acid phenylalanine, causing damage to the brain.

Physiological dependence: A condition in which a person's body requires the intake of some substance, without which it will become ill.

Plaque: Generally refers to a build-up of some substance. The fatty material and other substances that form on the lining of blood vessels are called plaque. Patches of scar tissue that form in areas where myelin tissue has been destroyed are also called plaque. Dental plaque is a thin, sticky film composed of sugars, food, and bacteria that cover teeth.

Platelet: A type of blood cell involved in the clotting of blood.

Pleural: Having to do with the membrane that surrounds the lungs.

Polyps: Small, abnormal masses of tissue that can form on the lining of an organ.

Polysomnograph: An instrument used to measure a patient's body processes during sleep.

Positron emission tomography (PET): A diagnostic technique that uses radioactive materials to study the structure and function of organs and tissues within the body.

Primary progressive: A form of multiple sclerosis in which the disease continually becomes worse.

Prion: A form of protein that can cause an infectious disease.

Process addiction: A condition in which a person is dependent on some type of behavior, such as gambling, shopping, or sexual activity.

Prodrome: A period of time during which certain symptoms signal the beginning of a disease.

Prophylactic: Referring to a treatment that prevents the symptoms of a condition from developing.

Protease inhibitors: The second major category of drug used to treat AIDS. They work by suppressing the replication of the HIV virus.

Protein: A type of chemical compound with many essential functions in the body, one of which is to build bones.

Psychological dependence: A condition in which a person requires the intake of some substance in order to maintain mental stability.

Psychosis: Extremely disordered thinking accompanied by a poor sense of reality.

Psychosocial therapy: Any means by which a trained professional holds interviews with a patient and tries to help that patient better understand himself or herself and the reasons for his or her thoughts and actions.

Psychotic disorder: A mental disorder characterized by delusions, hallucinations, and other symptoms indicating a loss of contact with the real world.

Pulmonary: Relating to the lungs.

Pulmonary function test: A test that measures the amount of air a patient can breath in and out.

Pulmonary hypertension: High blood pressure in the arteries and veins associated with the lungs.

Pulp: The soft, innermost layer of a tooth.

Purge: To rid the body of food by vomiting, the use of laxatives, or some other method.

Purified protein derivative (PPD): A substance injected beneath the skin to see whether a person presently has or has ever had the tubercle bacillus.

Q

Quadriplegia: Paralysis of both arms and both legs.

Quinine: One of the first successful treatments for malaria, derived from the bark of the cinchona tree.

R

Rad: A unit once used to measure the amount of damage done to tissue by ionizing radiation, now replaced by the gray.

Radial keratotomy (RK): A surgical procedure in which the shape of the cornea is changed in order to correct myopia.

Radiation: Energy transmitted in the form of electromagnetic waves or subatomic particles.

Radiation therapy: Treatment that uses high-energy radiation, like X rays, to treat cancer.

Radical mastectomy: Surgical removal of an entire breast along with the chest muscles around the breast and all the lymph nodes under the arm.

Radioactive isotope: A substance that gives off some form of radiation.

Radiotherapy: Treatment of a disease using some form of radiation, such as X rays.

Radon: A radioactive gas that occurs naturally and is often found in the lower levels of buildings.

Rash: A spotted pink or red skin condition that may be accompanied by itching.

Recessive gene: A form of a gene that does not operate in the presence of a dominant form of the same gene.

Reconstructive surgery: A medical procedure in which an artificial breast is created to replace the breast removed during a mastectomy.

Rectum: The lower part of the digestive system from which solid wastes are excreted.

Red blood cells: Blood cells that carry oxygen from the lungs to the rest of the body.

Reduction: The restoration of a body part to its original position after it has been displaced, such as during a fracture.

Refraction: The bending of light waves as they pass through a dense substance, such as water, glass, or plastic.

Relapse: A reoccurrence of a disease.

Relapsing-remitting: A form of multiple sclerosis in which symptoms appear for at least twenty-four hours and then disappear for a period of time.

Rem: An older unit used to measure the amount of damage done to tissue by ionizing radiation, now replaced by the sievert.

Renal: Relating to the kidneys.

Resorption: The process by which the elements of bone are removed from bone and returned to the body.

Respiratory system: The nose, tonsils, larynx, pharynx, lungs, and other structures used in the process of breathing.

Restless leg syndrome: A condition in which a patient experiences aching or other unpleasant sensations in the calves of the legs.

Retina: A thin membrane at the back of the eyeball that receives light rays that pass through the eyeball and transmits them to the optic nerve.

Rhabdovirus: The virus that causes rabies.

Rhinovirus: A type of virus that can cause the common cold.

RICE: The term stands for the program of rest, ice, compression, and elevation that is recommended for treating tendinitis.

Rickets: A condition caused by the deficiency of certain minerals, including vitamin D and calcium, causing abnormal bone growth.

S

Salmonella: A bacteria that commonly causes food poisoning, most often from poultry, eggs, meat, and milk.

Scald: A burn caused by a hot liquid or steam.

Scoliometer: A tool for measuring the amount of curvature in a person's spine.

Screening: Using a test or group of tests to look for some specific medical disorder.

Sebum: An oily material produced by sebaceous glands that keeps the skin moist.

Secondary progressive: A form of multiple sclerosis in which a period of relapses and remissions is followed by another period in which the disease becomes progressively worse without improvement.

Secondhand smoke: Smoke that someone inhales after it is exhaled by another person.

Sedative: A substance that calms a person. Sedatives can also cause a person to feel drowsy.

Seizure: A convulsion; a series of involuntary muscular movements that alternate between contraction and relaxation.

Selective serotonin reuptake inhibitors (SSRIs): A class of drugs used to reduce depression.

Semen: A white fluid produced by the male reproductive system that carries sperm.

Seminal vesicles: The organs that produce semen.

Senile plaque: Deposits that collect inside the brain cells of people with Alzheimer's disease.

Sensory hearing loss: Hearing loss that occurs in the inner ear, auditory nerve, or brain.

Serotonin: An important neurotransmitter in the brain.

Shigella: A bacterium that grows well in contaminated food and water, in crowded living conditions, and in areas with poor sanitation. It is transmitted by direct contact with an infected person or with food that has been contaminated by an infected person.

Shingles: A disease that causes a rash and a very painful nerve inflammation. An attack of chickenpox eventually gives rise to shingles in about 20 percent of the population.

Shock: A life-threatening condition that results from low blood volume due to loss of blood or other fluids.

Sickle cell: A red blood cell with an abnormal shape due to the presence of an abnormal form of hemoglobin.

Sievert (Sv): A unit used to measure the amount of damage done to tissue by ionizing radiation.

Sigmoidoscopy: A medical procedure in which a doctor looks at the rectum and lower colon through a flexible lighted instrument called a sigmoidoscope.

Silicosis: A disease of the lungs caused by inhaling fine particles of sand.

Skin graft: A surgical procedure in which dead skin is removed and replaced by healthy skin, usually taken from elsewhere on the patient's own body.

Sleep disorder: Any condition that interferes with sleep. The American Sleep Disorders Association has identified eighty-four different sleep disorders.

Somnambulism: Also called sleepwalking, it refers to a range of activities a patient performs while sleeping, from walking to carrying on a conversation.

Spasm: A contraction of the muscles that can cause paralysis and/or shaking.

Spastic: A condition in which muscles are rigid, posture may be abnormal, and control of muscles may be impaired.

Sphygmomanometer: An instrument used to measure blood pressure.

Spinal cord: A long rope-like piece of nervous tissue that runs from the brain down the back.

Spinal transection: A complete break in the spinal column.

Spirometer: An instrument that shows how much air a patient is able to exhale and hold in his or her lungs as a test to see how serious a person's asthma is and how well he or she is responding to treatment.

Spondylosis: Arthritis of the spine.

Sputum: Secretions produced inside an infected lung. When the sputum is coughed up it can be studied to determine what kinds of infection are present in the lung.

Staphylococcus aureas: A bacteria that causes food poisoning, commonly found on foods that are kept at room temperature.

Staphylococcus: A class of bacteria found on human skin and mucous membranes that can cause a variety of infectious diseases.

Streptococcus: A class of bacteria that causes a wide variety of infections.

Stem cells: Immature blood cells formed in bone marrow.

Steroids: A category of naturally occurring chemicals that are very effective in reducing inflammation and swelling.

Stimulant: A substance that makes a person feel more energetic or awake. A stimulant may increase organ activity in the body.

Stress test: An electrocardiogram taken while a patient is exercising vigorously, such as riding a stationary bicycle.

Subarachnoid hemorrhage (SAH): Loss of blood into the subarachnoid space, the fluid-filled area that surrounds brain tissue.

Subdural hematoma: An accumulation of blood in the outer part of the brain.

Substance addiction: A condition in which a person is dependent on some chemical substance, such as cocaine or heroin.

Substantia nigra: A region of the brain that controls movement.

Succimer (Chemet): A chemical agent used to remove excess lead from the body.

Symptomatic epilepsy: A form of epilepsy for which some specific cause is known.

Synovial fluid: A fluid produced by the synovial membranes in a joint that lubricates the movement of the bones in the joint.

Synovial membrane: A membrane that covers the articular capsule in a joint and produces synovial fluid.

Syphilis: A sexually transmitted disease that can cause sores and eventually lead to brain disease, paralysis, and death.

Systemic treatment: A form of treatment that affects the whole body.

Systolic blood pressure: Blood pressure exerted by the heart when it contracts (beats).

T

T-cells: Lymphocytes that originate in the thymus gland. T-cells regulate the immune system's response to infections, including HIV.

Tartar: Plaque that has become hardened and attached to the tooth surface.

Temporal bones: The bones that form the right and left sides of the skull.

Tendon: A tough, rope-like tissue that connects muscle to bone.

Tennis elbow: A form of tendinitis that occurs among tennis players and other people who engage in the same movement of the elbow over and over again.

Testosterone: A male sex hormone.

Thermal burns: Burns caused by hot objects or by fire.

Thoracentesis: A procedure for removing fluids from the pleural space by inserting a long, thin needle between the ribs.

Throat culture: A sample of tissue taken from a person's throat for analysis. The culture is often taken by swiping a cotton swab across the back of the throat.

Thrombolytic: Capable of dissolving a blood clot.

Thrombosis: The formation of a blood clot.

Thyroid: An organ that controls a number of important bodily functions.

Tic: A muscular contraction or vocal sound over which a patient has very little control.

Tinea capitis: Scalp ringworm; a fungal infection of the scalp.

Tinea corporis: Scientific name for body ringworm, a fungal infection of the skin that can affect any part of the body except the scalp, feet, and facial area.

Tinea cruris: An fungal infection that affects the groin and can spread to the buttocks, inner thighs, and external genitalia; also called "jock itch."

Tinea unguium: Ringworm of the nails; a fungal infection that usually begins at the tip of a toenail.

Tissue plasminogen activator (tPA): A substance that dissolves blood clots in the brain.

Tolerance: The ability of a body to endure a certain amount of a substance that had previously been too much for it to tolerate.

Tonic phase: The stage of a grand mal seizure in which muscles become rigid and fixed.

Tonometer: A device used to measure intraocular pressure in the eyeball.

Tonsillectomy: A surgical procedure to remove the tonsils.

Tonsils: Oval-shaped masses of lymph gland tissue located on both sides of the back of the throat.

Toxic dilation of the colon: An expansion of the colon that may be caused by inflammation due to ulcerative colitis.

Toxin: A poison.

Trachea: The windpipe, extending from the larynx (the voice box) to the lungs.

Traction: The process of placing an arm or leg bone, or group of muscles under tension by applying weights to them in order to keep them in alignment while they heal.

Tranquilizers: Drugs that help a person to calm down.

Transcutaneous electrical nerve stimulation: A procedure in which mild electrical currents are used to stimulate nerves in order to prevent the transmission of pain messages in the body.

Translocation: A condition in which a piece of one chromosome breaks off and becomes attached to another chromosome.

Tretinoin: A drug that increases the rate at which skin cells are formed and die.

Triglyceride: A type of fat.

Trimester: Three months. Often used to refer to one third of a woman's pregnancy.

Trisomy: A condition in which three identical chromosomes, rather than two, are matched with each other.

Tumor: A mass or lump of tissue made of abnormal cells.

Twelve-step program: A plan for overcoming an addiction by going through twelve stages of personal development.

Tympanic membrane: A thin piece of tissue between the external ear and the middle ear.

U

Ulcer: An open wound in the skin or mucous membrane that is usually sore and painful.

Ultrasound test: A medical procedure in which a sound wave is transmitted into a pregnant woman's womb. The reflections produced from the sound wave can be studied for the presence of abnormalities in a fetus.

Ultraviolet (UV) light: A naturally occurring part of ordinary sunlight that may, under some circumstances, have beneficial effects in curing certain medical disorders.

Urethra: The tube through which the bladder empties to the exterior of the body.

V

Vaccine: A substance that causes the body's immune system to build up resistance to a particular disease.

Varicella-zoster immune globulin (VZIG): A substance that can reduce the severity of chickenpox symptoms.

Varicella-zoster virus: The virus that causes chickenpox and shingles.

Variola: The virus that causes smallpox. The only two small samples of variola that remain on Earth are being stored in two separate research laboratories.

Varivax: A vaccine for the prevention of chickenpox.

Vasodilator: Any drug that causes a blood vessel to relax.

Vector: An animal that transmits an infectious agent, such as a virus, from one animal to another animal.

Vector-borne disease: A disease transferred from one organism to another by means of a third organism, such as an insect or tick.

Ventricle: One of the two lower chambers of the heart.

Vertebrae: Bones that make up the spinal column.

Virus: A very small organism that can live only within a cell and that can cause some form of disease.

Volume reduction surgery: A surgical procedure in which damaged portions of a patient's lung are removed to make it easier for the patient to use healthy parts of the lung to get the oxygen needed for ordinary functioning.

Voluntary muscle: A muscle under a person's conscious control.

W

Wasting Syndrome: A progressive loss of weight and muscle tissue caused by AIDS.

White blood cells: Blood cells that fight invading organisms, such as bacteria and viruses.

Withdrawal: The process by which a person adjusts to the absence of some substance or activity to which he or she has become addicted.

X

X rays: A kind of high-energy radiation that can be used to take pictures of the inside of the body, to diagnose cancer, or to kill cancer cells.

Research and Activity Ideas

The following research and activity ideas are intended to offer suggestions for complementing science and health curricula, to trigger additional ideas for enhancing learning, and to suggest cross-disciplinary projects for library and classroom use.

Disease graph: Different environments create different opportunities for diseases to spread. Obtain current data for your city or county on occurrences of a disease such as rabies or lyme disease or a condition such as asthma. Create a graph that compares the number of outbreaks in urban areas with the number in rural areas. If there are differences, brainstorm some of the environmental factors that may be causing such differences.

Public service announcement: Choose a disease or disorder and write a public service announcement that would appear on television to inform people about the condition. Your ad should include information about symptoms, warn of risk factors, mention current treatments, and dispel any myths that are associated with the disease. Record the public service announcement using a video camera or present it in class.

Geographic study: Different parts of the world often face unique challenges in controlling diseases. Choose two different countries with different cultures and environments. Find out what the top five health concerns are in each country. For each one, determine the major risk factors. Discuss what aspects of the culture or the environment may be increasing the incidences of these diseases in each country.

Disease transmission: With a group of five to eight people choose one daily activity that you will act out. This could be going to the grocery store, going through the lunch line at school, playing a game, or going out to dinner. Assign each person a role in the activity. Choose one player who will be infected with a contagious disease, such as influenza. Coat that person's hands with flour. Act out the scene as realistically as possible. At the end of the scene, note how many other players have flour on themselves and how many places the ill person left his or her germs.

Diabetic diet: Research the dietary requirements of a person with diabetes. Keep a food diary for two days, recording everything you eat. Examine how your eating habits would have to change if you had diabetes. What foods couldn't you have eaten? What might you have to eat more of?

AIDS risk factors: What are some of the myths about the transmission of AIDS? Choose five activities sometimes incorrectly thought to be risk factors for contracting AIDS. For each myth give the scientific reasons that the activity does not put one at risk of contracting AIDS.

The following Web sites offer many more research and activity ideas as well as interactive activities for students:

The American Museum of Natural History: Infection, Detection, Protection. http://www.amnh.org/explore/infection/smp_index.html

Cool Science for Curious Kids. http://www.hhmi.org/coolscience/

The Gateway to Educational Materials. http://thegateway.org/index1/SubjectIndex.html#health

Newton's Apple®. http://ericir.syr.edu/Projects/Newton/index.html

The University of Arizona. The Biology Project: An Online Interactive Resource for Learning Biology. http://www.biology.arizona.edu/

WNET School. http://www.wnet.rog/wnetschool

SICK!

*Diseases and
Disorders,
Injuries and
Infections*

INFECTIOUS MONONUCLEOSIS

DEFINITION

Infectious mononucleosis (pronounced MON-o-NOO-klee-O-siss) is a contagious (catching) illness caused by the Epstein-Barr virus (EBV). The virus most commonly infects the liver, lymph nodes, and mouth. Mononucleosis is usually not a serious disease. However, its major symptoms—fatigue and lack of energy—can linger for several months. Infectious mononucleosis is also known as "mono" or "the kissing disease."

INFECTIOUS MONONUCLEOSIS IS ALSO KNOWN AS "MONO" OR "THE KISSING DISEASE."

DESCRIPTION

Anyone can have infectious mononucleosis. However, the disease is most common in young adults between the ages of fifteen and thirty-five. It is especially common among teenagers. The rate of mononucleosis among college students has been estimated at 15 percent. The disease is often not recognized when it occurs in young children.

In people who are otherwise healthy, mononucleosis usually lasts about four to six weeks. In people with weakened immune systems, the disease may last much longer. AIDS patients (see AIDS entry) and people who have had

WORDS TO KNOW

Herpes viruses: A group of viruses that cause cold sores, chickenpox, shingles, and other diseases.

Reye's syndrome: A very serious, rare disease, most common in children, believed to be caused by aspirin.

organ transplants often have weakened immune systems. In such cases, serious complications may develop after a bout of mononucleosis.

CAUSES

The EBV that causes mononucleosis is related to the herpes viruses (see herpes infections entry). The herpes viruses are responsible for infectious diseases such as cold sores, chickenpox (see chickenpox entry), and shingles. Most people are exposed to EBV at some point in their lives. The virus is spread through contact with saliva from an infected person. It can be transferred by coughing, sneezing, kissing, or sharing of drinking glasses or eating utensils.

SYMPTOMS

The most prominent symptoms of mononucleosis are weakness and fatigue. Some other common symptoms include:

- Sore throat and/or swollen tonsils
- Fever and chills
- Nausea and vomiting
- Decreased appetite
- Swollen lymph nodes in the neck and armpits
- Headaches or joint pain
- Enlarged spleen
- Jaundice
- Skin rash

Serious complications of mononucleosis include an enlarged spleen or inflamed liver. In rare cases, the spleen may rupture (break open), producing sharp pains on the left side of the abdomen. This symptom calls for immediate medical attention. Other symptoms of a ruptured spleen include light-headedness, rapid heartbeat, and difficulty breathing. Other rare complications include damage to the heart, brain, or the body's red blood cells.

Symptoms usually do not appear until four to seven weeks after exposure to EBV. Even though symptoms have not appeared, an infected person is still contagious. That is, he or she can pass the disease on to another person. An infected person remains contagious for up to five months after symptoms have disappeared.

EBV is actually not very contagious. People can live in close contact with an infected person without catching the disease as long as they do not have direct contact with that person's saliva.

DIAGNOSIS

The symptoms of mononucleosis are similar to those of other diseases. If mononucleosis is suspected, a doctor may conduct a complete physical examination. The examination will usually include a test known as the "Monospot" antibody blood test. This test can pick out chemicals in a person's blood that the body has produced to fight off mononucleosis. Other blood tests are also available to confirm a diagnosis of mononucleosis.

TREATMENT

The most effective treatment for mononucleosis is rest because a person's body needs time to fight off the infection. Individuals with mild cases may not require bed rest, but they should restrict their physical activity. In any case, vigorous physical activity, such as athletics or heavy lifting, should be avoided. Such activities can cause the spleen to rupture, making the condition much more serious.

Swollen tonsils and neck glands are symptoms of infectious mononucleosis. (© 1992. Reproduced by permission of Amethyst/Custom Medical Stock Photo.)

Treatments are available for the symptoms of mononucleosis. For example, drinking water and fruit juices can help relieve the sore throat and dehydration that often accompany mononucleosis. Gargling with salt water or taking throat lozenges may also relieve discomfort. Over-the-counter medications, such as acetaminophen (pronounced uh-see-tuh-MIN-uh-fuhn, trade name Tylenol) or ibuprofen (pronounced i-byoo-PRO-fuhn, trade name Advil), may relieve symptoms such as fever and headache. Aspirin should not be given to children because it may cause Reye's syndrome (see Reye's syndrome entry), a serious illness.

Antibiotics are not effective in curing mononucleosis. However, they may be helpful in treating some symptoms of the disease. For example, they may help relieve the discomfort of the sore throat that often occurs with mononucleosis. Cortisone can also be used to reduce swelling and inflammation in the throat and tonsils.

PROGNOSIS

Most people recover from mononucleosis in about two to three weeks. They are then able to resume their normal activities, especially if they rested during their illness. A patient may not feel completely recovered, however, for a period of up to three months after being cured.

One of the most common problems in treating mononucleosis is that people are eager to return to their usual activities too quickly. When that happens, the disease may return. Once the disease has completely run its course, a person cannot be reinfected.

PREVENTION

There is no guaranteed way to avoid becoming infected with EBV. However, some simple rules of good hygiene can reduce a person's chance of catching the disease. For example, one should avoid sharing utensils and drinking glasses with someone who has cold symptoms.

FOR MORE INFORMATION

Books

Silverstein, Alvin, Virginia Silverstein, and Robert Silverstein. *Mononucleosis.* Hillside, NJ: Enslow Publishers, 1994.

Smart, Paul. *Everything You Need to Know About Mononucleosis.* New York: Rosen Publishing Group, 1998.

Zonderman, Jon. *Mononucleosis and Other Infectious Diseases.* New York: Chelsea House Publishers, 1989.

Organizations

National Institute of Allergy and Infectious Diseases. Building 31, Room 7A-50, 31 Center Drive, MSC 2520, Bethesda, MD 20892–2520. http://www.niaid.nih.gov.

INFLUENZA

DEFINITION

Influenza is a highly infectious disease that affects the respiratory (breathing) tract. It is also known as the flu or grippe. The disease is caused by a virus. When inhaled, the virus attacks cells in the upper part of the respiratory system and causes symptoms such as fatigue, fever and chills, a hacking cough, and body aches. Influenza can also lead to other, more serious infections.

The disease known as stomach flu is not really a form of influenza. The influenza virus normally does not attack the stomach or intestines. Stomach flu is instead caused by other organisms, such as the salmonella or E. coli bacteria.

DESCRIPTION

The flu is often confused with the common cold (see common cold entry), but it is actually much more serious. The annual death toll due to influenza and its complications averages twenty thousand in the United States alone. Sometimes, a flu epidemic sweeps across a wide part of the world, killing large numbers of people. An epidemic is a sudden, rapid spread of a disease through a large geographical area. In 1918–19, a form of influenza known as the Spanish flu spread throughout the world. The death toll from the epidemic was estimated at twenty million to forty million people. About five hundred thousand of those deaths occurred in the United States.

Influenza outbreaks occur on a regular basis. An influenza epidemic occurred in 1957 and again in 1968. The first of these outbreaks was

WORDS TO KNOW

Common cold: A mild infection of the upper respiratory tract caused by viruses.

Epidemic: A widespread outbreak of a disease.

Reye's syndrome: A potentially fatal illness in children believed to be associated with the use of aspirin.

known as the Asian flu. The second was called the Hong Kong flu. About seventy thousand Americans died of the Asian flu and about thirty-four thousand from the Hong Kong flu.

Influenza has been known for more than 2,500 years. The ancient Greek physician Hippocrates was one of the earliest writers to describe the condition. Throughout most of history, people blamed the disease on a number of factors, including various kinds of bacteria and "bad air." In 1933, however, researchers found the real cause of the disease: a virus.

Three types of influenza viruses have now been discovered: types A, B, and C. Type A virus can infect many different kinds of animals, including humans, pigs, horses, and birds. Viruses B and C infect only humans. Influenza A is responsible for most cases of the disease in humans. Types B and C are less common and produce a milder form of infection.

CAUSES

Influenza is caused by the transmission of a flu virus from an infected person to an uninfected person. The virus can be transmitted by sneezing, coughing, sharing of eating and drinking utensils, and direct contact.

SYMPTOMS

The first symptoms of infection appear one to four days after the virus has entered a person's body. They include headache, dry cough, and chills. These symptoms are followed quickly by overall achiness and a fever that may run as high as 104°F (40°C). As the fever declines, nasal (nose) congestion and a sore throat become noticeable. The flu leaves an individual very tired and weak. A person with the flu may not return to normal for several days or even a few weeks.

A magnified image of an influenza virus budding on the surface of an infected cell. (Reproduced by permission of CNRI/Science Photo Library, National Audubon Society Collection/Photo Researchers, Inc.)

A flu infection often leads to more serious complications. These complications are often caused by bacteria that get into the lower respiratory tract. The signs of a secondary (follow-up) infection often appear just as the person seems to be recovering from the flu. These signs include a high fever, chills, chest pains, and a cough that produces a thick, yellowish sputum (discharge from the throat). If these symptoms appear, medical treatment should be sought.

Secondary infections also affect the sinus or ears. The flu can also worsen heart and lung problems and certain other chronic diseases. For this reason, an attack of the flu can be especially serious for elderly people.

DIAGNOSIS

The symptoms of a flu infection are familiar to all medical workers. Doctors and nurses can usually diagnose the disease simply by examining a patient. Tests are available to identify the flu virus and the various forms in which it occurs, but these tests are seldom needed for the purpose of diagnosis. Some tests may be necessary to diagnose secondary infections. For example, a doctor may take a throat culture to identify a throat infection.

TREATMENT

Influenza cannot be cured. The usual course of action is to allow the body to heal itself. Various treatments are available to help relieve symptoms, however. For example, a person should get plenty of bed rest and drink lots of fluids. A steam vaporizer can make breathing easier. Painkillers help relieve the aches and pains of the flu. Children should not be given aspirin, however. Aspirin has been shown to cause a rare condition known as Reye's syndrome (see Reye's syndrome entry), which can be fatal.

Flu patients often do not feel hungry. However, they should be encouraged to eat as normally as possible. Patients should not try to return to normal activities too soon. Overactivity can cause a return of the infection or secondary infections.

Drugs

Patients sometimes ask their doctor for antibiotics to cure the flu. But antibiotics have no effect on the flu virus. They can be used, however, to treat secondary infections.

There are many over-the-counter (nonprescription) medications for the treatment of flu symptoms. Medications that include alcohol should be avoided, however. Alcohol has a tendency to reduce the amount of water in a person's body. The best medicine is often an analgesic (painkiller), such as acetaminophen (pronounced uh-see-tuh-MIN-uh-fuhn, trade name Tylenol) or naproxen (pronounced nuh-PROKS-suhn, trade name Aleve).

Two antiviral drugs are available for the treatment of influenza in the United States. They are recommended for people with weak immune systems or people who are allergic to the flu vaccine. These two drugs are amantadine hydrochloride (pronounced uh-MANT-uh-deen HIE-druh-KLOR-ide, trade names Symmetrel, Symadine, Amantadine-hydrochloride) and rimantadine hydrochloride (pronounced ruh-MAN-tuh-deen HIE-druh-KLOR-ide, trade name Flumandine). Both drugs are effective against type A viruses only. These should be used with care because they both have serious side effects.

Alternative Treatment

A number of alternative treatments have been recommended for the treatment of influenza. In most cases, there is little scientific evidence for the success of these treatments.

- **Acupuncture and acupressure.** Practitioners believe that these two techniques can stimulate natural resistance, relieve nasal congestion and headaches, reduce fever, and soothe coughs. Acupuncture is a Chinese ther-

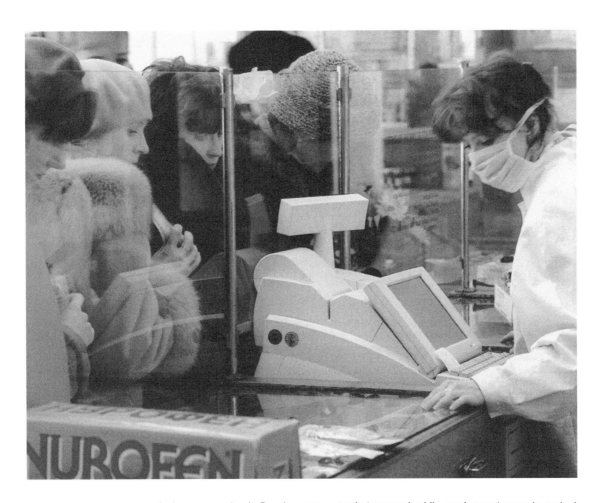

A pharmacy worker in Russia wears a respiratory mask while serving customers to protect herself from a flu epidemic in 1999. (Reproduced by permission of AP/Wide World Photos)

apy that uses fine needles to pierce the body; acupressure involves applying pressure to certain points in the body.

- **Aromatherapy.** Aromatherapists recommend gargling daily with one drop each of tea tree oil and lemon in a glass of warm water. Two drops of tea tree oil in a hot bath may help ease some symptoms. A few drops of the oils of eucalyptus (pronounced yoo-kuh-LIP-tus) or peppermint can be added to a steam vaporizer. They may help clear chest and nasal congestion.
- **Herbal remedies.** Echinacea (pronounced ek-i-NAY-see-uh) has been recommended to improve a person's immune system. Certain herbs, such as goldenseal and garlic, are thought to be able to kill viruses. A number of herbs can be used to treat the symptoms of influenza. For example, boneset may counteract aches and fever, and yarrow or elder flower may combat chills.
- **Homeopathy.** Homeopathic practitioners recommend a variety of herbs to treat the symptoms of the flu. These include Gelsemium (pronounced jel-SEE-mee-uhm) for the treatment of chills, headache, and nasal congestion;

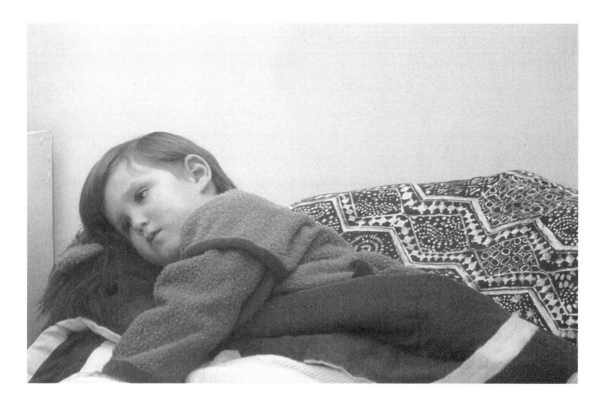

Often confused with a common cold, the flu is actually a much more serious infection. It causes aches, fever, and leaves an individual very tired and weak. (© 1991 Keith. Reproduced by permission of Custom Medical Stock Photo.)

Bryonia (pronounced brie-OH-nee-uh) for muscle aches, headaches, and dry cough; and poison ivy for restlessness, chills, hoarseness, and achy joints.

- **Hydrotherapy.** Taking a hot bath may help a person recover from the flu more quickly: The higher a person's body temperature, the more quickly the virus is likely to die. Hydrotherapists recommend that a person drink a cup of yarrow or elder flower tea while taking a bath: These herbs cause a person to sweat.

- **Vitamins.** Some people believe that large doses of vitamin C can help prevent the flu. They suggest increasing the amount of vitamin C once a flu infection has started.

PROGNOSIS

Healthy people under the age of sixty-five seldom experience serious, long-term consequences from a flu infection. Older people and people who are chronically ill are at risk for secondary infections, but they often recover from the flu quickly and completely. The high recovery rate from influenza should not be misleading. The infection can still be very serious. About 1 in 1,000 cases will actually lead to the patient's death.

PREVENTION

Vaccines are now available to help prevent influenza infections. The composition of these vaccines is changed every year. A vaccine is designed to protect people against three specific influenza viruses—the viruses thought to be most likely to infect people in a given year. Scientists may or may not make good guesses as to the "most likely" flu viruses. When they are successful, the vaccine can be 70 percent to 90 percent effective in people under the age of sixty-five.

The U.S. Centers for Disease Control and Prevention recommend that people get a flu vaccine injection each year before the flu season starts. In the United States, flu season usually runs from late December to early March. Adults usually need only one dose of the vaccine. Children under the age of nine who have not previously been vaccinated will need two doses one month apart.

Side effects from influenza vaccinations are rare. People who have never had influenza may experience about two days of discomfort. They may have a slight fever, feel tired, and experience achy muscles.

Certain people should not have influenza vaccinations. They include infants under the age of six months and people who are allergic to eggs. These people can be given the antiviral drugs described if necessary. However, certain groups of people are strongly advised to be vaccinated. These groups include:

- All people over the age of sixty-five
- Residents of nursing homes and other health-care facilities, regardless of age
- Adults and children who have chronic heart or lung problems, such as asthma (see asthma entry)
- Adults and children who have other kinds of chronic diseases, such as diabetes (see diabetes mellitus entry), severe anemia (see anemias entry), blood disorders, or kidney problems
- Children and teenagers who are on long-term aspirin therapy
- Women who are in the last two-thirds of their pregnancy and women who are nursing
- People with weakened immune systems, such as AIDS patients (see AIDS entry), people who have received organ transplants, and patients receiving various types of medical treatments, such as chemotherapy or radiation therapy
- Anyone who has regular contact with people in any of the above groups, such as teachers, health-care personnel, and family members
- Travelers to foreign countries

An individual need not be in one of the at-risk groups to receive a flu vaccination. Anyone who wants to avoid the discomfort of an influenza attack may receive the vaccine.

FOR MORE INFORMATION

Books

Brody, Jane E. *Jane Brody's Cold and Flu Fighter.* New York: W. W. Norton & Company, 1995.

Inlander, Charles B., and Cynthia K. Moran. *77 Ways to Beat Colds and Flu.* New York: Walker & Company, 1994.

Silverstein, Alvin, Virginia Silverstein, and Robert Silverstein. *Common Cold and Flu.* Hillside, NJ: Enslow Publishers, Inc., 1994.

Periodicals

Novitt-Moren, Anne. "Holiday's Biggest Spoilers: Colds and Flu." *Current Health* (December 1997): p. 6.

Saul, Helen. "Flu Vaccines Wanted: Dead or Alive." *New Scientist* (February 18, 1995): p. 26.

Organizations

Centers for Disease Control and Prevention. 1600 Clifton Road NE, Atlanta, GA 30333. (888) CDC-FACTS. http://www.cdc.gov.

INSOMNIA

DEFINITION

Insomnia is the inability to get an adequate amount of sleep. The difficulty can be in falling asleep, remaining asleep, or both. Insomnia is a common disorder that affects millions of people. It can be caused by many different conditions, diseases, and circumstances.

DESCRIPTION

Insomnia is a very common condition that probably affects most people at one time or another. However, it tends to occur more often in certain groups of people. For example, it is more common in women and older adults. People who are divorced, widowed, or separated seem to have the problem more often than those who are single or married.

Short-term, or transient, insomnia usually lasts no more than a few days. Long-term, or chronic, insomnia lasts for more than three weeks. Long-term insomnia is more of a problem. People who are deprived of sleep for extended periods of time are at risk to themselves and others. They are unable to concentrate normally while conducting daily activities. As a result, they are more likely to have accidents at work or while driving. They may also become moody and depressed. Chronic insomnia may also lead to immune disorders. The body's immune system fights off foreign invaders like bacteria and viruses. When a person does not get enough sleep, his or her immune system does not function properly, leaving them open to infection and disease.

CAUSES

Transient insomnia is often caused by a temporary, upsetting incident in a person's life. For example, an argument with a loved one, a brief illness, or jet lag can cause the disorder. This form of insomnia usually does not require medical treatment. When the incident is resolved, a person's ability to sleep returns.

Chronic insomnia is caused by one or more of the following factors:

- A medical condition or a treatment for a medical condition
- Use of certain substances, such as caffeine, alcohol, and nicotine

WORDS TO KNOW

Biofeedback: A technique that enables a person to gain some control over involuntary body functions.

Sleep disorder: Any condition that interferes with sleep. The American Sleep Disorders Association has identified eighty-four different sleep disorders.

- A psychiatric (mental) condition, such as depression or anxiety
- Stress, such as sadness caused by the loss of a loved one or a job
- Changes in one's sleep patterns, as when one's job shift has been changed
- Breathing problems, such as snoring
- Jerky leg movements that occur when a person is just falling asleep
- Nightmares or feelings of panic during sleep

Sometimes insomnia can be caused by the problem itself. That is, a person worries so much about falling asleep that he or she can't get to sleep. The more one worries about falling asleep, the harder it is to do.

SOMETIMES A PERSON WORRIES SO MUCH ABOUT FALLING ASLEEP THAT HE OR SHE CAN'T GET TO SLEEP. THE MORE ONE WORRIES ABOUT FALLING ASLEEP, THE HARDER IT IS TO DO.

SYMPTOMS

Some people with insomnia have trouble falling asleep. Others are able to fall asleep but wake up in the middle of the night and have trouble falling back asleep. Or they doze off but sleep very lightly. People with insomnia wake up in the morning tired and unrested. They continue to be exhausted throughout the day. These sleep patterns are common among the elderly and among those who are depressed (see depressive disorders entry).

Sometimes sleep patterns are reversed. For example, a person may find it difficult to stay awake during the day and may take many naps. Then, at night, they find it hard to go to sleep or to stay asleep.

DIAGNOSIS

Insomnia can be diagnosed easily by listening to a patient's symptoms. A doctor may ask the patient to keep records of his or her daily activities. This record can help the doctor determine the factors causing insomnia. For example, someone who eats just before going to bed may experience insomnia. Changing that person's eating patterns may cure the insomnia. A doctor may also conduct a physical examination to see if there are physical reasons for the insomnia.

People with chronic insomnia may need additional medical help. Some doctors specialize in treating sleep disorders. They can conduct additional tests and suggest treatment for more serious cases.

TREATMENT

Treatment of insomnia first requires finding out the factors that are causing the problem. Removing those factors often leads to a solution for insomnia.

Change in Behavior

People can try a number of things to relieve their insomnia. They should go to bed only when sleepy and use the bedroom only for sleep. Other activities, such as reading, watching television, or snacking, should take place in a different room. If they are unable to go to sleep, they should go into another room and do something relaxing, like reading. Watching television is usually not a relaxing activity as television programs often make people more excited. People should go back to bed only when they feel tired.

People with insomnia should set the alarm and get up at the same time every morning, whether or not they had a good night's sleep. In this way, they establish a regular sleep-wake pattern. They should avoid taking naps during the day. If a nap is necessary, it should be taken early in the afternoon for no more than thirty minutes.

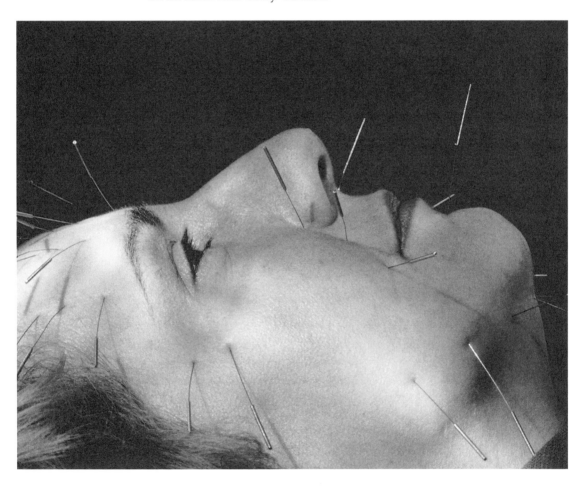

Acupuncture is an alternative treatment shown to be helpful for insomnia. (Reproduced by permission of Phototake, NYC)

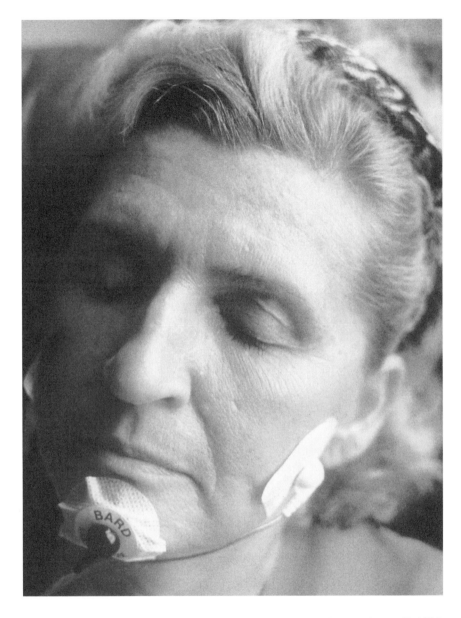

Biofeedback is used to treat insomnia by teaching patients relaxation techniques. (© 1992 Peter Berndt, M.D., P.A. Reproduced by permission of Custom Medical Stock Photo.)

One successful form of treatment is called sleep-restriction therapy. A person first determines how long he or she can sleep at night. The person then remains in bed no longer than that length of time. Each night, the time spent in bed is increased slightly. Under this program, the person gets a little more tired each night, and his or her chance of sleeping improves.

Drug Therapy

The simplest way to deal with insomnia is to use drugs. Sedatives, tranquilizers, and anti-anxiety drugs can help a person sleep, but the use of drugs has some serious side effects. First, they may become habit-forming. A person may get to the point where sleep is possible only if he or she takes the drugs. Also, drugs become less effective over time. A person may have to take more and more of a drug to get the same result. Also, drugs can make a person feel groggy during the day. To avoid these problems, drugs should be used to treat insomnia only with a doctor's advice and under very strict supervision.

Other Measures

Relaxing before going to bed can help a person fall asleep faster. People can learn to substitute pleasant thoughts for unpleasant ones. This technique can reduce the effect of depression, anxiety, and other feelings that prevent people from sleeping properly. Audiotapes can also help a person relax.

Changes in diet and exercise routines can help. Certain foods tend to interfere with sleep and should be avoided in the evening. These foods include coffee, tea, colas, and chocolate (all of which contain caffeine), and alcohol. Alcohol makes a person sleepy at first, but a few hours later it has the opposite effect.

Maintaining a comfortable bedroom temperature, reducing noise, and eliminating light are also helpful. Regularly scheduled morning or afternoon exercise can relax the body.

Alternative Treatment

Many alternative treatments have been suggested for treating the symptoms of insomnia and its underlying causes. Practicing relaxation techniques before bed can help a person fall asleep and sleep more deeply. These techniques include meditation; breathing exercises; and a warm bath that contains rose, lavender, marjoram, or chamomile.

Eating a healthy diet rich in calcium, magnesium, and B vitamins can also be beneficial. Eating a high-protein snack like yogurt before going to bed is also recommended. Some people find that a cup of herbal tea made with chamomile, hops, or St. John's wort helps them relax. Acupuncture (a Chinese therapy that involves the use of fine needles) and biofeedback (therapy that involves behavior modification) have also proved helpful.

PROGNOSIS

While short-term insomnia is disruptive to a person's natural balance, it can usually be solved by the methods described, and is therefore not considered a serious condition. However, chronic insomnia may lead to some serious secondary problems. If not treated, long-term sleep disturbance may lead to injuries due to lack of concentration, or possibly to a weakened immune system, which leaves a person at risk for infection or disease.

PREVENTION

The best way to prevent insomnia is to develop a healthy lifestyle. This includes a balance of rest, recreation, and exercise. People should also learn how to manage stress in their lives. A healthy diet can also reduce the risk of insomnia.

FOR MORE INFORMATION

Books

Bruno, Frank Joe. *Get a Good Night's Sleep: Understand Your Sleeplessness—And Banish It Forever!* New York: Macmillan General Reference, 1997.

Davies, Dilys. *Insomnia: Your Questions Answered.* New York: Penguin USA, 1999.

Idzikowski, Chris. *The Insomnia Kit: Everything You Need for a Good Night's Sleep.* New York: Penguin USA, 1999.

Simpson, Carolyn. *Coping With Sleep Disorders.* New York: Rosen Publishing Group, 1996.

Organizations

American Sleep Disorders Association. 6301 Bandel Road, Suite 101, Rochester, MN 55901. http://www.asda.org.

IRRITABLE BOWEL SYNDROME

DEFINITION

Irritable bowel syndrome (IBS) is a common intestinal condition. Its cause is unknown and there is currently no cure. IBS is characterized by abdominal pain, changes in bowel movements, gassiness, nausea, and other symptoms.

DESCRIPTION

Irritable bowel syndrome is a poorly understood condition even though, by some estimates, as many as 30 percent of Americans have had IBS at one time in their life. IBS is responsible for more time lost at work and school than any other medical problem except the common cold. It is a major reason that patients see gastroenterologists (doctors who specialize in the digestive system; pronounced GAS-troe-EN-tuh-ROL-uh-jist). Yet no more than half of the people who experience IBS ever see a doctor.

IBS normally does not appear until after adolescence. It affects women about twice as often as men. Researchers do not know the reason for these patterns.

CAUSES

The food a person eats passes through various stages of digestion. In the stomach and small intestine, food is changed into a liquid. In the large intestine (colon), water and salts in this liquid pass through the walls of the colon into the bloodstream. The semisolid material that remains is passed on to the rectum.

Food is passed through the digestive system by means of peristalsis (pronounced per-i-STOL-sis). Peristalsis is a wave-like series of movements made by muscles in the walls of the digestive system. Peristalsis in the colon usually occurs only after meals.

In people who have IBS, peristalsis occurs in unusual patterns. It may go on for extended periods of time, or it may take place much more slowly than usual. In the first case, watery solids are continually passed to the rectum, which results in diarrhea. In the second case, very dry solids are passed to the rectum, which leads to constipation. Irritable bowel syndrome is any condition in which the colon does not function normally.

Certain foods seem to cause IBS in some people. They include chocolate, milk products, caffeine, and large quantities of alcohol. Some individuals are affected by very specific foods. Stress is also related to IBS. People who have IBS are likely to develop symptoms when they feel anxious. Researchers do not yet know why this connection exists.

WORDS TO KNOW

Peristalsis: Periodic waves of muscular contractions that move food through the digestive system.

Rectum: The lower part of the digestive system from which solid wastes are excreted.

SYMPTOMS

Some typical symptoms of IBS include the following:

- Abdominal pain
- Diarrhea and/or constipation
- Cramps
- Gassiness
- Bloating

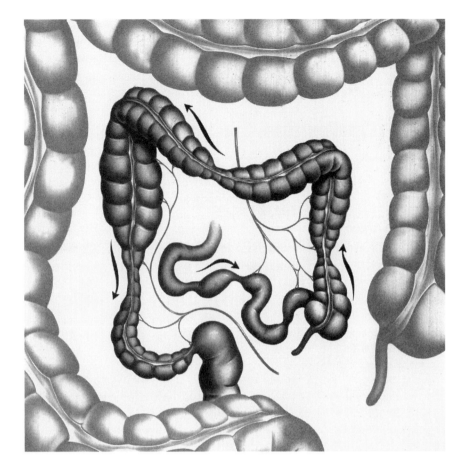

Illustration of the large intestine with irritable bowel syndrome. Darker center shows abnormal colon, showing areas of constriction which cause constipation, and areas of distention which causes diarrhea. (© 1995 John Bavosi/Science Photo Library. Reproduced by permission of Custom Medical Stock Photo.)

• Nausea
• A strong desire to defecate (have a bowel movement)
• A feeling that the bowels are not empty after a bowel movement

DIAGNOSIS

Many medical conditions produce symptoms similar to irritable bowel syndrome. A doctor needs to make sure that another condition is not causing the patient's symptoms. Eliminating other causes usually requires taking a medical history and conducting a general physical examination. Laboratory tests may also be needed. A stool sample can be tested for the presence of blood or parasites that may be causing an infection in the colon.

When other possible causes have been eliminated, a doctor may diagnose IBS. A positive diagnosis is based on a set of standards known as the Rome criteria. According to the Rome criteria an individual must have experienced continuous or recurrent symptoms for a period of three months. The diagnosis may also rate one of three levels for the disorder: mild, moderate, or severe.

About 70 percent of all patients have mild IBS. The symptoms of mild IBS are slight and do not interfere with the patient's daily life. Moderate IBS may interfere with some normal activities. It may also cause the patient some psychological problems. This level of IBS is seen in about 25 percent of all patients. Severe IBS causes a severe disruption of a patient's life. In some cases, patients suffer constant and intense pain. They usually cannot live normal lives or hold regular jobs. About 5 percent of all patients with IBS have this form of the disorder.

PSYCHOLOGICAL COUNSELING MAY BE HELPFUL IN TREATING IBS. THE PURPOSE OF COUNSELING IS TO HELP PATIENTS REDUCE ANXIETY AND LEARN TO DEAL WITH THE PAIN AND OTHER SYMPTOMS OF IBS.

TREATMENT

The treatment recommended for IBS depends on the severity of the disorder. Patients with mild or moderate symptoms should identify foods that lead to the symptoms of IBS and avoid them. Over-the-counter medications can be used to control both diarrhea and constipation. If those medications do not work, other drugs can be prescribed. Drugs are also available to control the abdominal pain that often accompanies IBS. People with constipation can sometimes be helped by setting specific times for meals and bowel movements.

Psychological counseling may also be helpful. The purpose of counseling is to help patients reduce anxiety and learn to deal with the pain and other symptoms of IBS. Patients with severe symptoms need more aggressive treatment. They may be given antidepressant drugs to help reduce the worst pain associated with the disorder.

Alternative Treatment

Alternative practitioners recommend a variety of techniques to help patients deal with stress. These techniques include yoga, meditation, hypnosis biofeedback, and reflexology. Reflexology is a form of foot massage that some people think relieves diarrhea, constipation, and other symptoms of IBS.

Certain herbal remedies are also thought to be helpful in controlling the symptoms of IBS. For example, ginger, buckthorn, and peppermint oil are recommended to avoid irritation in the upper part of the digestive tract.

Chamomile, valerian, rosemary, and lemon balm are thought to calm the digestive system and prevent abnormal peristaltic movements.

PROGNOSIS

Irritable bowel syndrome is not a life-threatening disorder. Nor is it likely to lead to more serious medical conditions, such as cancer (see cancer entry). In the majority of patients, the symptoms of IBS never disappear. However, those symptoms can usually be treated effectively and the condition is viewed as a temporary, if annoying, inconvenience.

PREVENTION

While there is no single known cause of IBS, there are some habits that an individual can develop to maintain good digestive health. Specifically, a well-balanced diet, low in fats, is recommended. Ensuring that your diet includes enough fiber is also a positive step; this means monitoring your intake of fresh fruits and vegetables, whole grains, and bran. Regular exercise, quitting smoking, and avoiding excessive amounts of caffeine are also encouraged.

FOR MORE INFORMATION

Books

Peikin, Steven R. *Gastrointestinal Health: A Self-Help Nutritional Program to Prevent, Cure, or Alleviate Irritable Bowel Syndrome, Ulcers, Heartburn, Gas, and Constipation,* revised edition. New York: HarperCollins, 1999.

Organizations

International Foundation for Functional Gastrointestinal Disorders. PO Box 17864, Milwaukee, WI 53217. (888) 964-2001. http://www.iffgd.org.

National Institute of Diabetes and Digestive and Kidney Diseases of the National Institutes of Health. 2 Information Way, Bethesda, MD 20892-3570. http://www.niddk.nih.gov.

JUVENILE ARTHRITIS

DEFINITION

Juvenile arthritis (JA) refers to a number of different conditions with two characteristics in common. First, they all strike children. Second, they all involve inflammation of the joints.

DESCRIPTION

Humans can move their head, arms, legs, fingers, and toes because of joints. A joint is a structure where two or more bones come together. The elbow, for example, is a joint at which bones in the upper and lower arm come together.

The space between the bones in a joint is occupied by a variety of other structures and fluids. These structures and fluids help the bones move more smoothly. One of the structures in a joint is the articular capsule. The articular capsule surrounds the bones that come together at a joint and the space between the joint. The articular capsule contains a thin covering called the synovial (pronounced si-NO-vee-uhl) membrane. The synovial membrane produces a clear liquid called synovial fluid that lubricates the space between the bones. The synovial fluid helps the bones slide across each other more easily.

WORDS TO KNOW

Articular capsule: A tough tissue that surrounds a joint and the bones that come together at the joint.

Joint: A structure that holds two or more bones together.

Synovial fluid: A clear liquid that fills the spaces between bones in a joint cavitiy and helps the bones move across each other more easily.

Synovial membrane: A membrane that covers the articular capsule in a joint and produces synovial fluid.

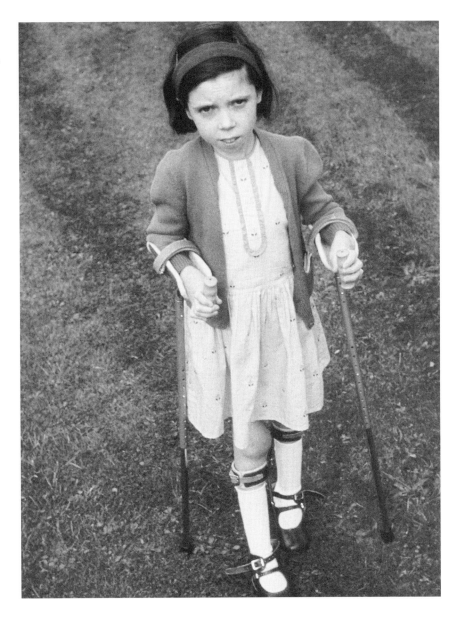

Juvenile arthritis is joint inflammation that affects children under the age of sixteen and that lasts for at least three to six months. The condition often goes through periods in which joints are very sore and painful and then return to normal. (© John Moss. Reproduced by permission of Photo Researchers, Inc.)

In juvenile arthritis, the synovial membrane becomes very inflamed. Instead of being thin and flexible, it becomes thick and stiff. This change occurs when white blood cells invade the membrane. The white blood cells release chemicals that cause inflammation and attack other structures in the joint. The bones, ligaments, and other structures in the joint are worn away and the joint can no longer move smoothly and easily. Bending and turning movements cause pain and discomfort.

Juvenile arthritis is a joint inflammation that affects a child under the age of sixteen and that lasts for at least three to six months. The condition often goes through periods in which joints are very sore and painful and then return to normal. After a while the inflammation returns and joints are once again sore and painful.

CAUSES

A number of possible causes for JA have been suggested. Some researchers feel that the disorder may have a genetic basis. It seems to occur more often in some families than in others. Other researchers think the disorder may be caused by an infectious agent, such as a bacterium or a virus, but no such agent has ever been found.

Some evidence suggests that JA may be an autoimmune disorder (see autoimmune disorder entry). An autoimmune disorder is one in which the body's immune system becomes confused. It behaves as if some normal part of a person's body is actually a foreign substance. The immune system then sets out to attack and destroy that part of the body. According to this explanation, a person's immune system mistakenly attacks his or her joints, causing the symptoms of juvenile arthritis.

SOME EVIDENCE SUGGESTS THAT JUVENILE ARTHRITIS MAY BE AN AUTOIMMUNE DISORDER.

SYMPTOMS

The most common symptoms of JA include pain, stiffness, redness, swelling, and warmth in a joint. Over time, the bones around an infected joint may grow too quickly or too slowly. As a result, a child's arms and legs may be of different lengths. A common consequence of JA is the condition known as contracture. Contracture is a shortening of muscle that occurs when the muscle is not used. Contracture occurs in JA patients because they find it painful to move, so their muscles are not exercised normally.

Five types of JA have been identified. Each type has its own specific symptoms. These five types are:

• **Pauciarticular JA.** Pauciarticular (pronounced paw-see-ar-TIK-yoo-luhr) JA is the most common and least severe form of JA and affects about 40 percent to 60 percent of all JA patients. Pauciarticular JA usually occurs in only four joints: the knee, ankle, wrist, and/or elbow. It usually does not interfere with the patient's growth. Less than 15 percent of patients with this form of JA end up with deformed joints. Some children with the disorder have swelling in a joint without pain. Others develop an inflammation of the eye that can lead to blindness if left untreated. Many children with pauciarticular JA recover completely within a few years of diagnosis.

• **Polyarticular JA.** About 40 percent of all cases of JA are polyarticular (pronounced pol-ee-ar-TIK-yuh-luhr). It occurs more commonly among girls than boys. Polyarticular JA usually develops before the age of three or after the age of ten and affects five or more joints at the same time. It occurs most commonly in the small joints of both hands and both feet, but it can also develop in larger joints, such as the elbow or knee. If the condition occurs in both knees at once, the patient's legs may grow at different rates so that one leg becomes longer than the other.

About half of all patients with polyarticular JA have arthritis of the spine and/or hip. Many patients with the disorder also have more general symptoms, such as anemia (low red blood cell count; see anemias entry), decreased growth rate, poor appetite, low-grade fever, and a slight rash.

This form of JA is most severe when it occurs during early adolescence. In some cases, the disorder may be an early form of an adult disorder known as rheumatoid arthritis (see arthritis entry). The disorder can be very serious because it destroys and deforms the joints.

Systemic onset JA. Systemic onset JA is also called Still's disease after the doctor who first described it. It occurs in 10 percent to 20 percent of patients with JA and is equally common in boys and girls. The disorder is usually first seen between the ages of five and ten. The initial symptoms of systemic onset JA do not occur in the joints. Instead, they are general symptoms, such as high fever, rash, loss of appetite, and weight loss. More serious symptoms may also develop, including pericarditis (inflammation of the sac surrounding the heart; pronounced per-i-kar-DIE-tiss), pleuritis (inflammation of the tissue lining the lungs; pronounced ploor-I-tuhs), and myocarditis (inflammation of the heart muscle; pronounced my-o-kar-DIE-tiss).

Typical symptoms of arthritis affecting the joints usually develop later in systemic onset JA. They generally show up in the wrists and ankles. Many children go through regular cycles when their condition becomes worse and then better. They may also develop polyarticular JA.

Spondyloarthropathy. Spondyloarthropathy (pronounced SPON-duh-lo-ar-THROP-uh-thee) is relatively rare. It occurs most commonly in boys older than eight. Arthritis develops first in the knees and ankles and then moves upward to include the hips and lower spine.

Psoriatic JA. Psoriatic (pronounced sore-ee-AT-ik) JA usually starts in fewer than four joints. However, it gradually spreads to include many joints, as in polyarticular JA. The hips, back, fingers, and toes are often affected. A skin condition known as psoriasis (pronounced suh-RIE-uh-sis) accompanies this form of JA. Psoriatic JA often becomes a serious, disabling problem.

DIAGNOSIS

Diagnosis is usually made on the basis of a patient's symptoms. Laboratory tests are often not very helpful because they do not show any indication of disease.

TREATMENT

The goal of treating JA is to decrease the inflammation in a joint. In this way, the patient retains better movement. Common medications used to reduce inflammation are the nonsteroidal anti-inflammatory drugs (NSAIDs), such as ibuprofen (pronounced i-byoo-PRO-fuhn, trade name Advil) and naproxen (pronounced nuh-PROKS-suhn, trade name Aleve). Steroid drugs can also be given by mouth or injection. Oral injections are helpful but have dangerous long-term side effects. Injections of steroids directly into a joint are often the best treatment.

Other drugs used to treat JA include methotrexate (pronounced meth-uh-TREK-sate), sulfasalazine (pronounced SULL-fuh-SAL-uh-zeen), penicillamine (pronounced pen-i-SIL-uh-meen), and hydroxychloroquine (pronounced hi-droks-ee-KLOR-uh-kween). Steroid eyedrops can be used to treat eye inflammations.

Physical therapy and exercise are often recommended to improve joint mobility and muscle strength. Occasionally, splints are used to rest painful joints and to prevent or improve deformed joints.

Alternative Treatment

Some practitioners recommend juice therapy for treating JA. Patients are encouraged to drink a mixture of fruit and vegetable juices, including carrots, celery, cabbage, cherries, lemons, beets, cucumbers, radishes, and garlic. Another alternative therapy is aromatherapy, in which the patient inhales vapors that include cypress, fennel, and lemon. Massage with oils such as rosemary, chamomile, camphor, juniper, and lavender can sometimes be helpful. Other types of therapy include acupuncture (a Chinese therapy that involves the use of fine needles) and acupressure (a Chinese therapy treatment during which pressure is applied to certain points in the body).

Some authorities believe that nutritional supplements can relieve the symptoms of JA. These supplements include large amounts of antioxidants (vitamins A, C, and E; zinc; and selenium) as well as B vitamins and minerals such as boron, copper, and manganese.

There is some evidence that JA can be caused by food allergies. Patients should identify any foods that increase their symptoms and exclude those foods from their diet.

PROGNOSIS

The prognosis for pauciarticular JA and spondyloarthropathy is quite good. It is not as good for polyarticular JA, which can sometimes lead to more serious forms of arthritis when the patient gets older, as well as to joint deformities. The prognosis for systemic onset JA depends on the organs affected. About 1 percent to 5 percent of all JA patients die of complications of the disorder, such as infection, inflammation of the heart, or kidney disease.

PREVENTION

Because so little is known about the causes of JA, there are no recommendations for avoiding the disorder.

FOR MORE INFORMATION

Books

Aldape, Virginia Tortorica. *Nicole's Story: A Book About a Girl With Juvenile Rheumatoid Arthritis.* Minneapolis, MN: Lerner Publications, 1996.

Organizations

American College of Rheumatology. 60 Executive Park South, Suite 150, Atlanta, GA 30329. (404) 633–1870. http://www.rheumatology.org.

Arthritis Foundation. 1330 West Peachtree Street, Atlanta, GA 30309. (404) 872–7100. http://www.arthritis.org.

National Institute of Arthritis and Musculoskeletal and Skin Diseases. http://www.nih.gov/niams.

Web sites

"Arthritis." [Online] http://arthritis.miningco.com (accessed on June 20, 1999).

KAPOSI'S SARCOMA

DEFINITION

Kaposi's sarcoma (KS; pronounced kuh-PO-seez sar-KO-muh) is a very rare form of cancer (see cancer entry). The word "sarcom" refers to any form of cancer that affects muscle, bone, liver, kidneys, lungs, spleen, bladder, and other organs and tissues. At one time, Kaposi's sarcoma was seen almost entirely in older men of Mediterranean or eastern European background. In the 1980s, however, it began to show up in young men with AIDS (see AIDS entry). Mild forms of the disease can be treated with topical (local) agents. More serious forms are treated with chemotherapy (treatment with drugs). KS is a major cause of death among people with AIDS.

DESCRIPTION

Scientists know of four forms of Kaposi's sarcoma. One form, called classical KS, affects older men of Mediterranean or eastern European background. The disease appears as pink, purple, or brown patches on the lower legs. These patches can be painful and ugly, but they are usually not life-threatening.

A second form of KS is called African endemic KS. It affects boys and men of any ethnic background. Its earliest symptoms are similar to those of classical KS. The cancer soon spreads, however, to tissues under the skin, the bones, and the lymph system. The disease is difficult to treat and often causes death within a few years of diagnosis.

Iatrogenic (pronounced eye-a-truh-JE-nik) KS is a third form of the disease. An iatrogenic disorder is one that develops because a patient is being treated for some other disease. Iatrogenic KS usually occurs in patients who have had a liver or kidney transplant. It is able to develop because these patients have taken drugs to suppress (restrain) their immune systems. Iatrogenic KS tends to disappear when these patients stop taking the drugs.

The fourth form of KS is AIDS-related KS. This form of KS appeared among gay men who developed AIDS in the 1980s. AIDS-related KS tumors first appear on the skin. But the disease may then spread to the head, neck, back, mouth, stomach and intestines, lymph nodes, and lungs. In its advanced stages, AIDS-related KS is very difficult to cure and can often cause death.

CAUSES

A variety of factors appear to lead to the development of KS:

- Genetic background. People with classic and African KS appear to possess an abnormal gene. Genes are chemical substances in the body that determine a person's physical and biological characteristics.
- Sex hormones. KS occurs far more often in men than in women. This suggests that sex hormones may have something to do with how the disease develops.
- Immune suppression. In many cases, the immune system may be strong enough to defend the body against KS. When the immune system is weakened, however, it loses that ability. People who are taking immunosuppressant drugs are, therefore, at risk for KS. So are people with AIDS, whose immune systems are often very badly damaged.
- Infectious agents that are sexually transmitted. Gay and bisexual men and intravenous drug users are all at high risk for AIDS. But gay and bisexual men are ten times more likely to develop KS than are intravenous drug users. That suggests that KS may be caused by some agent that is transmitted sexually. Further support for this idea comes from the fact that the rate of KS cases among gay and bisexual men has dropped dramatically as safer sex practices have become more widespread.

Researchers have already found viruses they think may cause KS. One of the most likely candidates is called human herpes virus 8. This virus belongs to the same family that causes cold sores and shingles. The virus has been found in samples of KS taken from patients with the disease. Additional studies are still needed to confirm this theory.

WORDS TO KNOW

African endemic Kaposi's sarcoma: A form of KS that affects boys and men, has symptoms like those of classic KS, and can spread rapidly and cause death.

AIDS-related Kaposi's sarcoma: A form of KS that occurs primarily in gay and bisexual men; it is much more dangerous than classic KS.

Classic Kaposi's sarcoma: A form of KS that usually affects older men of Mediterranean or eastern European background.

Iatrogenic Kaposi's sarcoma: A form of KS that develops in people who have had organ transplants and are taking immunosuppressant drugs.

SYMPTOMS

The symptoms of KS are quite visible and take the form of pink, purple, or brown patches that usually first appear on the lower legs.

DIAGNOSIS

KS can often be diagnosed simply by the appearance of the lesions (blotches) on a patient's skin. An unexplained cough or chest pain, or unexplained stomach or intestinal pain or bleeding, may suggest that the disease has spread to internal organs. A visual diagnosis of KS is usually confirmed with a biopsy. A biopsy is a process by which a small sample of tissue is taken from a patient. The sample is studied under a microscope to see what kinds of cells are present. KS cells have a very distinctive appearance that a scientist can recognize.

TREATMENT

There is no single best treatment for KS. The choice of treatment depends on the type of KS a patient has and how far it has spread. Doctors sometimes use a combination of treatments to obtain the best possible results. Some common treatments include:

Topical Therapy

Topical therapy is used when there are few lesions and the disease seems to be progressing slowly. In such a case, a doctor may freeze the lesions, which kills them. Radiation therapy can also be used on individual lesions. Radiation therapy involves the use of some form of radiation, such as X rays, to kill cancer cells.

Systemic Chemotherapy

In systemic chemotherapy, a patient is given drugs that enter his or her bloodstream and are carried throughout the body. The drugs can thus attack and kill cancer cells in all parts of the body. Doctors have found that a combination of cancer-killing drugs often works better than a single drug. Some commonly used drugs include vinblastine (pronounced vin-BLAS-teen), bleomycin (pronounced blee-uh-MYS-uhn), and doxorubicin (dok-suh-ROO-buh-suhn).

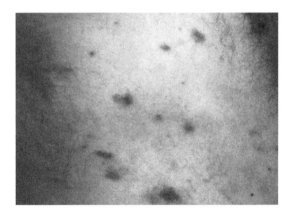

The symptoms of Kaposi's sarcoma are quite visible and take the form of pink, purple, or brown patches on the skin that usually first appear on the lower legs. (Reproduced by permission of Custom Medical Stock Photo)

Antiviral Therapy

A number of drugs have been developed for the treatment of AIDS. Some of these drugs also appear to be effective against KS. Among the most promising of these drugs is a group of chemicals known as protease inhibitors. Some widely used antiviral drugs (drugs that kill viruses) have not, however, been effective in treating KS. These drugs include acyclovir (pronounced a-SI-klo-veer) and ganciclovir (pronounced gan-SI-klo-veer).

Other Treatments

A number of other treatments for KS are being studied. These include:

Alpha-interferon. Alpha-interferon is a chemical produced naturally in the body that fights infectious agents. It has been tested as a treatment for KS by injecting it directly into lesions.

- **Retinoids.** Retinoids are related to vitamin A. They have long been used to treat acne (see acne entry) and other skin diseases (see skin disorders entry). Some researchers believe that they also may be effective against KS lesions.
- **Laser therapy.** Laser therapy is similar to radiation therapy except that it uses laser light instead of X rays or other forms of radiation. Laser therapy has had limited success in destroying small lesions.

Alternative Treatment

There is little evidence that any form of alternative treatment is effective against KS. Some practitioners recommend the use of herbal medicines and special diets.

WHAT ARE INTERFERONS?

Infections are caused by bacteria, viruses, fungi, and other organisms. Doctors now have a number of tools to fight most of these disease-causing agents. For example, many bacterial infections can be cured by antibiotics. Viral infections, however, are a more difficult problem. Scientists have discovered relatively few drugs that will kill viruses. Some of the most promising of these drugs belong to a group known as the interferons.

Interferons were discovered in 1957 by the Scottish virologist Alick Isaacs and the Swiss virologist Jean Lindenmann. While studying influenza, Isaacs and Lindenmann made an unexpected discovery. Viruses in a cell had a way of preventing other viruses from entering the same cell. The viruses originally present in the cell produced a protein (chemical) that killed newly-arrived viruses. Isaacs and Lindenmann called the protein interferon because it "interfered" with the presence of other viruses.

At first, scientists thought that only one kind of interferon existed. But they have now discovered more than two dozen. Alpha-interferon is one type. It is being used to treat patients with Kaposi' sarcoma. Scientists are now investigating ways in which they will be able to make interferons work for them in fighting a number of diseases, including cancer.

PROGNOSIS

The prognosis for KS differs significantly for various forms of the disease. Patients with classic KS stand a good chance of complete recovery if they receive treatment soon enough. The prognosis for African endemic KS is not very good. The disease tends to spread rapidly and causes death within a relatively short period of time. Milder forms of AIDS-related KS can often be controlled. If the disease spreads to internal organs, however, prognosis is much less certain.

PREVENTION

There are no known methods for preventing classic and African endemic KS. AIDS-related KS can be prevented if those who are at risk for the disease (primarily gay and bisexual men) practice safer-sex methods. These methods prevent the spread of the infectious agent—whatever it is—from an infected to a noninfected person.

FOR MORE INFORMATION

Organizations

American Academy of Dermatology. 930 N. Meacham Road, PO Box 4014, Schaumburg, IL 60173. (847) 330-0230; (888) 462–3376. http://www.aad.org.

Gay Men's Health Crisis. 119 West 24th Street, New York, NY 10011. (212) 367-1000. http://www.gmhc.org.

LARYNGITIS

DEFINITION

Laryngitis (pronounced lar-uhn-JIE-tiss) is an inflammation of the larynx, resulting in hoarseness of the voice.

DESCRIPTION

The larynx is the upper portion of the trachea (pronounced TRAY-kee-uh), or windpipe. When a person breathes in, air passes into the nose or mouth. It then travels down the trachea into the lungs. The larynx also contains the vocal cords, used in making sounds. When air passes over the vocal cords, it causes them to vibrate. That vibration produces sound.

In laryngitis, the lower part of the larynx, including the vocal cords, is swollen and inflamed. The vocal cords can still vibrate, but not in their normal manner. The sound produced is husky. Laryngitis is a very common problem. It often occurs during an upper respiratory (breathing) tract infection, such as a common cold (see common cold entry).

CAUSES

In the vast majority of cases, laryngitis is caused by a virus. The virus is often the same one that causes a common cold or influenza (the flu; see influenza entry). In very rare cases, the disease is caused by a bacterium, such as the one

WORDS TO KNOW

Larynx: The part of the airway between the pharynx and trachea.

Trachea: The part of the airway that leads into the bronchial tubes in the lungs.

that also causes tuberculosis (see tuberculosis entry). In people with weakened immune systems, such as those with AIDS (see AIDS entry), laryngitis can be caused by a fungus.

SYMPTOMS

The symptoms of laryngitis are similar to those of the common cold. They include a sore, scratchy throat; fever; runny nose; achiness; and tiredness. A person may have trouble swallowing and may experience coughing and wheezing. The most characteristic symptom of laryngitis, however, is a hoarse and raspy voice.

In very rare cases, swelling of the larynx can cause constriction (shrinking or blockage) of the airways. This problem is usually serious only in young children, whose airways are small.

DIAGNOSIS

A common clue used to diagnose laryngitis is the recent occurrence of a cold or the flu followed by hoarseness. The throat usually appears red and somewhat swollen. The doctor will usually listen to the patient's chest and back with a stethoscope. A harsh, wheezing sound is an indication of laryngitis.

THE DOCTOR WILL USUALLY LISTEN TO THE PATIENT'S CHEST AND BACK WITH A STETHOSCOPE. A HARSH, WHEEZING SOUND IS AN INDICATION OF LARYNGITIS.

Chronic (persistent) laryngitis may suggest the presence of tuberculosis. In such a case, a doctor can use an instrument known as a laryngoscope (pronounced luh-RING-guh-skope) to look directly into the patient's airway. The presence of redness, swelling, nodules (small lumps), and sores indicates the possibility of tuberculosis.

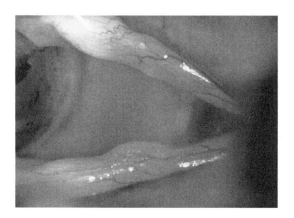

An endoscopic view of vocal cords with laryngitis. (Reproduced by permission of Custom Medical Stock Photo)

TREATMENT

Since laryngitis is usually caused by a virus, there is no cure for the disease. Treatment is aimed at relieving its symptoms. Gargling with warm salt water, taking pain relievers, using a moist air vaporizer, and getting plenty of rest are usually the best practices to follow.

When laryngitis is more serious, which is rare, it needs special treatment. For example, an infant who has trouble breathing may temporarily require an artificial airway. A person with tubercular laryngitis requires the combination of medications used to treat tuberculosis itself.

Alternative Treatment

One kind of alternative treatment is aromatherapy. In aromatherapy, the patient breathes fumes of special mixtures with soothing properties. For laryngitis, these mixtures may contain lavender, frankincense, thyme, or sandalwood. Special solutions for gargling can be made with a variety of herbs, including sage, yarrow, or licorice.

Some practitioners recommend the use of echinacea (pronounced ek-i-NAY-see-uh) to strengthen the immune system. Herbs believed to kill viruses, such as usnea (pronounced US-nee-uh), have also been suggested. Homeopathic remedies are recommended based on the patient's symptoms. Some people may get relief by placing cold compresses (pads) on the throat.

PROGNOSIS

Prognosis for laryngitis is excellent. Recovery is complete and usually occurs within a week.

PREVENTION

Most people get at least one cold or other upper respiratory tract infection a year. About the only way to avoid these infections is to wash one's hands well and often and to avoid contact with people who have colds. The same rules hold true for laryngitis. By avoiding colds and similar infections, the chances of developing laryngitis are greatly reduced.

FOR MORE INFORMATION

Books

Stoffman, Phyllis. *The Family Guide to Preventing and Treating 100 Infectious Diseases.* New York: John Wiley & Sons, 1995.

Organizations

American Academy of Otolaryngology-Head and Neck Surgery, Inc. One Prince Street, Alexandria, VA 22314-3357. (703) 836-444.

LEAD POISONING

DEFINITION

Lead poisoning occurs when a person swallows lead or breathes in its fumes. The result can be damage to the brain, nerves, and many other parts of the body. Acute lead poisoning occurs when a person takes in a large amount of lead over a short period of time. Acute lead poisoning is rare. Chronic lead poisoning occurs when small amounts of lead are taken in over a longer period. Chronic lead poisoning is a common problem among children.

DESCRIPTION

Lead can damage almost every system in the body. It can also cause hypertension (high blood pressure; see hypertension entry). Lead poisoning is especially harmful to fetuses and young children because it damages body systems that are still developing.

The seriousness of lead damage depends on two factors: the amount of lead that gets into the body and the length of time it remains there. Over the long term, lead poisoning in children can lead to learning disabilities (see learning disorders entry), behavior problems, and mental retardation (see mental retardation entry). At very high levels, lead poisoning can cause seizures, coma, and even death.

The U.S. Agency for Toxic Substances and Disease Registry estimates that one out of every six children in the United States has a high level of lead in his or her blood. One of the most common sources of lead is paint used on walls in homes. At one time, most paint contained lead. As paint gets older, it tends to peel off the walls. Because young children are inclined to put things into their mouths, they often eat these chips of paint. This problem will be less serious in the future—house paints are no longer permitted to contain lead, but old lead paint is still present in many homes.

Another common source of lead is gasoline fumes in the air. Lead compounds were once added to gasoline to make it burn more efficiently. The lead escaped into the air when the gasoline was burned. People inhaled the lead, and it got into their bloodstreams. Today, lead compounds can no longer be used in gasoline.

WORDS TO KNOW

Chelation therapy: Treatment with chemicals that bind to a poisonous metal and help the body quickly eliminate it.

Dimercaprol (BAL): A chemical agent used in chelation therapy.

Edetate calcium disodium (EDTA calcium): A chemical agent used in chelation therapy.

Succimer (Chemet): A chemical agent used to remove excess lead from the body.

Lead also gets into people's bodies through water pipes. Water pipes were once made of lead. As water passed through the pipes, it picked up small amounts of lead. When people drank that water, the lead got into their bodies. Plumbers now use copper or plastic tubing rather than lead pipes to prevent this problem.

CAUSES

Lead was once widely used in paints, gasoline, water pipes, and other products. Scientists did not realize how dangerous lead was to the human body. Since finding out how harmful lead can be, governments have banned the use of lead in most products. Some sources still pose a problem, however. These include:

- Lead-based paints. Paints in older homes are still the most common source of exposure to lead among preschool children.
- Dust and soil. Lead from gasoline fumes and from factory smokestacks eventually settles out of the air and becomes part of the soil. When people handle the soil or eat foods grown in it, they may absorb lead into their bodies.
- Drinking water. The pipes used in homes built before 1930 were usually made of lead. Drinking water in older homes may therefore contain lead.
- Jobs and hobbies. Many occupations and leisure-time activities bring people into contact with lead. Such activities include making pottery or stained glass, refinishing furniture, doing home repairs, and using indoor firing ranges for gun practice.
- Foods and containers. Foods canned in the United States contain no lead, but foods imported from other countries may be shipped in cans that are sealed with lead compounds. Also, certain kinds of glassware and ceramic dishes are made with lead compounds.
- Folk medicines. Certain types of home remedies that people have used for many years contain lead. These remedies include alarcon, azarcon, bali goli, coral, greta, liga, and pay-loo-ah.

SYMPTOMS

Scientists continue to learn more about lead poisoning. One of their newest discoveries is that very low levels of lead, once thought to be harmless, can be damaging over long periods of time. Even though a child seems healthy, he or she may have enough lead in the blood to cause chronic lead poisoning. Some symptoms of chronic lead poisoning include:

- Learning disabilities (see learning disorders entry)
- Hyperactivity (very high levels of activity)
- Mental retardation (see mental retardation entry)

- Slowed growth
- Hearing loss (see hearing loss entry)
- Headaches (see headache entry)

Lead poisoning can also affect adults. Some symptoms of the disorder among adults include high blood pressure, digestive problems, nerve disorders, memory loss, and muscle and joint pain. In addition, it can lead to difficulties during pregnancy and cause reproductive problems in both women and men.

Acute Lead Poisoning

Acute lead poisoning is less common than chronic lead poisoning. People who work around lead in their jobs, for example, are at risk for taking in large amounts of lead in a short period of time. In such cases, some of the symptoms that may develop include:

- Severe abdominal (stomach) pain
- Diarrhea
- Nausea and vomiting
- Weakness of the limbs
- Seizures
- Coma

DIAGNOSIS

A medical worker may be able to diagnose lead poisoning based on the described symptoms. The only positive test for the disorder, however, is a blood test. The U.S. Centers for Disease Control and Prevention (CDC) recommends that all children be tested for lead at twelve months of age. A blood test is important because children with lead in their blood may not show any symptoms. CDC also recommends a second blood test at the age of two years. For children known to be at risk, the CDC recommends a blood test at six months. Some states require blood tests for lead at these or other ages.

Children at Risk

Children are regarded as being at risk for lead poisoning if:

- They live in or regularly visit a house built before 1978 in which chipped or peeling paint is present.
- They live in or regularly visit a house that was built before 1978 where remodeling is planned or under way.
- They have a brother or sister, housemate, or playmate who has been diagnosed with lead poisoning.
- They live with an adult whose job or hobby involves exposure to lead.
- They live near an active lead smelter (factory), battery-recycling plant, or other industry that releases lead into the environment.

Adults at Risk

Adults whose work or hobbies expose them to lead should also have regular blood tests. These activities include:

- Working with glazed pottery or stained glass
- Furniture refinishing
- Home renovation
- Target shooting at indoor firing ranges
- Battery reclamation
- Precious metal refining
- Radiator repair
- Art restorations

TREATMENT

The first step in treating lead poisoning is to avoid further contact with lead. For adults, this usually means making changes at work or in hobbies. For children, it means finding and removing sources of lead in the home. In most states, the public health department can help inspect the home and find sources of lead.

If the problem is lead paint, a professional with special training should remove it. Home owners should not try to do this job themselves. Scraping or sanding lead paint creates large amounts of dust that can poison people in the home. The dust can stay around long after the work is completed. People living in the home should leave until the cleanup has been finished by the professional.

Chelation Therapy

If blood levels of lead are high, the doctor may also prescribe chelation (pronounced kee-LAY-shun) therapy. The word "chelation" comes from the Greek word for "claw." Chemicals used in chelation therapy take hold of lead in the bloodstream, like a crab grabs an object with its claw. The lead can then be washed out of the blood.

The U.S. Food and Drug Administration (FDA) has approved three chemicals for use in chelation therapy. Edetate calcium disodium (EDTA calcium) and dimercaprol (BAL; pronounced die-muhr-KAP-rol) are usually injected with a shot. Or they can be added directly to the bloodstream with an intravenous (into the vein) line. Succimer (trade name Chemet) can be taken in pill form.

Alternative Treatment

No forms of alternative treatment have proved effective in treating lead poisoning. Increasing the amount of calcium, zinc, iron, and protein in the

Lead based paints are the most common source of exposure to lead among preschool children. (Photograph by Robert J. Huffman, Field Mark Publications. Reproduced by permission.)

diet may be of some help. They tend to reduce the amount of lead taken into the bloodstream. Some practitioners believe that nutritional, herbal, and homeopathic medicines can help the body recover from lead poisoning after the source of lead has been found and eliminated.

PROGNOSIS

If chronic lead poisoning is caught early, serious damage can be limited by reducing future exposure to lead and getting proper medical treatment. If acute lead poisoning reaches the stage of seizures and coma, there is a high risk of death. The long-term effects of lower levels of lead can also be permanent and severe.

PREVENTION

Lead poisoning can often be prevented by steps such as the following:

- Keep areas where children play as clean and dust-free as possible.
- Wash baby pacifiers and bottles when they fall on the floor. Wash toys and stuffed animals often.
- Make sure children wash their hands before meals and at bedtime.

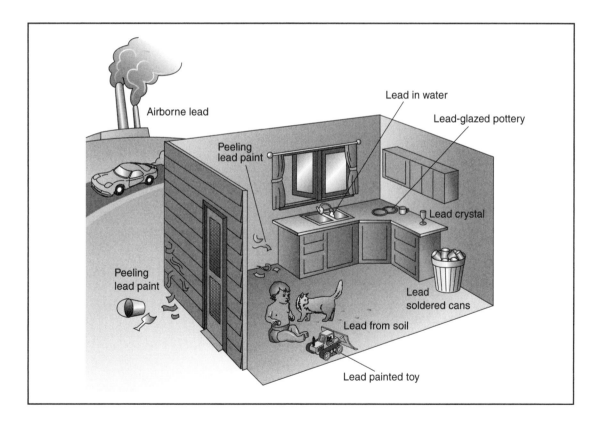

Possible sources of lead poisoning. (Reproduced by permission of Electronic Illustrators Group)

- At least twice a week, mop floors and wipe windowsills and other surfaces on which children might chew. Use a solution of powdered dishwasher detergent in warm water.
- Plant bushes next to an older home with painted exterior walls to keep children at a distance.
- Have household tap water tested to find out if it contains lead.
- Use water only from the cold-water tap for drinking, cooking, and making baby formula. Water from the hot-water tap tends to contain higher levels of lead.
- If the cold water hasn't been used for six hours or more, run it for several seconds before using it. The longer water sits in pipes, the more lead it tends to dissolve.
- If you work with lead in your job or hobby, change your clothes before you go home.
- Do not store food in open cans, especially imported cans.
- Do not store or serve food in pottery meant for decorative use.

FOR MORE INFORMATION

Books

Centers for Disease Control and Prevention. *Screening Young Children for Lead Poisoning: Guidance for State and Local Public Health Officials.* Atlanta, GA: CDC, 1997.

Kessel, Irene, and John W. Graef. *Getting the Lead Out: The Complete Resource on How to Prevent and Cope With Lead Poisoning.* New York: Plenum Press, 1997.

Stapleton, Richard M. *Lead Is a Silent Hazard.* New York: Walker & Company, 1995.

Upton, Arthur, C., and Eden Graber, eds. *Staying Healthy in a Risky Environment: The New York University Medical Center Family Guide.* New York: Simon & Schuster, 1993.

Periodicals

Krucoff, Carol. "Lead Alert." *Child* (August 1996): pp. 64–65+.

Organizations

National Center for Environmental Health. Centers for Disease Control and Prevention. Mail Stop F-29, 4770 Buford Highway NE, Atlanta, GA 30341-3724. (888) 232-6789. http://www.cdc.gov/nceh/ncehhome.htm.

Office of Water Resources Center. Environmental Protection Agency. Mail Code (4100), Room 2615 East Tower Basement, 401 M St. SW, Washington, DC 20460. (800) 426-4791. http://www.epa.gov/ow/.

Web sites

"Lead Poisoning Prevention Outreach Program." *National Safety Council's Environmental Health Center.* [Online]. http://www.nsc.org/ehc/lead.htm (accessed on October 22, 1999).

LEARNING DISORDERS

DEFINITION

Learning disorders are academic problems experienced by children and adults of average to above-average intelligence. Learning disorders involve problems with reading, writing, mathematics, or a combination of these three skills. These difficulties can interfere with a person's ability to do schoolwork, as well as his or her daily activities. Learning disorders are also referred to as learning disabilities.

DESCRIPTION

Learning disorders affect about two million children between the ages of six and seventeen, or about one out of every twenty schoolchildren. These children have problems learning new information, remembering that information, and knowing how to use the information. The three main types of learning disorders are reading disorders, mathematics disorders, and writing disorders.

Reading Disorders

Reading disorders are the most common type of learning disorder. Children with reading disorders have difficulty recognizing letters and words and remembering what they mean. They also have trouble understanding the sounds and letter groups that make up words. Because of these problems, children with reading disorders often cannot understand materials they read.

Mathematics Disorders

Children with mathematics disorders often have problems recognizing numbers. For example, they may not remember how to use numbers in counting. They have trouble understanding how numbers can apply to everyday situations. Mathematics disorders are often diagnosed in the first few years of elementary school. It is during this period that children first begin to learn mathematical concepts such as addition and subtraction. Children with mathematics disorders often have reading and writing disorders as well.

Writing Disorders

Children with writing disorders have problems with the basic skills of writing such as spelling, punctuation, and grammar. They often have one other type of learning disorder as well—either a reading disorder or a mathematics disorder.

CAUSES

The brain is divided into various sections that control different behaviors. Some parts of the brain control the ability to speak; others, the ability to understand the spoken word or to recognize what words and numbers mean. In people with learning disorders, one or more of these sections may not function normally.

Some learning disorders may be inherited. Children from families with a history of learning disorders are more likely to develop disorders them-

A child's performance in school may offer clues to the presence of a learning disorder. (© 1992 Kevin Beebe. Reproduced by permission of Custom Medical Stock Photo.)

selves. Learning disorders can also be caused by medical conditions. For example, a blow to the head or a brain infection can damage certain parts of the brain, leading to a learning disorder.

SYMPTOMS

A child's performance in school may offer clues to the presence of a learning disorder. Some children earn high scores on intelligence tests, suggesting that the child should do well in school, but the grades that he or she receives may be far below what those tests predict. This may be a sign of a learning disorder.

A child's schoolwork may also display symptoms of a learning disorder. A boy or girl may confuse words, switch words and letters around, or add or omit syllables from words. These symptoms suggest the presence of a reading disorder.

Symptoms of a writing disorder may often be seen in the kind of written work a student produces. The work may be filled with spelling, grammatical, punctuation, and other errors. The child's handwriting may also be poor.

Children with mathematical disorders often cannot count in the correct sequence. They may not be able to name numbers and perform mathematical operations, such as addition and subtraction.

DIAGNOSIS

The first step in diagnosing a learning disorder is a complete medical, psychological, and educational examination. The purpose of this examination is to rule out other conditions with symptoms similar to those of learning disorders. For example, a child with mental retardation (see mental retardation entry), attention-deficit/hyperactivity disorder (see attention-deficition/hyperactivity disorder entry), or an unusually poor educational background may show the symptoms of a learning disorder. These conditions are different from a learning disorder and need to be treated differently.

If no medical problems are found, the child can take a series of psychological and educational tests. Some of the tests commonly used include the Wechsler Intelligence Scale for Children, the Woodcock-Johnson Psycho-educational Battery, and the Peabody Individual Achievement Test-Revised. These tests measure the child's native intelligence as well as his or her mental achievements.

TREATMENT

Once a learning disorder has been diagnosed, an individual education plan (IEP) is developed for the child. An IEP outlines the kind of instructional program that is likely to help the child overcome his or her learning problems. It may involve special instruction within a regular classroom or assignment to a special-education class. All IEPs also provide for annual retesting to measure the child's progress.

An IEP for a child with a reading disorder may focus on helping the child recognize the sounds and meanings of letters and words. As the child progresses, instruction shifts to improving his or her ability to understand words and sentences, to remember what he or she has read, and to learn how to study more efficiently.

Students with writing disorders are often encouraged to keep a journal—a daily record of their activities. They often find it easier to express their thoughts by using a computer rather than paper and pencil. Children with mathematical disorders are often given number problems from everyday life. For example, they are taught how to balance a checkbook or compare prices on a shopping trip.

PROGNOSIS

The high school dropout rate for children with learning disorders is almost 40 percent. Many of these children are never properly diagnosed or given appropriate instruction. As a result, they never become fully literate.

THE HIGH SCHOOL DROPOUT RATE FOR CHILDREN WITH LEARNING DISORDERS IS ALMOST 40 PERCENT.

Learning disorders can also lead to other problems. Children may become frustrated and discouraged. They may not learn how to get along with other children and become aggressive and troublesome.

The prognosis is good for children who are diagnosed early in their school years. Early diagnosis allows the development of IEPs that help them overcome their disorder. Most people who receive proper educational and vocational training can complete college and find a satisfying job.

See also: Dyslexia.

FOR MORE INFORMATION

Books

Hallowell, Edward. *When You Worry about the Child You Love.* New York: Simon & Schuster, 1996.

Harris, Jacqueline L. *Learning Disorders.* New York: Twenty First Century Books, 1995.

Osman, Betty B. *Learning Disabilities and ADHD: A Family Guide to Living and Learning Together.* New York: John Wiley & Sons, 1997.

Organizations

National Center for Learning Disabilities (NCLD). 381 Park Avenue South, Suite 1401, New York, NY 10016. (212) 545-7510; (888) 575–7373. http://www.ncld.org.

Learning Disabilities Association of America (LDA). 4156 Library Road, Pittsburgh, PA 15234-1349. (412) 341-1515. http://www.ldanatl.org.

The National Institute for Literacy. 1775I Street, Suite 730, Washington, DC 20006. (800) 228-8813. http://www.nifl.gov.

Web sites

"LD Online: Learning Disabilities Information and Resources." [Online] *The Interactive Guide to Learning Disabilities for Parents, Teachers, and Children.* http://www.ldonline.org (accessed on October 22, 1999).

LEUKEMIA

DEFINITION

Leukemia (pronounced loo-KEE-mee-uh) is a form of cancer (see cancer entry) in which the body produces too many white blood cells. Many forms of leukemia have been identified. They are divided into two general types: acute and chronic. An acute condition comes on fairly quickly. A chronic disorder develops more slowly over time.

DESCRIPTION

Blood contains three types of cells: red blood cells, white blood cells, and platelets (pronounced PLATE-lits). Each type of cell has a special function in the body. Red blood cells carry oxygen from the lungs to the rest of the body. White blood cells fight invading organisms, such as bacteria and viruses. Platelets are involved in the process of blood clotting.

All blood cells form in the soft tissue that fills the center of bones. This tissue is called bone marrow. All three types of blood cells arise out of a primitive type of cell known as a stem cell. A stem cell can develop into a red blood cell, a white blood cell, or a platelet, depending on conditions.

leukemia

Leukemia is caused by the overproduction of white blood cells. This has two effects on the body. First, the white blood cells may not mature properly as they develop. They may lack the ability to kill foreign bodies in the bloodstream. This defect seriously damages the immune system and the body loses its ability to fight off infections.

Second, so many white blood cells may form that they pack the bone marrow until there is not enough room for red blood cells and platelets to develop. Without red blood cells, the body's cells do not get enough oxygen, and the condition known as anemia (see anemias entry) develops. Anemia is characterized by general weakness, headache, pale skin, and dizziness. It can become a life-threatening disorder. Without platelets, blood cannot clot properly and simple injuries can lead to serious blood loss.

There are three types of white blood cells. Each has a special role to play in the immune system. The three types are granulocytes (pronounced GRAN-yuh-lo-site), lymphocytes (pronounced LIM-fuh-sites), and monocytes (pronounced MON-uh-sites). Leukemia may result in the overproduction of any one type of white blood cell. Each type of leukemia is named for two characteristics:

- Whether it is acute or chronic
- Whether it affects granulocytes, lymphocytes, or monocytes

For example, one form of leukemia develops very slowly. It results in the overproduction of granulocytes. That form of leukemia is called chronic granulocytic leukemia. The same disease is also known by another name, chronic myelogenous (pronounced my-uh-LAJ-uh-nuhs) leukemia.

WORDS TO KNOW

Acute: A condition that comes on fairly quickly.

Bone marrow: Soft, spongy material found in the center of bones.

Bone marrow biopsy: A procedure by which a sample of bone marrow is removed and studied under a microscope.

Bone marrow transplantation: A procedure in which healthy bone marrow is injected into a leukemia patient's bones.

Chronic: A condition that develops slowly and lasts a long time or is reoccuring.

Immune system: A network of organs, tissues, cells, and chemicals designed to fight off foreign invaders, such as bacteria and viruses.

Lumbar puncture: A procedure in which a thin needle is inserted into the space between vertebrae in the spine and a sample of cerebrospinal fluid is withdrawn for study under a microscope.

Platelets: Blood cells that assist in the process of blood clotting.

Red blood cells: Blood cells that carry oxygen from the lungs to the rest of the body.

Stem cells: Immature blood cells formed in bone marrow.

White blood cells: Blood cells that fight invading organisms, such as bacteria and viruses.

Another form of leukemia occurs rapidly. It results in the overproduction of lymphocytes. That form of leukemia is called acute lymphocytic leukemia.

Leukemias account for about 2 percent of all cancers. It is the most common form of cancer among children. For that reason, leukemia is sometimes called a disease of childhood. However, leukemias affect nine times as many adults as children. Half of all cases of the disease occur in people over sixty. The incidence of acute and chronic leukemias is about the same.

CAUSES

No one knows what causes leukemia. Researchers have strong suspicions about four possible causes, however. They are radiation, chemicals, viruses, and genetic factors.

- **Radiation.** The term "radiation" refers to various forms of energy, such as X rays and ultraviolet (UV) light found in sunlight. Radiation can tear chemicals apart, thus damaging or destroying cells. Some researchers believe that exposure to radiation can cause some forms of leukemia.
- **Chemicals.** Some types of chemicals are known to be carcinogens (pronounced car-SIN-o-genz). A carcinogen is anything that can cause cancer. Chemicals can cause cancer by damaging cells and the substances within them.
- **Viruses.** Some researchers believe that some types of leukemia are viral infections. A virus is a very small organism that can cause a disease. The link between viruses and leukemia is strong in some cases, but it has not been proved.
- **Genetics.** Leukemia tends to occur in some families more commonly than in others. This suggests that at least some forms of leukemia may be hereditary.

SYMPTOMS

The symptoms of leukemia are generally vague. A patient may experience all or some of the following symptoms:

- Weakness or chronic fatigue
- Fever of unknown origin
- Unexplained weight loss
- Frequent bacterial or viral infections

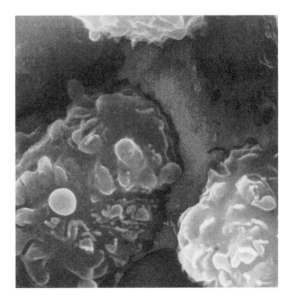

Acute myelogenous leukemia cancer cells. (Photograph by Robert Becker. Reproduced by permission of Custom Medical Stock Photo.)

- Headaches
- Skin rash
- Bone pain with no known cause
- Easy bruising
- Bleeding from gums and nose
- Blood in urine or stools
- Enlarged lymph nodes and/or spleen
- Fullness in the stomach

DIAGNOSIS

The first step in diagnosing leukemia occurs when a patient sees a doctor for one or more of the described symptoms. The doctor must then try to find the cause of these symptoms. The doctor first performs tests to rule out other medical conditions.

The first specific test for leukemia is likely to be a blood test. A blood test shows the relative amounts of red and white blood cells. An unusually large number of white blood cells might suggest the possibility of leukemia.

A more specific test is a bone marrow biopsy. A bone marrow biopsy is conducted with a long, thin needle that is inserted into the marrow of a bone. A bone in the hip or chest is usually chosen for this procedure. A sample of

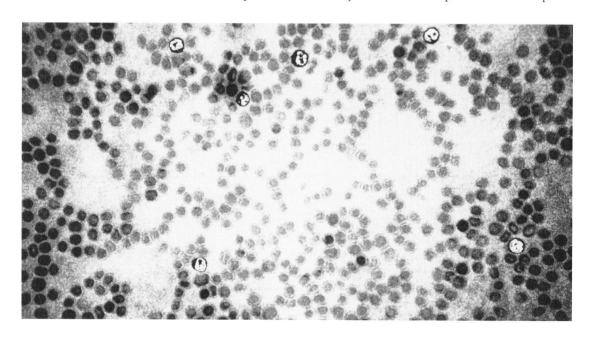

Chronic lymphocytic leukemia cells magnified 400 times. (© 1999. Reproduced by permission of Custom Medical Stock Photo.)

the bone marrow is removed and studied under a microscope. The presence of abnormal blood cells is the basis for diagnosing leukemia.

If there is still doubt, an additional test may be performed. This test is a lumbar puncture (spinal tap). In a lumbar puncture, a thin needle is inserted into the space between vertebrae in the patient's spine. A sample of cerebrospinal fluid is withdrawn. Cerebrospinal fluid is a liquid that surrounds the tissues in the brain and spine. The presence of abnormal blood cells indicates that the patient has leukemia.

TREATMENT

Treatment of leukemia takes place in two steps. The goal of the first step is to bring the disease into remission. Remission means two things. First, no symptoms of the disease remain. Second, no abnormal white blood cells can be found in bone marrow. Two forms of treatment are used in this first step: chemotherapy and radiation.

Chemotherapy involves the use of certain chemicals that can kill cancer cells. These chemicals may be given orally (by mouth) or intravenously (through a vein in the arm).

Radiation involves the use of high-energy rays, such as X rays, to kill cancer cells. A common source of radiation used to treat leukemia is the radioactive element cobalt 60. A radioactive element is an element that gives off high-energy radiation. A patient is placed on a table beneath a small piece of cobalt 60 contained in a large machine. The energy given off by the cobalt 60 is aimed at the patient's body. It kills cancer cells and may lead to remission.

THE NATIONAL BONE MARROW DONOR REGISTRY

Bone marrow transplantation (BMT) works only under very special circumstances. Specifically, bone marrow from a donor and a patient must match very closely. Usually this means the donor must be related to the patient, but not always. Sometimes non-relatives will also have very close matches. The question is how to find those non-relatives.

The task is not as easy as making a public announcement on the radio or television or in the newspaper. Experts estimate that the chance of the bone marrow of two unrelated people matching is somewhere between 1 in 10,000 to 1 in 20,000. How can doctors find that very rare person who can donate bone marrow to a patient?

Until the 1980s, there was no good answer to that question. Then, bone marrow transplant registries started springing up around the world. A bone marrow transplant registry is an office that keeps records of people's bone marrow types. In the United States, the National Bone Marrow Donor Registry (NBMDR) was created in 1986. People who wish to be considered as bone marrow donors must have a blood test. The results of that test are recorded at the NBMDR. When a leukemia patient needs a BMT, records are searched at the NBMDR. With luck, a good match is found and a bone marrow transplant can be conducted.

Once remission has been achieved, treatment moves to the second step. The goal of this step is to treat the patient's bone marrow. Unless the bone marrow is changed, it will continue to produce abnormal white blood cells and the leukemia will eventually return.

The usual method for treating bone marrow is with a bone marrow transplantation. In a bone marrow transplantation, healthy bone marrow is injected into the patient's bones. If the transplantation is successful, the new bone marrow will start producing normal blood cells and the basic cause of leukemia will have been corrected.

Bone marrow transplantation is a difficult procedure. The bone marrow injected into a patient must be very similar to his or her own bone marrow. For this reason, close relatives may be the only people who can donate bone marrow for the procedure.

If foreign bone marrow is used for transplantation, the patient's immune system will attack it as if the transplanted bone marrow is a bacterium, virus, or some other disease-causing organism. In the process, the patient's immune system may start to kill off the cells in his or her body. There are drugs that can prevent this type of immune system reaction, but the drugs are quite dangerous and have serious side effects.

Alternative Treatment

Many alternative treatments are available that may prove helpful in combating the side effects of traditional cancer therapies. These alternatives, however, should not replace prescribed cancer treatments; rather, they are suggested to work in conjunction with conventional treatment.

Body work therapy such as acupuncture (Chinese therapy involving the use of fine needles), acupressure (Chinese therapy that involves applying pressure to certain points in the body), reflexology, and massage may help calm the patient and reduce stress. Relaxation techniques such as yoga and meditation may relieve nausea and discomfort. An exercise program, designed in consultation with a physician, may help promote physical and mental strength. A well-balanced diet high in fresh fruits and vegetables and whole grains and low in fats, sugar, and alcohol is suggested for overall well-being.

MEDICAL PROGRESS HAS GREATLY IMPROVED THE PROGNOSIS FOR LEUKEMIA. MORE AND MORE PATIENTS FACE THE POSSIBILITY NOT ONLY OF REMISSION BUT ALSO A CURE.

PROGNOSIS

The prognosis for various forms of leukemia varies widely. Three important factors are the patient's age and general health, and the time since diagnosis. That is, younger patients who are otherwise in good health have the best chance for survival if their leukemia is diagnosed early.

Prognosis also varies depending on the form of leukemia. In general, patients with chronic forms of the disease tend to live longer than those with acute forms. The average survival rate for patients with chronic leukemia is about nine years. By contrast, only about half of all patients with acute myelogenous leukemia survive five years. For acute lymphocytic leukemia, the survival rate is even less.

Medical progress has greatly improved the prognosis for leukemia over the past thirty years. Surgeons are becoming much more proficient at bone marrow transplantations. As a result, more and more patients face the possibility not only of remission but also a cure.

PREVENTION

Until the cause or causes of leukemia are found, there is no way to prevent the disease.

FOR MORE INFORMATION

Books

Dollinger, Malin. *Everyone's Guide to Cancer Therapy.* Toronto: Somerville House Books, Ltd., 1994.

Murphy, Gerald P. *Informed Decisions: The Complete Book of Cancer Diagnosis, Treatment and Recovery.* Atlanta, GA: American Cancer Society, 1997.

Siegel, Dorothy Schainman, and David E. Newton. *Leukemia.* New York: Franklin Watts, 1994.

Organizations

American Cancer Society. 1599 Clifton Road NE, Atlanta, GA 30329. (800) 227–2345. http://www.cancer.org.

Cancer Care, Inc. 1180 Avenue of the Americas. New York, NY 10036. (800) 813–HOPE. http://www.cancercareinc.org.

Cancer Research Institute. 681 Fifth Avenue, New York, NY 10022. (800) 992–2623. http://www.cancerresearch.org.

Leukemia Society of America, Inc. 600 Third Avenue, New York, NY 10016. (800) 955-4572. http://www.leukemia.org.

National Cancer Institute. 31 Center Drive, Bethesda, MD 20892–2580. (800) 4–CANCER. http://www.nci.nih.gov.

Web sites

Oncolink. [Online] University of Pennsylvania Cancer Center. http://cancer.med.upenn.edu (accessed on October 13, 1999).

LICE

DEFINITION

Lice are small, insect-like parasites. Parasites are animals that live off other animals. Lice live on the human body, most commonly on the skin, hair, and genital area. They feed on human blood and lay their eggs on body hair and in clothing. The word "lice" is plural for the word "louse."

DESCRIPTION

Lice do not cause dangerous infections. However, they may carry organisms that cause more serious diseases, such as trench fever and typhus. Lice tend to be a problem primarily in overcrowded areas or areas that have inadequate facilities for bathing and laundry. They are often a problem among the homeless or in military or refugee camps. All humans are equally at risk to attack by lice, but elderly people are more prone to develop complications from lice attacks.

WORDS TO KNOW

Crabs: A slang term for pubic lice.

Infestation: A situation in which large numbers of organisms come together in a single area.

Lindane: A chemical used in the treatment of lice infestations.

Malathion: An insecticide that is sometimes used in the treatment of clothing and bedding belonging to people who have lice.

Nits: The eggs produced by head or pubic lice.

Permethrin: A medication used to treat head lice.

CAUSES

The three common types of lice infestation are head lice, body lice, and pubic lice. Head lice can be transmitted by sharing hats, combs, or hairbrushes. Epidemics of head lice are very common among school-age children. An epidemic is the rapid spread of a disease across a wide geographical area. Head lice do not cause typhus or other serious diseases.

The head louse is about .06 inches (.15 centimeters) in length and can usually be seen by examining the patient's scalp. The louse reproduces by laying eggs, which are attached to the base of hairs close to the scalp. Nits (a name for the eggs and young lice) hatch in three to fourteen days. After they hatch, they must feed on blood within a day. If they do not, they die. Head lice may spread to the eyebrows, eyelashes, and facial hair in adults. They are usually isolated to the scalp in children.

Body lice are about the same size as head lice, but are more difficult to see. They tend to spend their lives in clothing, only coming to the skin to feed. People who wear the same clothes day after day are at risk for lice infestations. The lice spread easily from person to person through close personal contact or sharing of bedding.

Pubic lice, also known as crabs, tend to infest the genital area. However, they may also spread to other parts of the body. Individuals contract pubic lice through intimate contact or by sharing bedding, towels, or clothing.

THE HEAD LOUSE IS ABOUT .06 INCHES IN LENGTH AND CAN USUALLY BE SEEN BY EXAMINING THE PATIENT'S SCALP. THE LOUSE REPRODUCES BY LAYING EGGS, WHICH ARE ATTACHED TO THE BASE OF HAIRS CLOSE TO THE SCALP.

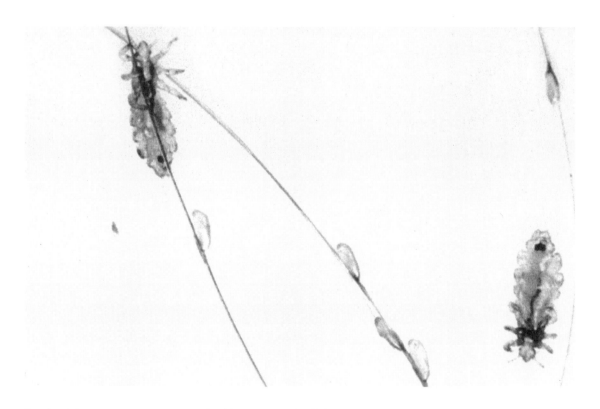

Two head lice and nits (eggs) on strands of human hair. (© 1990 David, National Medical. Reproduced by permission of Custom Medical Stock Photo.)

SYMPTOMS

The most common symptom of a lice infestation is intense itching. The itching is caused by a toxin (poison) present in the saliva of lice. Repeated bites can lead to severe inflammation of the skin. Scratching lice bites can often cause injury to the skin. Other symptoms of lice infestation depend on the body part in which the lice occur.

Head lice often produce intense itching. A patient may actually scratch the skin open. When that happens, a bacterial infection may develop. An attack of head lice often causes swelling of the neck glands as well.

Body lice also cause intense itching. Their bites may first appear as small, red pimples. Eventually, the pimples develop into a rash that covers the skin. If body lice are not treated, complications may develop, including headaches, fever, and bacterial infections.

Pubic lice may be difficult to see, but scratches made by an itching patient are usually easily visible. Small dark-brown specks on a person's underwear are also a sign of pubic lice. The specks are matter excreted by the lice. Less commonly, pubic lice may cause the formation of small bluish spots on the patient's body, especially the thighs.

DIAGNOSIS

Doctors can often easily diagnose lice with a visual examination. The lice are large enough to be seen with the naked eye or through a magnifying glass. Brown specks on the patient's underwear are another sign of lice. The patient may also have bruised skin where he or she has been scratching. Lice nits are also easy to see. They can be found at the base of hairs near the skin.

Final diagnosis may involve ruling out other medical problems. For example, ordinary dandruff sometimes looks like an infestation of head lice. Scabies also resembles body lice. Scabies is a skin condition caused by tiny organisms called skin mites. Differences among diseases can usually be detected with a microscope. Blood and other laboratory tests are not useful in making these distinctions.

TREATMENT

Treatment for lice involves two steps. First, a chemical is used to kill the adult lice. Two common products used for this are lindane (trade name Kwell) and permethrin (trade name Nix). Both products are strong chemicals and care must be used in applying them to the hair or skin.

The second step in treatment is removing nits. If left in place, the nits may survive and mature to become young lice. The easiest way to remove nits is with a fine-tooth comb or tweezers. In most cases, a single treatment destroys all lice and nits. If necessary, a second treatment can be applied a week later.

Treatment also involves washing the patient's clothing and bedding in hot water. These objects should then be ironed with a hot iron. Clothing and bedding can also be treated with an insecticide, such as malathion powder.

Alternative Treatment

Some practitioners of holistic medicine believe that lice can be treated with a mixture of oil of pennyroyal, garlic, and distilled water. The mixture is applied once a day for three days.

PROGNOSIS

In the vast majority of cases, there are no serious long-term effects from a lice infestation. The patient recovers completely with no bodily damage. In rare cases, patients may develop complications, such as typhus or trench fever.

PREVENTION

There are no vaccines or skin treatments to protect a person against lice. The most people can do is follow a few simple rules to reduce the risk of contracting (getting) lice. These rules include:

- Teaching school-age children the basics of good hygiene. This includes the importance of not lending or borrowing combs, brushes, or hats.
- Notifying and treating the sexual partners of adults who have pubic lice.
- Checking homeless people, elderly patients who are unable to care for themselves, and other high-risk individuals before they are admitted to a hospital. In this way, other patients in the hospital may be protected from lice.

FOR MORE INFORMATION

Books

Bakalar, Nick. *Wiping Out Head Lice.* New York: Signet, 1997.

Copeland, Lennie. *The Lice-Buster Book: What to Do When Your Child Comes Home With Head Lice!* New York: Warner Books, 1996.

Lassieur, Allison. *Head Lice.* New York: Franklin Watts, 2000.

LUNG CANCER

DEFINITION

Lung cancer is a disease in which the cells of lung tissues grow uncontrollably and form tumors. A tumor is a mass or lump of tissue made of abnormal cells.

DESCRIPTION

Lung cancer is the leading cause of death from cancer among both men and women in the United States. Experts estimate that 28 percent of all cancer deaths—about 160,000—are caused by lung cancer. It is further estimated that at least 172,000 new cases of lung cancer are diagnosed each year.

Lung cancer is rare among children and young adults. It is usually found in people older than fifty. The average age at diagnosis is sixty. There are two kinds of lung cancer, primary and secondary. Primary lung cancer starts in the lungs. Secondary lung cancer starts somewhere else in the body; cancer cells then spread to the lungs and start a new infection. When cancer cells travel from one area of the body to another it is called metastasis (pronounced muh-TASS-tuh-siss). When this happens, a cancer is said to have metastasized (pronounced muh-TASS-tuh-sized).

CAUSES

By far the major cause of lung cancer is tobacco smoking. Ninety percent of all cases of lung cancer are thought to be caused by smoking. Other factors that may lead to lung cancer include:

- Exposure to asbestos and toxic chemicals. Asbestos is a naturally occurring mineral that was once used widely in many applications. For example, home and office insulation was once made of asbestos. Scientists now know that asbestos fibers can cause lung cancer. Studies show that people who work with asbestos are seven times more likely to die of lung cancer. A variety of other chemicals can also cause lung cancer, including arsenic, compounds of chromium and nickel, mustard gas, vinyl chloride, and emissions from coke ovens.
- Radon gas. Radon is a gas given off by radioactive materials. A radioactive material is a substance that gives off radiation and turns into a new substance. Radon gas is often formed in rocks that contain radioactive materials. It escapes from those rocks and gets into the air. It is often found in the basements of homes, office buildings, and factories built over such rocks.

A person who smokes and is exposed to radon gas has the highest risk for lung cancer.

- Lung disorders. The lungs can be damaged by a variety of diseases and disorders. Among these are tuberculosis (see tuberculosis entry), pneumonia (see pneumonia entry), silicosis (pronounced sil-i-KO-siss), and berylliosis (pronounced buh-ril-ee-O-suhs). The last two diseases are caused by inhaling certain minerals. These diseases and disorders can scar lung tissue. Such scarring may later develop into tumors.
- Family history. People with relatives who have had lung cancer are at slightly higher risk for contracting (getting) lung cancer.

SYMPTOMS

The most common symptoms of lung cancer include:

- A cough that does not go away
- Chest pain
- Shortness of breath
- Persistent hoarseness
- Swelling of the neck and face
- Significant weight loss that cannot be explained by other factors
- Fatigue and loss of appetite
- Bloody or brown-colored sputum
- Unexplained fever
- Recurrent lung infections, such as bronchitis (see bronchitis entry) or pneumonia

DIAGNOSIS

The first step in diagnosing lung cancer is a medical history and a physical examination. An important part of the medical history involves questions about smoking. A patient who smokes is at high risk for lung cancer.

The primary purpose of the physical examination is to rule out other disorders with similar symptoms. For example, many respiratory problems can cause hoarseness and coughing. The doctor needs to be certain that none of these problems is responsible for the patient's symptoms.

WORDS TO KNOW

Berylliosis: A disease of the lungs caused by inhaling small particles of the element beryllium.

Biopsy: A procedure in which a small sample of tissue is removed and then studied under a microscope.

Chemotherapy: A method of treating cancer using certain chemicals that can kill cancer cells.

Metastasis: The process by which cancer cells travel from one area of the body to another.

Primary lung cancer: Cancer that starts in the lungs.

Radiation therapy: The use of high-energy radiation to treat cancer.

Radon: A radioactive gas that occurs naturally and is often found in the lower levels of buildings.

Secondary lung cancer: Cancer that starts somewhere else in the body and then spreads to the lungs.

Silicosis: A disease of the lungs caused by inhaling fine particles of sand.

Sputum: Material that is coughed up from the passageways of the lungs.

Tumor: A mass or lump of tissue made of abnormal cells.

Imaging techniques may also be used. A chest X ray may show the presence of unusual masses in the lungs. A computed tomography (CT) scan or magnetic resonance imaging (MRI) test may provide further information about the size, shape, and location of any tumors.

Sputum analysis may be ordered to study materials coughed up by the patient. This test can detect at least 30 percent of all lung cancers. An important feature of a sputum test is that it can detect cancer in its earliest stages.

The most conclusive test for lung cancer is a lung biopsy. A biopsy is a procedure in which a small sample of tissue is removed. The sample is then studied under a microscope. Cancer cells can be identified under a microscope because of their distinctive appearance.

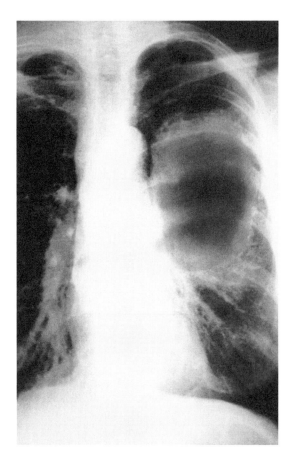

X ray showing cancer in the left lung (right side of image). (Reproduced by permission of Custom Medical Stock Photo)

TREATMENT

Treatment of lung cancer depends on the type of cancer, its location, and its stage of development. The patient's age, general health, and medical history are also taken into account. The three most common forms of treatment are surgery, radiation, and chemotherapy.

Some types of lung cancer cannot be treated surgically. For example, surgery is not an option if the cancer has already metastasized. The type of surgery performed depends on how far the cancer has spread. If it is still limited to one area of the lung, only that area is removed. In many cases, however, the cancer has already spread to other parts of the lung. The next most aggressive step is to remove one lobe of the lung. The right lung has three lobes, and the left lung has two. The lungs can continue to function if one lobe is removed. The most drastic surgery involves the removal of the whole lung, followed by a lung transplantation. This procedure is used only when cancer has spread throughout the entire lung.

Radiation is also used to treat lung cancer. Radiation involves the use of high-energy rays to kill cancer cells. In most cases, the radiation comes from radioactive materials. Radioactive materials are substances that give off high-energy radiation, similar to X rays. The radiation can be given either externally or internally. If it is given externally, the radioactive source is placed above the patient's body in the area of the cancer. Radiation from the source penetrates the body and destroys cancer cells. Radiation can also be given internally by implanting the source directly in the patient's body.

Radiation can also be used prior to surgery. In this case, the purpose of the radiation treatment is to shrink the tumor. Radiation may also be given following surgery. The purpose in this case is to destroy any cancer cells that may remain after the surgery.

Chemotherapy is the use of chemicals that kill cancer cells. These chemicals can be given either orally (by mouth) or intravenously (into the bloodstream). Chemotherapy is often used when cancer has spread beyond the lungs. The chemicals spread throughout the patient's body and attack cancer cells wherever they occur. As with radiation, chemotherapy may be given either before or after surgery.

Both radiation and chemotherapy have a number of unpleasant side effects. Radiation may cause tiredness, skin rashes, upset stomach, diarrhea, sore throat, difficulty swallowing, and loss of hair. Chemotherapy also causes nausea, vomiting, hair loss, anemia (general weakness due to low blood count; see anemias entry), and weakening of the immune system.

Alternative Treatment

Many alternative treatments are available that may prove helpful in combating the side effects of traditional cancer therapies. These alternatives, however, should not replace prescribed cancer treatments; rather, they are suggested to work in conjunction with conventional treatment.

Body work therapy such as acupuncture (Chinese therapy involving the use of fine needles), acupressure (Chinese therapy that involves applying pressure to certain points in the body), reflexology, and massage may help calm the patient and reduce stress. Relaxation techniques such as yoga and meditation may relieve nausea and discomfort. An exercise program, designed in consultation with a physician, may help promote better breathing and stronger chest muscles. A well-balanced diet high in fresh fruits and vegetables and whole grains and low in fats, sugar, and alcohol is suggested for overall well-being.

PROGNOSIS

The prognosis for lung cancer depends very much on how early the condition is discovered. If it is treated in its earliest stages, about half of all patients survive at least five years after initial diagnosis. The problem is that only 15 percent of lung cancers are found in an early stage. Overall, the five-year survival rate for all forms of lung cancer is 14 percent.

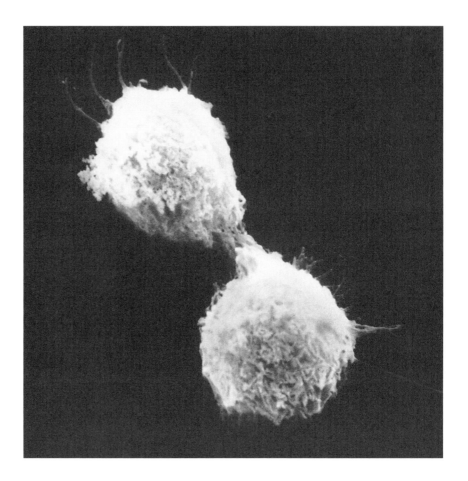

A magnified image of lung cancer cells. (© J.L. Carson. Reproduced by permission of Custom Medical Stock Photo.)

PREVENTION

In the vast majority of cases, lung cancer is relatively easy to prevent. People who do not smoke or who stop smoking are at very low risk for contracting the disease. Some authorities suspect that secondhand smoke may also pose a threat for lung cancer. Secondhand smoke is smoke that a person breathes in from another person's cigarette, cigar, or pipe.

Other ways to prevent lung cancer are to avoid contact with chemicals that can cause the disease (such as asbestos) and to have one's home checked for radon gas. Home test kits for radon are available. They are easy to use and can tell in a matter of minutes whether radon is present in a building.

FOR MORE INFORMATION

Books

Morra, Marion E., and Eve Potts. *Choices*. New York: Avon Books, 1994.

Organizations

American Cancer Society. 1599 Clifton Road NE, Atlanta, GA 30329. (800) 227–2345. http://www.cancer.org.

American Lung Association. 1740 Broadway, New York, NY 10019-4374. (800) 586-4872. http://www.lungusa.org.

Cancer Care, Inc. 1180 Avenue of the Americas. New York, NY 10036. (800) 813–HOPE. http://www.cancercareinc.org.

Cancer Research Institute. 681 Fifth Avenue, New York, NY 10022. (800) 992–2623. http://www.cancerresearch.org.

National Cancer Institute. 31 Center Drive, Bethesda, MD 20892–2580. (800) 4–CANCER. http://www.nci.nih.gov.

National Coalition for Cancer Survivorship. 1010 Wayne Avenue, 5th Floor, Silver Springs, MD 20910. (301) 650–8868.

Web sites

Oncolink. [Online] University of Pennsylvania Cancer Center. http://cancer.med.upenn.edu (accessed on October 13, 1999).

LUPUS

DEFINITION

Lupus is a disease in which a person's immune system attacks the body's own organs and tissues (see autoimmune disorders entry). The complete medical name for lupus is systemic lupus erythematosus (SLE; pronounced LOO-puhs er-uh-THEM-uh-tuhs).

DESCRIPTION

The immune system is a network of cells and tissues that protect the body against foreign organisms, such as bacteria and viruses. One mechanism used by the immune system is the release of antibodies. Antibodies are molecules that attack and destroy foreign organisms. For each type of organism, the immune system produces a special kind of antibody.

In a patient who has lupus, the immune system functions incorrectly. It thinks that the body's own cells are foreign organisms and releases antibodies to attack these cells the way it would attack bacteria and viruses. This causes tissues to become inflamed (red and swollen). They may even be killed by the attacking antibodies.

Lupus occurs in both males and females of all ages, but it is much more common in women. About 90 percent of all lupus cases occur in women. The majority of these women are of childbearing age. African Americans are more likely to develop lupus than Caucasians (whites).

CAUSES

The cause of lupus is unknown. Some researchers think that heredity may be a factor. Environmental factors also may be involved. In some cases, the symptoms of lupus become worse after exposure to sunlight, alfalfa sprouts, and certain medications. On rare occasions, a form of lupus can be caused by medications. Some drugs used to treat heart problems are among these medications. The lupus usually disappears when the person stops taking the drug.

SYMPTOMS

The symptoms of lupus vary in seriousness. Sometimes they are quite mild, and sometimes they are quite severe. Typical symptoms include fever, fatigue, muscle pain, decreased appetite, and weight loss. The spleen and lymph nodes are often swollen. Other areas that may be affected by lupus include:

- **Joints.** Joint pain and disorders, such as arthritis (see arthritis entry), are common. About 90 percent of all lupus patients have such problems.
- **Skin.** Lupus may cause skin rashes on any part of the body. They usually occur on the face, scalp, chest, ears, back, arms, and legs. When they occur in the mouth, they form ulcers (open sores). Hair loss is common.
- **Lungs.** Lupus may cause inflammation of the pleura, the tissue that lines the lungs. The patient may experience coughing and shortness of breath.
- **Heart and circulatory system.** Lupus may cause inflammation of the tissue surrounding the heart (pericarditis; pronounced per-i-kar-DIE-tiss) or of the heart itself (myocarditis; pronounced my-o-kar-DIE-tiss). When this happens, various heart problems may develop,

WORDS TO KNOW

Autoimmune disorder: A condition in which a person's immune system mistakes the body's own tissues for foreign invaders and begins to make antibodies against them.

Immune system: A network of cells and tissues that work together to protect the body against foreign invaders, such as bacteria and viruses.

Psychosis: Extremely disordered thinking accompanied by a poor sense of reality.

such as an irregular heartbeat (arrhythmia; pronounced uh-RITH-mee-uh), heart failure, and even sudden death. Blood clots often form in the blood vessels. These blood clots can break loose and cause a stroke (see stroke entry) or other complications.

- **Nervous system.** Headaches, seizures, personality changes, and psychosis (confused thinking) may occur.
- **Kidneys.** During a lupus attack, the body's kidney cells may begin to die. When this happens, the kidney can no longer filter blood. Toxins (poisons) may build up in the kidney, causing it to stop functioning.
- **Gastrointestinal (digestive) system.** Patients may experience nausea, vomiting, diarrhea, and abdominal (stomach) pain. The lining of the stomach may also become inflamed.
- **Eyes.** The eyes may become red, sore, and dry. Inflammation of nerves in the eye may cause vision problems and blindness.

DIAGNOSIS

Lupus is usually difficult to diagnose, especially since many of its symptoms are similar to other diseases, such as rheumatoid arthritis (see arthritis entry) and multiple sclerosis (see multiple sclerosis entry). There is no one test that can be used to diagnose the disease. Blood tests can be used to look for certain kinds of antibodies. The most dependable of these tests may be correct 70 percent to 80 percent of the time.

Many doctors rely on a standard created by the American Rheumatism Association to diagnose lupus. According to this standard, a patient has to have four of eleven symptoms to be diagnosed with lupus. Those symptoms are:

- Butterfly rash, a distinctive type of facial rash
- Discoid rash, another distinctive type of facial rash
- Unusual sensitivity to light
- Ulcers in the mouth
- Arthritis
- Inflammation of the lining of the lungs or the lining around the heart
- Kidney damage
- Seizures or psychosis
- Low numbers of red blood cells or certain types of white blood cells
- The presence of certain kinds of immune cells
- The presence of certain kinds of antibodies

TREATMENT

Treatment of lupus depends on how serious a patient's case is. Mild cases may involve rashes and moderate pain. These cases can be treated with nonsteroidal anti-inflammatory drugs, such as aspirin and ibuprofen (pronounced i-byoo-PRO-fuhn, trade names Motrin, Advil). More serious rashes and joint problems may be treated with drugs also used to treat malaria (see malaria entry).

More serious symptoms may have to be treated with steroids. Steroids can reduce inflammation and swelling. They have some serious side effects, however, so they must be used with caution.

The most seriously ill patients may be treated with immunosuppressant drugs. Immunosuppressant drugs cause the immune system to shut down partially or completely. These drugs also have very serious side effects. With a weakened immune system, a patient is at risk for many other kinds of infections.

Other lupus treatments are designed for specific systems affected by the disease. For example, substances that thin the blood can be used if blood clots have formed. A person whose kidneys have begun to fail may require kidney dialysis or even a kidney transplantation. Kidney dialysis is a process in which a machine artificially cleanses a person's blood.

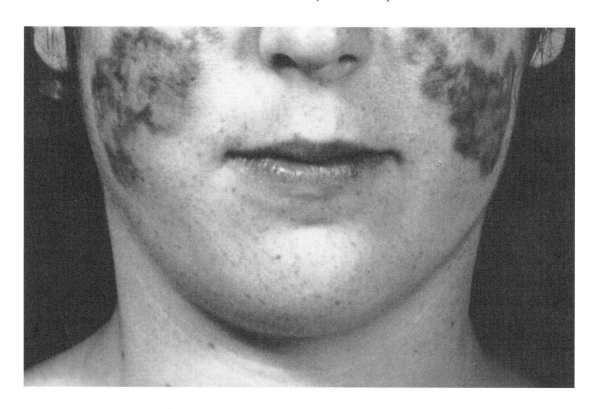

Lupus can cause skin rashes on any part of the body. One that often occurs on the face is called a butterfly rash. (© 1993 NMSB. Reproduced by permission of Custom Medical Stock Photo.)

Alternative Treatment

A number of alternative treatments have been suggested to help reduce the symptoms of lupus. These include acupuncture and massage for relieving the pain of sore joints and muscles. Patients can be taught to relax with techniques such as meditation and yoga. Hydrotherapy (water therapy) may also promote relaxation.

Proper nutrition may be an important factor in treating the symptoms of lupus. Some cases of the disease may be triggered by certain types of foods. Wheat, dairy products, and soy are the most common causes of the disease. Avoiding these foods may reduce the symptoms of lupus.

Some practitioners recommend nutritional supplements, such as vitamins B, C, and E, and minerals, such as magnesium, selenium, and zinc. They think these supplements may improve the general health of patients with lupus. Vitamin A can also be used to treat facial rashes.

Herbalists believe that certain herbs help relieve specific symptoms of lupus. They think that herbs can also help people develop a healthier outlook on life.

PROGNOSIS

The prognosis for lupus depends primarily on two factors: the systems affected and the degree of inflammation. Some patients experience mild symptoms or no symptoms at all over long periods of time. About 90 percent to 95 percent of all patients with lupus are still alive two years after diagnosis. Up to 75 percent of all patients survive twenty years or more.

The most common causes of death in the early years of lupus are infectious diseases and kidney failure. For people who have had the condition longer, the most common cause of death is blood clots.

PREVENTION

There is no way to avoid developing lupus. However, patients with the condition can often avoid the worst symptoms of the disease by maintaining a healthy diet, getting plenty of rest, avoiding stress, exercising regularly, and decreasing exposure to the sun. Patients can try to find out what factors seem to worsen their symptoms and then avoid those factors as much as possible.

FOR MORE INFORMATION

Books

Aaseng, Nathan. *Autoimmune Diseases.* New York: Franklin Watts, 1995.

Lahita, Robert G., and Robert H. Phillips. *Lupus: Everything You Need to Know.* Garden City Park, NY: Avery Publishing Group, 1998.

Wallace, Daniel J. *The Lupus Book.* New York: Oxford University Press, 1995.

Periodicals

Mann, Judy. "The Harsh Realities of Lupus." *Washington Post* (October 8, 1997): p. C12.

Umansky, Diane. "Living with Lupus." *American Health for Women* (June 1997): p. 92+.

Organizations

American College of Rheumatology. 1800 Century Place, Suite 250, Atlanta, GA 30345. (404) 633-3777. http://www.rheumatology.org

Lupus Foundation of America, Inc. 1300 Piccard Drive, Suite 200, Rockville, MD 20850–4303. (800) 558-0121. http://www.lupus.org.

Lupus Network. 230 Ranch Drive, Bridgeport, CT 06606. (203) 372-5795.

LYME DISEASE

DEFINITION

Lyme disease is caused by the bacterium *Borrelia burgdorferi* (*Bb*). The bacterium is carried by ticks and is transmitted to humans through a tick bite. The disease is named for the town of Lyme, Connecticut. It was in Lyme that the disease was first discovered in 1975, after a series of unexplained cases of arthritis developed.

WORDS TO KNOW

Cerebrospinal fluid (CSF): Fluid found around the brain and spinal cord. CSF provides nutrients to the cells of the nervous system and provides a cushion for the structures of the nervous system.

Larva: An immature form of an organism.

Latency: A period during which a disease-causing organism is inactive but not dead.

Nymph: A stage of development between the most immature and the adult stages of life.

Vector-borne disease: A disease transferred from one organism to another by means of a third organism, such as an insect or tick.

DESCRIPTION

Lyme disease is a vector-borne disease. A vector is an organism that carries a disease from one organism to another. In this case, the vector is the tick. The tick carries the bacterium *B. burgdorferi* in its blood and saliva. When the tick bites a human, it leaves some of its saliva, along with the bacterium, in the human's bloodstream. The bacterium begins to reproduce and spread. Eventually it causes the symptoms of Lyme disease.

Lyme disease accounts for about 90 percent of all reported vector-borne diseases in the United States. Nearly one hundred thousand cases of the disease were reported between 1982 and 1996. The true number of cases is difficult to estimate accurately. Some experts think that there are many more cases of the disease than are actually reported.

CAUSES

A tick passes through three stages of development: larva, nymph, and adult. The larva is an immature form of the tick. It hatches from eggs laid on the ground in summer. Larvae attach themselves to small animals and birds and feed on their blood. At this point, the larvae are no threat to humans.

Eventually, larvae develop into nymphs. Nymphs feed off humans. It is at this stage of a tick's life that it is the greatest threat. A nymph can transmit Lyme disease if it bites a human. A nymph is too small to be seen easily seen, and as a result, people may be bitten without realizing it.

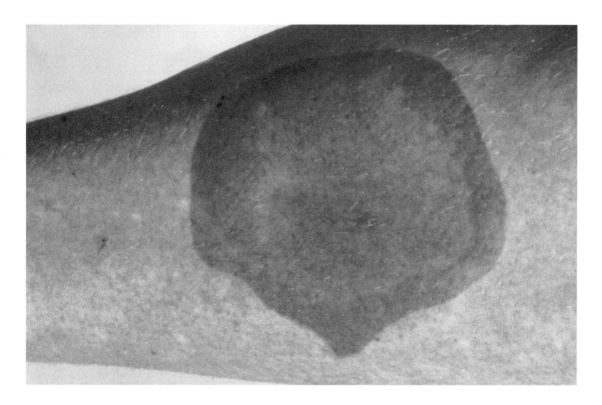

The first sign of Lyme disease is usually a rash around the site of the tick bite. It may be warm or itchy. (© 1993 Science Photo Library. Reproduced by permission of Custom Medical Stock Photo.)

Adult ticks feed off humans, mice, and deer. They are sometimes called deer ticks. They can still transmit Lyme disease, but they are larger and easier to see. They are thus less of a threat to humans, who can pick them off quite easily.

The *Bb* bacterium spreads quickly once it reaches the human bloodstream. It can usually be found in the cerebrospinal fluid (CSF) only twelve hours after a tick bite. Cerebrospinal fluid is the fluid found in the spinal column.

SYMPTOMS

The way symptoms develop following a tick bite varies widely among individuals. Some people have no symptoms at all. Others have a serious at-

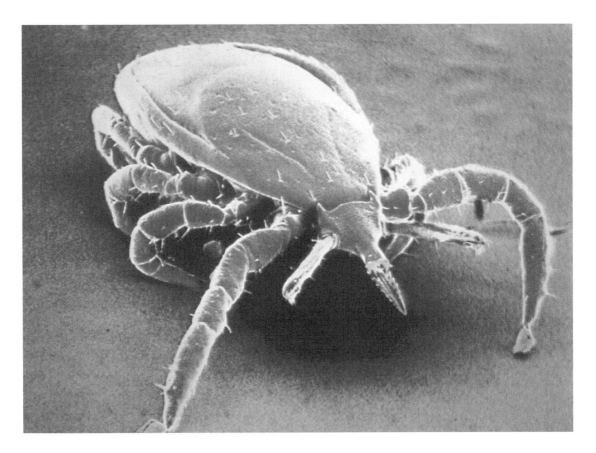

Magnification of a mature deer tick, a carrier for Lyme disease. (Reproduced by permission of CNRI/Phototake NYC)

tack that appears quickly and then disappears. Still others develop a chronic (long-lasting) form of the disease.

One factor that complicates the symptoms of Lyme disease is the latency of the bacterium. Latency means that the bacterium can become inactive for long periods of time. It has not died, but it does not cause any symptoms. Then, at some later date, the bacterium becomes active again and symptoms reappear.

Early, Localized Lyme Disease

The first sign of Lyme disease is usually a rash around the site of the tick bite. It may be warm or itchy. In many cases, the patient may not even notice the rash. Over the next three to thirty days, the rash expands. The center of the rash may clear up, forming a bull's-eye pattern. Or the center may become red.

Other early symptoms of a Lyme infection include headache, fever, chills, fatigue, muscle and joint pain, and swelling of the lymph nodes.

Late, Chronic Lyme Disease

Many cases of Lyme disease go unnoticed and untreated. In such cases, new symptoms may appear a few weeks, months, or even years after the tick bite. These symptoms include:

- Fatigue, forgetfulness, confusion, changes in mood, irritability, and numbness
- Disorders of the nervous system, such as unexplained pain and paralysis of the facial muscles
- Arthritis and other problems with muscles and bones

DIAGNOSIS

One problem in diagnosing Lyme disease is that its symptoms are similar to other disorders. The first task facing a doctor is to eliminate other possible explanations for a patient's symptoms. The doctor will perform tests to ensure that the patient does not have chronic fatigue syndrome (see chronic fatigue syndrome entry), multiple sclerosis (see multiple sclerosis entry), or some other disease with symptoms similar to those of Lyme disease.

An important aid in diagnosing Lyme disease is a geographical factor. Currently, Lyme disease occurs much more frequently in some parts of the United States than in others. The disease is quite rare in the Rocky Mountain states, for example, but relatively common in the Northeastern states. A doctor is aided in making a diagnosis if he or she can find out what part of the country the patient was in when he or she was bitten by a tick.

TREATMENT

Lyme disease is caused by a bacterium, so it can be treated with antibiotics. In general, the earlier treatment begins, the greater the chance of success. The deciding factor is often the appearance of the characteristic rash. The usual treatment is an oral antibiotic, such as doxycycline (pronounced dok-si-SIE-kleen) or amoxicillin (pronounced uh-MOK-sih-SIL-in), given for twenty-one days.

Some doctors are cautious about the use of antibiotics with Lyme disease. In many instances, doctor prescribe antibiotics for ailments when they are really not needed. The problem with this practice is that bacteria may become resistant to antibiotics and are no longer killed by drugs that were once effective. Some doctors therefore wait until they are certain that a patient has Lyme disease before prescribing an antibiotic.

Alternative Treatment

A common goal of alternative treatments for Lyme disease is to strengthen overall body health. Practitioners may recommend vitamin and nutritional supplements for this purpose. In addition, some herbs are thought to be effective in treating bacterial diseases like Lyme disease. A popular choice for this purpose is the western herb spilanthes.

A NEW LYME DISEASE VACCINE

The U.S. Food and Drug Administration (FDA) has given its approval to a new Lyme disease vaccine. The approval for the vaccine, which is being manufactured by the U.S. pharmaceutical company SmithKline Beecham, came on December 21, 1998. The vaccine was one of two new products being tested. The other vaccine was being tested by the French firm of Pasteur Merieux Connaught.

Some authorities have questioned whether a vaccine for Lyme disease is really needed. They point out that the disease can be diagnosed and treated quite easily. Members of the Lyme Disease Foundation have argued, however, that the vaccine will bring relief to countless people who may be exposed to the disease.

PROGNOSIS

The vast majority of patients who receive early treatment recover completely from Lyme disease. The key is that patients remain on the prescribed course of medication as directed by the doctor. Stopping medication too soon can cause relapses and reoccurrence of the disease.

A very small number of patients do not respond well to treatment. In the worst cases, people have died of the disorder. However, this is rare.

PREVENTION

Researchers are currently testing vaccines against Lyme disease. Until they are approved, the best way to prevent Lyme disease is to avoid contact with ticks that carry *Bb*. Some general recommendations for people who spend time outdoors include:

- Use bug repellents containing the chemical DEET.
- Wear light-colored clothing in order to see ticks better.
- Tuck pant legs into socks or boot tops.
- Check children and oneself frequently for ticks.

Tick removal is an important step in avoiding infection. Some hints about tick removal include:

- Using tweezers, grasp the tick as near to the skin as possible.
- Pull the tick straight back steadily and slowly.
- Do not try to make the tick back out by using petroleum jelly, alcohol, or a lit match.
- Place the tick in a closed container or flush it down the toilet.
- See a doctor if any sort of rash appears three to thirty days after the tick bite.

FOR MORE INFORMATION

Books

Territo, J., and D. V. Lang. *Coping with Lyme Disease: A Practical Guide to Dealing with Diagnosis and Treatment.* New York: Henry Holt, 1997.

Vanderhoof-Forschne, K. *Everything You Need to Know about Lyme Disease and Other Tick-Borne Disorders.* New York: John Wiley & Sons, 1997.

Organizations

Lyme Disease Foundation, Inc. One Financial Plaza, 18th Floor, Hartford, CT, (800) 886-LYME. http://www.lyme.org.

The Lyme Disease Network of New Jersey, Inc., 43 Winton Road, East Brunswick, NJ 08816. http://www.lymenet.org.

MALARIA

DEFINITION

Malaria is a serious, infectious disease spread by certain kinds of mosquitoes. It is common in tropical climates and is characterized by chills, fevers, and an enlarged spleen. These symptoms reappear again and again. The disease can be treated with medication, but it tends to come back even after being cured. Malaria is endemic in many developing countries. An endemic disease is one that occurs frequently in a particular location. Isolated, limited outbreaks of malaria sometimes occur in the United States.

DESCRIPTION

Malaria is not a serious problem in the United States. Over the past ten years, only about 1,200 cases have been reported each year in this country. In most cases, a person was infected outside the United States while traveling on business or on vacation.

Malaria is a far more serious problem in other parts of the world. Between 300 million and 500 million people in Africa, India, Southeast Asia, the Middle East, the South Pacific, and Central and South America have the disease. About two million people die of the disease every year. Most of these deaths occur in southern Africa.

A person can have malaria more than once. In some parts of Africa, people have up to forty

MALARIA IS A SERIOUS PROBLEM IN CERTAIN PARTS OF THE WORLD. BETWEEN 300 MILLION AND 500 MILLION PEOPLE IN AFRICA, INDIA, SOUTHEAST ASIA, THE MIDDLE EAST, THE SOUTH PACIFIC, AND CENTRAL AND SOUTH AMERICA HAVE THE DISEASE.

bouts of malaria during their lifetime. Malaria is becoming a more serious problem because the organisms that cause the disease are growing resistant to the drugs used to treat it.

CAUSES

Malaria is caused by four different kinds of parasites belonging to the plasmodium family. A parasite is an organism that lives off another organism. Animals can also get malaria, but malaria cannot be passed from humans to animals or from animals to humans.

Malaria is transmitted by female mosquitoes that carry the parasite in their bodies. When the mosquito bites a human, it injects a small amount of its saliva into the human's bloodstream. The saliva contains parasites that travel through the person's bloodstream to his or her liver. There, the parasites reproduce. Eventually, they leave the liver and travel back into the bloodstream. Once in the bloodstream, they begin to cause the symptoms of malaria.

Malaria cannot be passed directly from one human to another. It can be transmitted by a mosquito. A mosquito may bite a person infected with the malaria parasite. When it sucks the person's blood, it takes in some of the parasites. If the same mosquito bites a second person, it may transfer those parasites to the uninfected person.

Malaria can also be transmitted through blood transfusions. If an infected person donates blood, the blood will contain malaria parasites. If the blood is put into another person's body, the parasites will also flow into his or her bloodstream. For this reason, blood donors are often screened for the malaria parasite before they are allowed to give blood.

The incubation period for malaria varies considerably. An incubation period is the time between the mosquito bite and the time symptoms of malaria begin to appear. The incubation period differs depending on the kind of parasite involved. For the most serious form of malaria, the incubation period is eight to twelve days. In some rare forms of malaria, the incubation period can be as long as ten months.

WORDS TO KNOW

Artemisinin: An antimalarial herb used for many years in China under the name qiinghaosu.

Chloroquine: An antimalarial drug first used in the 1940s as a substitute for quinine, and still widely used in Africa because of its relatively low cost.

Mefloquine: An antimalarial drug developed by the U.S. Army in the early 1980s.

Quinine: One of the first successful treatments for malaria, derived from the bark of the cinchona tree.

Sulfadoxine/pyrimethamine (trade name Fansidar): An antimalarial drug developed in the 1960s, often used in areas where quinine and chloroquine are no longer effective.

SYMPTOMS

A person infected with malaria passes through three stages of very distinctive symptoms. The first stage is characterized by uncontrollable shivering for an hour or two. In the next stage, the patient's temperature rises quickly. It may reach 106°F (41°C) for a period of up to six hours. In the third stage, the patient begins to sweat profusely, and his or her temperature drops rapidly.

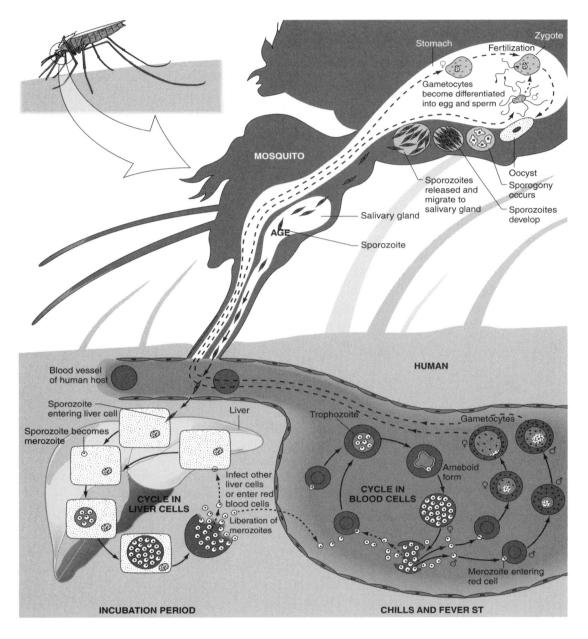

Diagram of mosquito biting a human, transmitting malaria. (Reproduced by permission of Hans and Cassady)

Other symptoms may accompany these stages. They include fatigue, severe headache, nausea, and vomiting. After the third stage, the patient often falls asleep from exhaustion.

The three stages are often repeated the following day, two days later, or at some later time. In many cases, a person experiences a repetition of the stages again and again during their lifetime. Some people go many years before the symptoms repeat.

The most serious forms of malaria can result in death in a matter of hours. The parasites attack a person's red blood cells and change their structure. The cells become very sticky and begin to clump together. As they do, they may block blood vessels in vital organs, such as the kidneys and spleen. These organs may no longer be able to function properly, and the patient may fall into a coma and die.

DIAGNOSIS

Malaria can be diagnosed with a blood test. A sample of a patient's blood is taken and studied under a microscope to detect the presence of parasites. Blood tests sometimes need to be repeated after a seventy-two-hour period to confirm the diagnosis.

AN ANCIENT ILLNESS

Malaria has been a known disease for centuries and was described in medical records from ancient China, India, and Greece. Doctors first believed that malaria was caused by poisonous vapors in the air. People who lived around swamps, bogs, and other wetlands were especially likely to get the disease. Therefore, it was presumed that it must be the "bad gases" given off by these watery regions. In fact, the name of the disease comes from two Italian words for "bad air": mal- ("bad") and -aria ("air").

The Romans are credited with one of the most successful attempts to eliminate malaria. They drained large areas of swampy land around the city, believing that they were cutting off the supply of "bad gases." In fact, they were destroying the wet areas in which malaria carriers (the mosquitoes) lived and bred.

The three stages of malaria can also be used to diagnose the disease. A person who lives in an area where malaria is common and who has chills, fever, and a very high temperature should have a blood test as quickly as possible.

Malaria is sometimes misdiagnosed in North America. The disease is not very common in this part of the world, and its symptoms are similar to those of the flu (see influenza entry). A doctor may think that a person has the flu when he or she really has malaria. This kind of misdiagnosis can result in the patient's death if he or she has a severe case of malaria.

TREATMENT

Malaria can be treated with drugs. However, treatment is complicated by a number of factors. First, each type of malaria requires a different drug. Second, the treatment depends on the region of the world in which the person was infected. The kinds of parasites living in different parts of the world respond in different ways to different drugs.

The classic treatment for malaria is quinine. Quinine is still effective in treating some forms of malaria in some parts of the world, but other parasites have developed a resistance to quinine.

If quinine is not effective, a variety of antibiotics can be tried. These include tetracycline (pronounced tet -ruh-SIE-kleen), clindamycin (pronounced klin-duh-MY-suhn, trade name Cleocin), mefloquine (pronounced MEF-luh-kwine, trade name Lariam), or sulfadoxine/pyrimethamine (pronounced sull-fuh-DOK-seen/pi-ruh-METH-uh-meen, trade name Fansidar). A modified form of quinine known as chloroquine (pronounced KLOR-uh-kween) can also be used. In some parts of the world, the parasite that causes the most serious form of malaria is resistant to all known drugs.

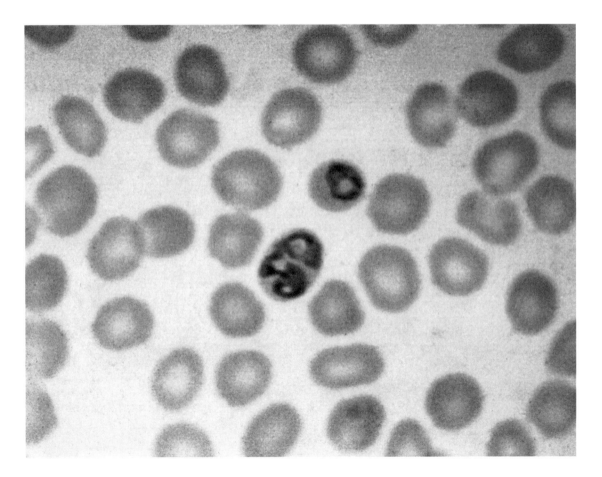

Blood cells infected with the parasite that causes malaria. (©1993 NMSB. Reproduced by permission of Custom Medical Stock Photo.)

Patients with very serious cases of malaria may require hospitalization and special treatments. These treatments may include intravenous fluids (fluids injected into the patient's bloodstream), blood transfusions, kidney dialysis, and oxygen therapy to help him or her breathe.

Alternative Treatment

The Chinese herb qinghao (known as artemesia in the West) has long been used to treat malaria. However, it is not approved for use in the United States and other parts of the developed world. Researchers are still concerned about the herb's possibly dangerous side effects.

Some practitioners suggest using certain herbs to protect against malaria and to strengthen the liver. These herbs include wormwood, goldenseal, Chinese goldenthread, and milk thistle.

PROGNOSIS

If treated in its early stages, malaria can be cured. Cures are more difficult for people who live in areas where malaria is endemic. These people may be bitten by mosquitoes and exposed to malaria parasites again and again and may never fully recover from the disease.

PREVENTION

Malaria can be prevented in one of two ways. First, a person can avoid being bitten by a mosquito carrying the malaria parasite. The World Health Organization (WHO) has been working to eliminate malaria for more than thirty years. Its approach has been to kill as many of the mosquitoes that cause malaria as possible. For some years, WHO was quite successful in this effort. It used DDT and other pesticides to kill mosquitoes. Unfortunately, mosquitoes have slowly become resistant to many pesticides. It has become more and more difficult to kill mosquitoes with the pesticides now available.

The second method for avoiding malaria is to take drugs that protect against the disease. These drugs kill parasites as soon as they enter the bloodstream. The problem is that antimalarial drugs are expensive. Most people in Africa, Asia, and other areas where malaria is common cannot afford them.

Scientists have long hoped to find a vaccine for malaria. With a vaccine, a person could be protected for a lifetime with one or a few shots. So far, however, researchers have had no success in producing such a vaccine.

People who travel in areas where malaria is common can protect themselves by wearing mosquito repellent. The compound known as DEET is one of the most effective repellents, but it can have harmful side effects, especially in children. It should be used only with caution.

Certain other preventive measures can also be followed, including:

- Staying indoors in well-screened areas between dusk and dawn
- Sleeping inside mosquito nets that have been soaked with mosquito repellent
- Wearing clothes that cover the entire body

People who plan trips to areas in which malaria is endemic should take antimalarial drugs as a preventive against contracting the disease. The drugs usually prescribed are chloroquine or mefloquine. A person starts taking the drugs a few days before leaving on the trip. He or she continues to take the drugs while on the trip and for at least four weeks after they return home.

FOR MORE INFORMATION

Books

Desowitz, Robert S. *The Malaria Capers: More Tales of Parasites and People, Research, and Reality.* New York: W. W. Norton, 1993.

Stoffman, Phyllis. *The Family Guide to Preventing and Treating 100 Infectious Illnesses.* New York: John Wiley & Sons, 1995.

Periodicals

Kristof, Nicholas D. "Malaria Makes a Comeback, Deadlier Than Ever." *New York Times* (January 8, 1997).

Mack, Alison. "Collaborative Efforts Under Way to Combat Malaria." *Scientist* (May 12, 1997): p. 1+.

Shell, Ellen Ruppel. "Resurgence of a Deadly Disease." *Atlantic Monthly* (August 1997).

Organizations

Centers for Disease Control Malaria Hotline. (770) 332-4555.

Centers for Disease Control Travelers Hotline. (770) 332-4559.

Malaria Foundation International. http://www.malaria.org.

MEASLES

DEFINITION

Measles is a viral infection (an infection caused by a virus). Its most characteristic feature is a reddish skin rash. Measles is also known as rubeola, five-day measles, or hard measles.

DESCRIPTION

Measles infections occur throughout the world. At one time, they reappeared in two- or three-year cycles, usually in the winter and spring. Today, there is a very effective measles vaccine. This vaccine has greatly reduced the occurrence of measles in many parts of the world.

Babies up to the age of eight months usually do not get measles. They receive special cells from their mothers that protect them against the disease. A person who has had measles will never get the disease again.

CAUSES

Measles is a very contagious disease. That is, it can be transmitted from one person to another very easily. The usual method of transmission is through coughing or sneezing. The virus that causes measles is contained in tiny droplets of moisture released when an infected person coughs or sneezes. A person who inhales those droplets will almost certainly develop measles.

The incubation period for measles is seven to eighteen days. The incubation period is the time between the moment the virus enters a person's body and the appearance of symptoms. A person is contagious (capable of passing on the infection) from three to five days before symptoms appear to about four days after the rash shows up.

SYMPTOMS

The first signs of measles are a fever, runny nose, red and runny eyes, and a cough. A few days later, a rash appears in the mouth. The rash consists of tiny white dots on a reddish bump. This rash is called Koplik's spots. They are important in diagnosing measles because they do not occur with other diseases. Koplik's spots are accompanied by a red, sore, swollen throat.

About two days after Koplik's spots appear, the measles rash begins. It first shows up on the head, face, and neck. It then travels to the abdomen and, finally, to the arms and legs. At first, the rash consists of flat, red patches. Eventually, bumps appear. The rash may or may not be itchy. As the rash develops, the patient's temperature begins to rise and may so as high as 105°F (40.5°C). Other symptoms include nausea, vomiting, diarrhea, and swollen lymph nodes. The patient usually feels very ill.

WORDS TO KNOW

Encephalitis: An infection of the brain that results in a high fever and swelling of the brain.

Koplik's spots: Tiny white spots on a reddish bump on the inside of the mouth that are a characteristic marker for measles.

The rash normally lasts about five days. As it fades, it becomes more brownish in color. The affected skin becomes dry and flaky.

A bout of measles leads to other infections in 5 percent to 15 percent of patients. Some of these infections are caused by bacteria. These include ear infections, sinus infections, and pneumonia (see pneumonia entry). Other infections are caused by viruses. Some common viral infections are croup, bronchitis (see bronchitis entry), laryngitis (see laryngitis entry), and viral pneumonia. Inflammation of the liver, appendix, intestines, and lymph nodes are other problems that may develop as a result of a measles infection. Less common complications include inflammation of the heart or kidney, loss of blood platelets (the blood cells that help blood clot; pronounced PLATE-lits), and recurrence of old tuberculosis (see tuberculosis entry) infections.

Probably the most serious complication of a measles infection is encephalitis (see encephalitis entry). Encephalitis is a brain infection that results in a very high fever and swelling of the brain. Symptoms of encephalitis include fever, headaches, sleepiness, seizures, and coma. People with encephalitis may suffer serious, long-term brain damage. Encephalitis occurs in about 1 out of every 1,000 cases of measles. About 10 percent to 15 percent of those who develop the disease die from it.

A very rare complication of measles is called subacute sclerosing panencephalitis. This disease can occur up to ten years after infection by the measles virus. It develops slowly over a period of years and causes massive destruction of the brain. It eventually results in death.

DIAGNOSIS

Measles is fairly easy to diagnose because of its characteristic symptoms. The presence of Koplik's spots is often the most important clue. The appearance of a rash that travels from the head and neck out to the arms and legs is also an important indicator of a measles infection.

In case of doubt, a variety of laboratory tests can be performed. These tests are used to identify the presence of the measles virus in body fluids, such as urine and mucus.

TREATMENT

There is no treatment that can kill the measles virus or stop the course of the disease.

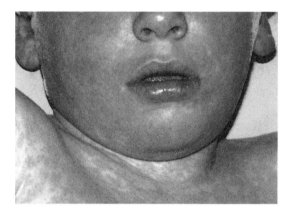

The measles rash starts on the head, face, and neck, and eventually spreads to the abdomen, arms, and legs. The rash may or may not be itchy. (Reproduced by Custom Medical Stock Photo)

Treatments instead are used to make a patient feel more comfortable during the disease. For example, acetaminophen (pronounced uh-see-tuh-MIN-uh-fuhn, trade name Tylenol) can relieve pain and fever. Aspirin, however, should never be given to children who have measles. Aspirin has been found to cause Reye's syndrome (see Reye's syndrome entry), a potentially fatal disease.

A cool-mist vaporizer may help relieve the cough that comes with measles. Patients should also drink lots of liquids. The patient should be watched carefully to make sure that complications do not appear. If they do, antibiotics may be used to treat bacterial infections.

Alternative Treatment

Some practitioners believe that certain herbs can strengthen the body's immune system. Purple coneflower (echinacea; pronounced ek-i-NAY-see-uh) is one such herb. Homeopathic support can also be effective in helping a person feel more comfortable during a measles infection.

Some of the symptoms of measles can be relieved by using various herbs, such as bupleurum, peppermint, witch hazel, chickweed, or eyebright (for sore eyes). A preparation made from empty cicada shells has also been recommended.

PROGNOSIS

The prognosis for a child who is otherwise in good health is usually very good. In developing countries, however, death rates from measles can reach 15 percent to 25 percent. The prognosis for adolescents and adults is less favorable. Women who contract the disease while pregnant may give birth to a baby with hearing problems.

The most serious consequence of a measles infection is encephalitis. One in 1,000 measles patients will develop encephalitis. Of this number, about 10 percent to 15 percent will die; 25 percent will suffer permanent brain damage.

PREVENTION

A highly effective vaccine is now available to prevent measles. The vaccine is usually given at about fifteen months of age. A repeat injection should be given at about ten or eleven years of age.

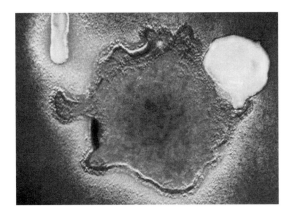

Measles virion seen through a microscope. (Reproduced by permission of Custom Medical Stock Photo)

FOR MORE INFORMATION

Books

Silverstein, Alvin, Virginia Silverstein, and Robert Silverstein. *Measles and Rubella*. Hillside, NJ: Enslow Publishers, Inc., 1997.

Stoffman, Phyllis. *The Family Guide to Preventing and Treating 100 Infectious Diseases*. New York: John Wiley & Sons, 1995.

Periodicals

Ramsey, Alison. "Childhood Diseases Are Back." *Reader's Digest* (February 1996): pp. 73+.

Organizations

Centers for Disease Control and Prevention. http://www.cdc.gov.

MENINGITIS

DEFINITION

Meningitis (pronounced meh-nen-JI-tiss) is an inflammation of the meninges (pronounced meh-NIN-jeez). The meninges are the thin layers of tissue that cover the brain and the spinal cord. Meningitis is most commonly caused by infection (by bacteria, viruses, or fungi). It can also be caused by bleeding into the meninges, cancer (see cancer entry), diseases of the immune system, and other factors. The most dangerous forms of meningitis are those caused by bacteria. The disease is very serious and can be fatal.

DESCRIPTION

Any time a part of the body is infected, it is likely to become inflamed and swollen. These symptoms are especially serious in the brain. The brain is enclosed in the skull, a bony structure that cannot change size. If the brain swells, it pushes outward against the skull. Brain cells may become squeezed and begin to die. Brain cells are some of the only kinds of cells in the body that do not regenerate (renew) themselves. Once they die, they cannot be replaced.

WORDS TO KNOW

Blood-brain barrier: Cells within the blood vessels of the brain that prevent the passage of toxic substances from the blood into the brain.

Cerebrospinal fluid (CSF): Fluid made in chambers of the brain that flows over the surface of the brain and the spinal cord. CSF provides nutrients to cells of the nervous system and provides a cushion for the structures of the nervous system.

Meninges: The three-layer membranous covering of the brain and spinal cord.

An infection in the brain can cause damage in a second way. Brain cells are very delicate. They require just the right balance of chemicals, including sugar, sodium, calcium, potassium, and oxygen. An infection can change the balance of chemicals in the brain. Brain cells may receive too much of one chemical or too little of another. This loss of chemical balance can also kill brain cells.

Meningitis is a serious medical problem because it is difficult to treat. Blood flows into the brain from the neck through a network of blood vessels. This network contains special cells that prevent many chemicals from passing into the brain. This system is known as the blood-brain barrier.

The blood-brain barrier prevents harmful substances from getting into the brain. The blood-brain barrier "knows" which substances the brain needs and which will damage brain cells.

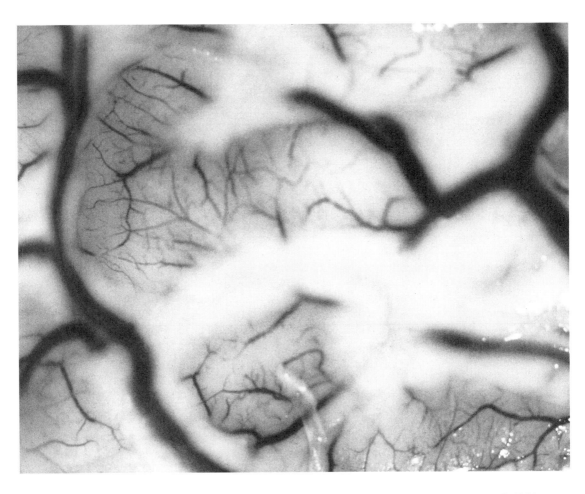

Brain tissue covered with thick white exudate (pus) from acute meningitis. (© 1994 Joseph R. Siebert, Ph.D. Reproduced by permission of Custom Medical Stock Photo.)

The problem is that the blood-brain barrier usually does not recognize drugs as "good" chemicals. It prevents them from passing into the brain, where they could help clear up an infection. Doctors often have to find other ways to treat the kinds of infection that cause meningitis.

CAUSES

Meningitis may be caused by bacteria, viruses, fungi, head injuries, infections in other parts of the body, and other factors. The type of meningitis a person is most likely to contract depends on his or her age, habits, living environment, and health status.

Bacteria are not the most common cause of meningitis. But they produce the most serious and most life-threatening forms of the disease. The most common kinds of meningitis in newborns are those caused by streptococci (pronounced STREP-tuh-KOK-see) bacteria. These bacteria pass from the mother to the child through the blood system they share before birth. The highest incidence (rate) of meningitis occurs in babies under the age of one month. Children up to the age of two years are also at relatively high risk for the disease.

BACTERIA ARE NOT THE MOST COMMON CAUSE OF MENINGITIS. BUT THEY PRODUCE THE MOST SERIOUS AND MOST LIFE-THREATENING FORMS OF THE DISEASE.

Adults are usually infected by a different kind of bacterium. This bacterium produces a form of meningitis that has some symptoms like those of pneumonia (see pneumonia entry).

One type of bacterium causes a contagious form of meningitis. A person with this form of meningitis can pass it to others with whom he or she comes into contact. Epidemics (mass infections) of meningitis have been known to occur in crowded day-care centers and military training camps.

Meningitis is often caused by a virus. The virus is usually the same one that causes other viral infections such as mumps (see mumps entry), measles (see measles entry), chickenpox (see chickenpox entry), rabies (see rabies entry), and herpes infections (like cold sores; see herpes infections entry).

A person's general health can also increase his or her risk of developing meningitis. For example, a person with a weakened immune system is at greater risk for meningitis than one who has a healthy immune system. People with AIDS (see AIDS entry) have damaged immune systems and are less able to fight off fungal infections. These fungal infections can lead to infections of the brain and meningitis.

People who have had their spleens removed are also at higher risk for meningitis. Spleen removal may be necessary to solve some other medical problem, such as cancer of the spleen. But it may also expose the patient to greater risk for meningitis.

The most common cause of meningitis is blood-borne spread. This term means that a person already has an infection in some other part of his or her body. If that infection is not treated properly, it can become more serious and start to spread through the body by way of the bloodstream. Normally, the blood-brain barrier would keep the infectious agents out of the brain. But if huge numbers of infectious agents accumulate in the blood, some of them may get through the blood-brain barrier. They will then be able to infect the meninges and cause meningitis. Infections that occur close to the brain, such as an ear or sinus infection, pose an especially high risk for meningitis.

Meningitis can also develop because of openings in the skull. These openings can occur because of a skull fracture or a surgical procedure. These openings provide a way for infectious agents to get into the brain because the blood-brain barrier cannot prevent the infection.

SYMPTOMS

The classic symptoms of meningitis include fever, headache, vomiting, sensitivity to light, irritability, severe fatigue, stiff neck, and a reddish-purple rash on the skin. If the infection is not treated quickly, more serious symptoms develop, including seizures, confusion, and coma.

These symptoms may not be present in very young babies or the elderly. The immune system of babies is usually not developed enough to fight off an infection of the meninges. So symptoms that accompany an immune re-

SARA ELIZABETH BRANHAM

Before the discovery of antibiotics, meningitis was a dreaded diseases. There was no way to stop its progress. Those who survived an attack of the disease were likely to be left blind, deaf, or mentally retarded. The disease was also feared because of the ease with which it spread. During World War I (1914–18), for example, meningitis often swept through groups of soldiers who lived and fought together. The only way to stop its spread was to isolate infected soldiers from others who were still healthy.

Important breakthroughs in the treatment of meningitis came as the result of the work of Dr. Sara Elizabeth Branham (1888–1962). Dr. Branham worked for many years at the National Institutes of Health. Initially, she was interested primarily in food poisoning caused by bacteria. But the tragedies of World War I encouraged her to focus on ways of treating meningitis.

When she began her research, the only treatment available for meningitis was antiserum obtained from horses. Horse antiserum is a chemical produced in horses when they have been exposed to meningitis bacteria. As horse antiserum lost its effectiveness, Dr. Branham developed another form of antiserum, produced in rabbits.

Finally, in 1937, Dr. Branham decided to try the newly discovered sulfonamide drugs on meningitis. The sulfonamides were the first antibiotics to be widely used. Dr. Branham found that they could be used effectively against the bacteria that cause meningitis. Largely as a result of her research, meningitis was kept under control during World War II (1939–45).

sponse, such as fever, are not observed. Seizures may be the only symptom of meningitis in young children. The same is true of older people who have other kinds of medical disorders that leave them in a weakened state.

DIAGNOSIS

The first clues that a person may have meningitis can be obtained from a simple physical examination. The doctor may try to move the patient's head in various directions. For a person with meningitis, these movements can be difficult and painful.

The standard test for diagnosing meningitis is called a lumbar puncture (LP), or spinal tap. An LP involves the insertion of a thin needle into the space between the vertebrae that make up the spine. A small sample of cerebrospinal fluid is removed. Cerebrospinal fluid (CSF) is a clear liquid present in the space between cells in the brain and the spinal cord. It serves a number of important functions. It provides a cushion for the brain and spinal cord, brings nutrients to these structures, and carries away waste products.

CSF normally contains certain fixed amounts of various chemicals, such as sugar, sodium, potassium, and calcium. An infection in the meninges will cause a change in these amounts. For example, bacteria "eat" sugar, so the presence of bacteria in the meninges causes a reduction in the amount of sugar in the CSF.

The presence of white blood cells in the CSF is also a clue to the presence of meningitis. The immune system produces white blood cells to fight off infections. A healthy body would normally not have white blood cells in the CSF. If they are present, the immune system is probably fighting an infection in the brain or spinal cord, such as meningitis.

TREATMENT

Meningitis infections caused by bacteria can be treated with antibiotics. Penicillin and cephalosporins (pronounced seff-a-lo-SPORE-inz) are commonly used. Special methods are necessary for giving these drugs, however, because of the blood-brain barrier. The usual procedure is to inject large quantities of an antibiotic directly into a person's bloodstream. If the concentration of drugs is high enough, some will get through the blood-brain barrier and into the meninges.

Antiviral and antifungal medications can be used similarly. Antiviral drugs usually do not kill viruses, but they can lessen some of the effects of the viruses.

Steroids may also be used to treat meningitis. Steroids tend to reduce inflammation and swelling, lessening possible harm to brain cells. The balance of sugar, sodium, potassium, calcium, and other substances in the CSF must also be carefully monitored. It may be necessary to inject one or more of these chemicals into the patient's body to maintain a proper balance.

PROGNOSIS

Viral meningitis is the least severe type of the disease. Patients usually recover with no long-term effects. Bacterial infections are far more serious and progress quickly. Very rapid treatment with antibiotics is necessary. If the infection is not halted, the patient may fall into a coma and die in less than a day.

Death rates for meningitis vary depending on the cause of the infection. Overall, the death rate from the disease is just less than 20 percent.

Long-term effects of meningitis are not unusual. For example, damage to cells in certain parts of the brain can cause deafness and/or blindness. Some patients develop permanent seizure disorders. These disorders may require lifelong treatment with antiseizure medications. Scarring of brain tissue can block normal flow of CSF. This condition may be serious enough to require the installation of shunt tubes, surgically implanted devices that help to restore normal circulation of CSF.

PREVENTION

There are no specific recommendations for avoiding meningitis. People should try to avoid developing any kind of infection that might spread to the meninges, especially those of the ear and sinus.

Some preventive treatments are available for specific types of meningitis. For example, there is a vaccine for individuals who have to be in areas where contagious meningitis exists. These individuals may also take antibiotics to protect them from infection by the bacterium that causes this form of the disease. A vaccine is available for one of the forms of meningitis that occurs in young children.

FOR MORE INFORMATION

Books

Stoffman, Phyllis. *The Family Guide to Preventing and Treating 100 Infectious Diseases*. New York: John Wiley & Sons, 1995.

Willett, Edward. *Meningitis*. Hillside, NJ: Enslow Publishers, Inc. 1999.

Periodicals

Meissner, Judith W. "Caring for Patients with Meningitis." *Nursing* (July 1995): pp. 50+.

Organizations

American Academy of Neurology. 1080 Montreal Avenue, St. Paul, MN 55116. (612) 695-1940. http://www.aan.com.

MENTAL RETARDATION

DEFINITION

Mental retardation is a developmental disability that is marked by lower-than-normal intelligence and limited daily living skills. Mental retardation is normally present at birth or develops early in life.

DESCRIPTION

Mental retardation is defined by two standards. The first standard is a person's level of intelligence. Intelligence levels are usually measured by special tests called intelligence tests. Intelligence tests provide a numerical ranking of a person's mental abilities. That ranking is called an intelligence quotient or, more commonly, an IQ. In general, a person with an IQ score of less than 75 is said to be retarded.

The second standard for mental retardation is adaptive skills. The term "adaptive skills" means how well a person can deal with the tasks of everyday life. These tasks include the ability to speak and understand; home-living skills; use of community resources; leisure, self-care, and social skills; self-direction; basic academic skills (reading, writing, and arithmetic); and work skills. A person is regarded as mentally retarded if he or she is unable to dress, feed, wash, or otherwise care for him- or herself; to hold a job; or to carry out most of the other tasks needed to get through an ordinary day.

Mental-health professionals classify patients into one of four levels of retardation.

Mild Mental Retardation

- IQ scores from 50 to 75
- Includes about 85 percent of the mentally retarded population
- Individuals in this group can often live on their own with community support.

Moderate Mental Retardation

- IQ scores between 35 and 50
- Includes about 10 percent of the mentally retarded population
- Individuals in this group can often lead relatively normal lives provided they receive some level of supervision. Such individuals often live in group homes with other mentally retarded people.

Severe Mental Retardation

- IQ scores between 20 and 35
- Includes about 3 percent to 4 percent of the mentally retarded population
- Individuals in this category can often master the most basic skills of living, such as cleaning and dressing themselves. They often live in group homes.

Profound Mental Retardation

- IQ scores of less than 20
- Includes about 1 percent to 2 percent of the mentally retarded population
- Individuals at this level can often develop basic communication and self-care skills. They often have other mental disorders.

WORDS TO KNOW

Adaptive skills: The ability to carry out a large variety of ordinary tasks required to live successfully in the world.

Fetal alcohol syndrome (FAS): A medical problem that affects a fetus and is caused by excessive drinking by the mother.

Genes: Chemical units found in all cells that carry the instructions telling cells how they are to perform.

Hydrocephalus: Accumulation of fluid in the brain; also known as "water on the brain."

Hyperthyroidism: A condition in which the thyroid gland produces too much thyroid hormone, causing a variety of medical problems.

Intelligence: The ability to learn and understand.

Intelligence quotient (IQ): A numerical measure of a person's intelligence.

Neural tube defect: A medical disorder in which a fetus's spine does not close normally.

CAUSES

In about one-third of all cases, the cause of mental retardation is not known. The remaining two-thirds of cases are thought to be caused by one of four factors: heredity, prenatal problems, childhood illnesses, and environmental factors.

Heredity

About 5 percent of mental retardation cases are caused by genetic factors. Genes are chemical units found in all cells. They carry the instructions that tell cells how they are to perform. In some cases, children inherit defective genes from their parents. These genes may interfere with the normal development of the child's brain. This may lead to mental retardation.

Prenatal Problems

The daily choices a pregnant woman makes may affect the mental health of her fetus. For example, fetal alcohol syndrome (FAS) affects about 1 in 600 children in the United States. Fetal alcohol syndrome is caused by excessive drinking by the mother during pregnancy and can lead to mental retardation in the fetus. Drug abuse and smoking during pregnancy may also cause mental retardation in the fetus.

Infections in the mother may lead to mental retardation of the fetus. The infections may spread to the fetus and damage its nervous system, including its brain. High blood pressure and blood poisoning in a pregnant woman may also cause brain damage in a fetus, leading to mental retardation.

Fetal damage may occur naturally, for unknown reasons. An example is the problem known as neural tube defect. In this disorder, the fetus's spine does not close normally. Fluids may collect in its brain, producing a condition known as hydrocephalus ("water on the brain"; pronounced hi-dro-SEF-uh-luhs). One possible result of hydrocephalus is mental retardation.

Childhood Illnesses

Children sometimes experience serious infections. These infections may spread to the brain and cause it to become inflamed and swollen. These changes can damage brain cells and bring about retardation. Childhood injuries can also lead to mental retardation. A blow to the head or a violent shaking by an adult may cause brain damage and mental retardation.

Environmental Factors

Children who might otherwise develop normally sometimes become mentally retarded because of the environment in which they live. Poverty, malnutrition, unhealthy living conditions, and inadequate medical care may all increase a child's risk for mental retardation. Children who are neglected or abused often do not develop normally. Their native intelligence never gets a chance to express itself, and they become retarded.

Another important environmental factor is lead poisoning (see lead poisoning entry). Young children sometimes eat paint that has flaked off the walls of their home. This paint may contain the element lead. Lead has many harmful effects on growing children, one of which is damage to the brain.

SYMPTOMS

The symptoms of mental retardation usually appear early in life. Children with the disorder tend to develop more slowly than normal. They may learn to sit up, to walk, to talk, and to perform other simple tasks later than average. Mental retardation is often accompanied by other symptoms as well. These symptoms include aggression, a tendency toward self-injury, and personality changes. As a child grows older, the best indication of mental retardation is the standard intelligence tests.

DIAGNOSIS

The first step in diagnosing mental retardation is a complete physical examination and medical history. Some forms of mental retardation are caused by treatable illnesses. Hyperthyroidism is an example. Hyperthyroidism is a condition in which the thyroid gland produces too much thyroid hormone. A child's mental disorder may be treated, then, by first treating the medical problem that caused it.

If medical problems are ruled out, the patient may then be given a series of intelligence tests. These tests are designed to determine the child's intelligence quotient. Some tests that are commonly used include the Stanford-Binet Intelligence Scale, the Wechsler Intelligence Scales, and the Kaufmann Assessment Battery for Children.

Final diagnosis may also include a series of interviews between a mental-health professional, the child, and the child's family.

TREATMENT

Some forms of mental retardation can be treated. These are cases that are caused by medical problems, such as hyperthyroidism. In most cases, however, no treatment can change a person's basic intellectual capabilities.

THE GOAL OF MOST TREATMENT PROGRAMS IS TO HELP MENTALLY RETARDED INDIVIDUALS DEVELOP THEIR INTELLECTUAL AND FUNCTIONAL SKILLS TO THE MAXIMUM POSSIBLE LEVEL.

The goal of most treatment programs is to help mentally retarded individuals develop their intellectual and functional skills to the maximum possible level. The federal government has recognized the importance of this goal. It allows for all mentally retarded children to have free testing and appropriate education and skills training from ages three to twenty-one.

Many retarded children now have the opportunity to attend special preschool programs and day schools. These programs and schools teach children basic skills, such as bathing and feeding themselves. They also provide educational programs, extracurricular activities, and social events developed especially for retarded children.

As mentally retarded individuals approach adulthood, they may receive training in independent living and job skills. The level of training they receive depends on the degree of retardation. Mildly retarded individuals can often acquire the skills needed to live on their own and hold an outside job. Moderate to profoundly retarded individuals usually require supervised community living.

Treatment may also include family therapy. The purpose of family therapy is to help family members understand the nature of mental retardation.

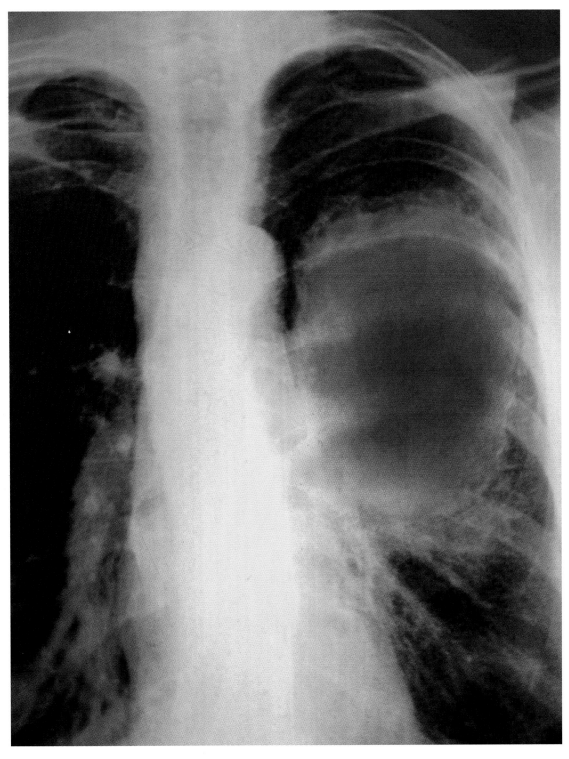

Colored X ray showing cancer in the left lung (right side of image). (Reproduced by permission of Custom Medical Stock Photo.)

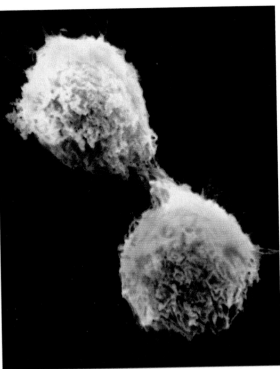

A magnified image of lung cancer cells. (© J. L. Carson. Reproduced by permission of Custom Medical Stock Photo.)

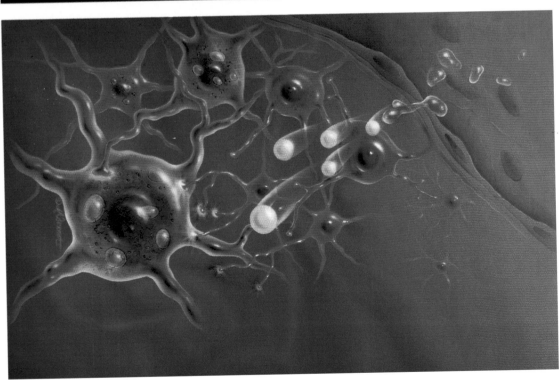

An illustration of Parkinson's disease at the cellular level. Parkinson's is caused by a disturbance in dopamine balance in the brain. (© 1996 Teri J. McDermott. Reproduced by permission of Custom Medical Stock Photo.)

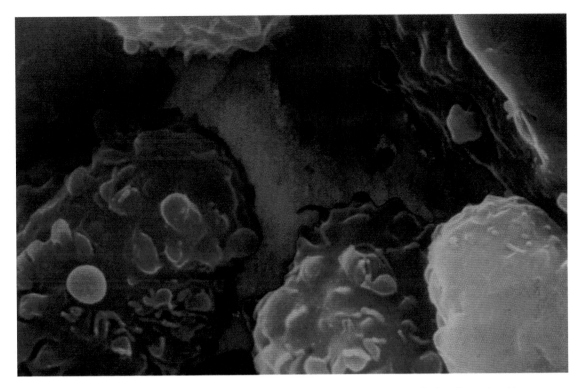

A magnified image of acute myelogenous leukemia cancer cells. (Photograph by Robert Becker. Reproduced by permission of Custom Medical Stock Photo.)

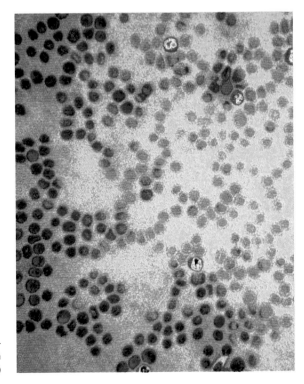

Chronic lymphocytic leukemia cells, colorized and magnified 400 times. (© 1999. Reproduced by permission of Custom Medical Stock Photo.)

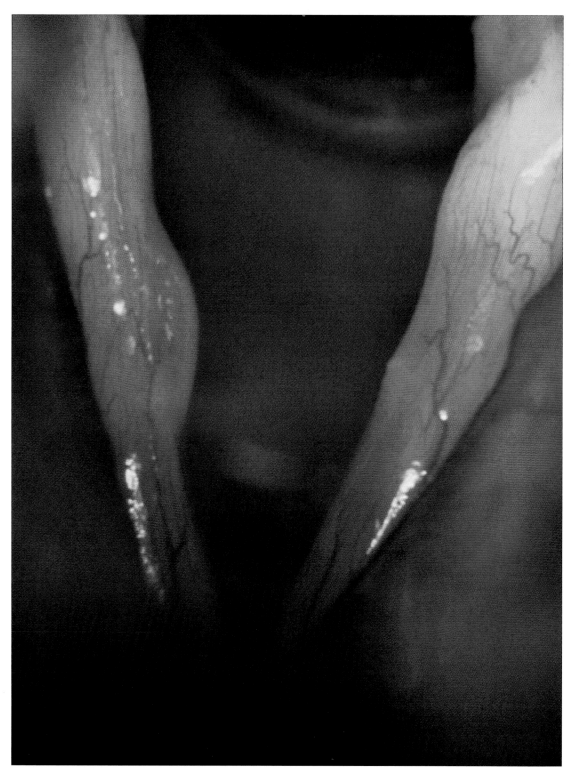

An endoscopic view of vocal cords with laryngitis. (Reproduced by permission of Custom Medical Stock Photo.)

A computer generated model of the outer protein coat of a polio virus. (© 1996 James M. Hegle, Harvard Medical School, Science Photo Library. Reproduced by permission of Custom Medical Stock Photo.)

The first sign of lyme disease is usually a rash around the site of the tick bite. The rash may be warm or itchy. (© 1993 Science Photo Library. Reproduced by permission of Custom Medical Stock Photo.)

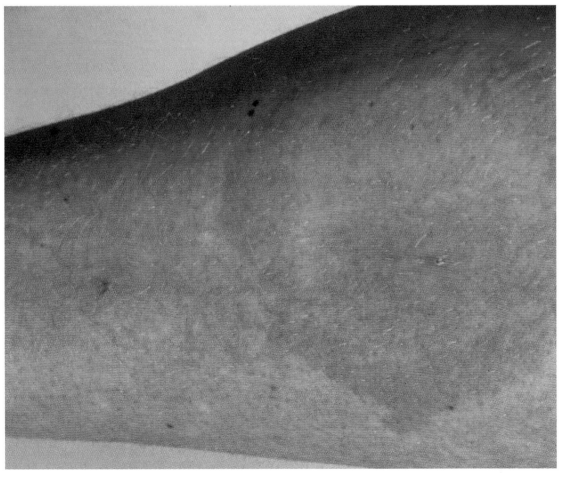

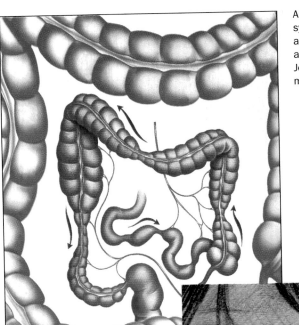

An illustration of the large intestine with irritable bowel syndrome. Red center shows abnormal colon, with areas of constriction which cause constipation, and areas of distention which cause diarrhea. (© 1995 John Bavosi/Science Photo Library. Reproduced by permission of Custom Medical Stock Photo.)

Most people experience moments of anxiety. But panic disorder is far more serious. It is a chronic, crippling condition that can have a devastating impact on a person's family, work, and social life. (© 1993 Andrew Bezear, Reed Business Publishing, Science Photo Library. Reproduced by permission of Custom Medical Stock Photo.)

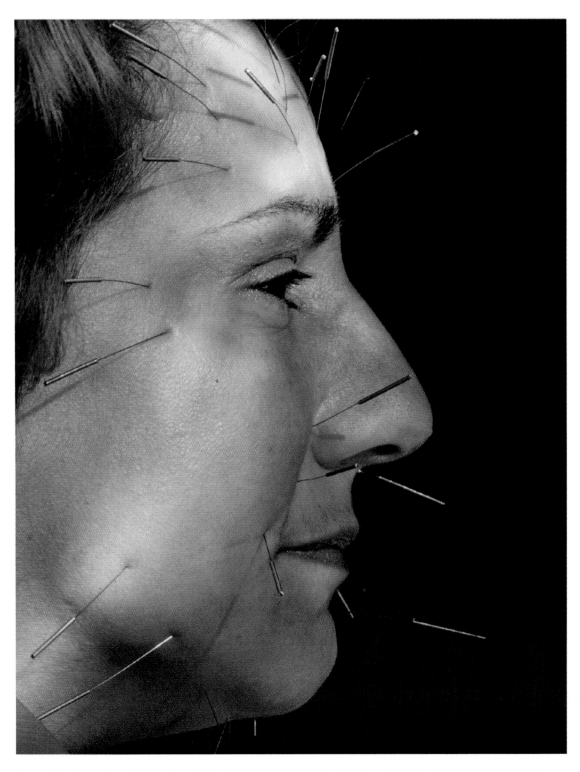

Acupuncture is an alternative treatment shown to be helpful for insomnia. (Reproduced by permission of Phototake, NYC.)

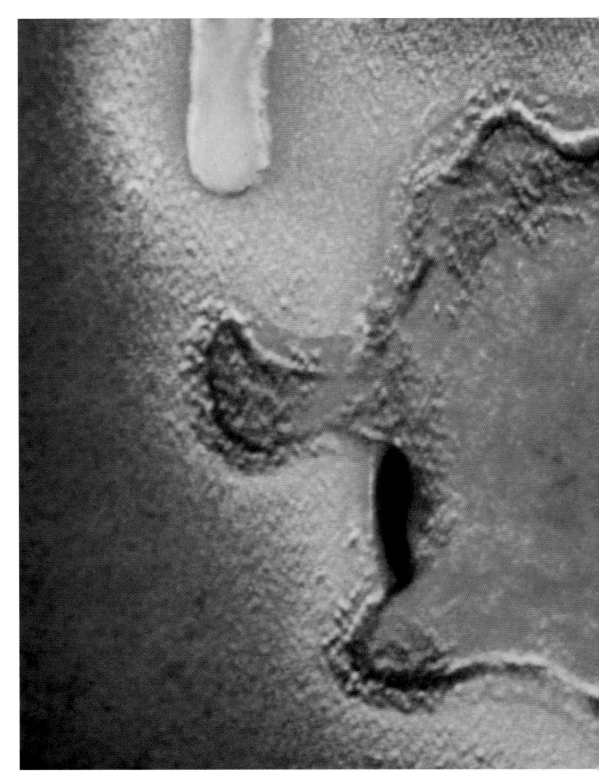

Measles virus seen through a microscope. (Reproduced by permission of Custom Medical Stock Photo.)

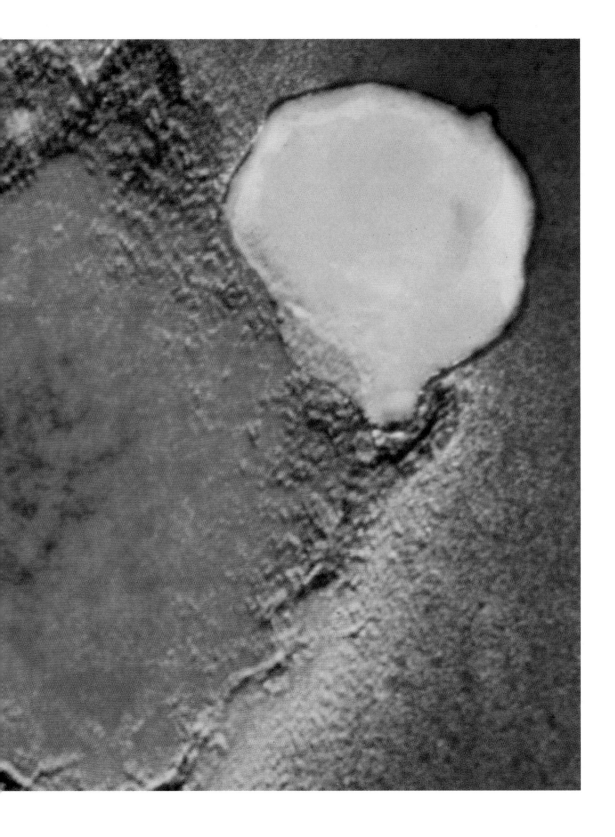

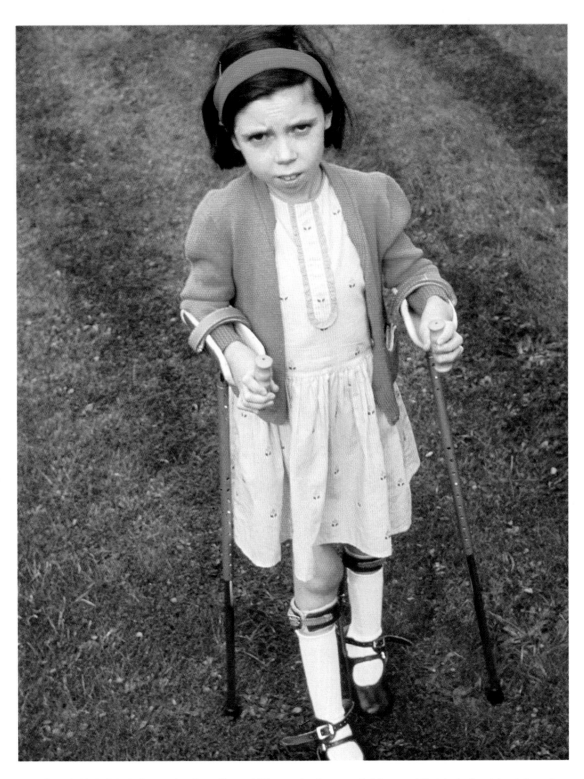

Juvenile arthritis is joint inflammation that affects children under the age of sixteen and that lasts for at least three to six months. (© John Moss. Reproduced by permission of Photo Researchers, Inc.)

A head louse and nits (eggs) on strands of human hair. (© 1990 David, National Medical. Reproduced by permission of Custom Medical Stock Photo.)

Lead-based paints are the most common source of exposure to lead among children. (Photograph by Robert J. Huffman, Field Mark Publications. Reproduced by permission.)

A close-up image of brain tissue covered with thick white exudate (pus) from acute meningitis. (© 1994 Joseph R. Siebert, Ph.D. Reproduced by permission of Custom Medical Stock Photo.)

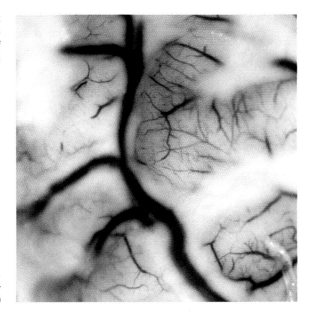

Acute meningitis, brain tissue with mucus in crevices. (© 1993 Joseph R. Siebert, Ph.D. Reproduced by permission of Custom Medical Stock Photo.)

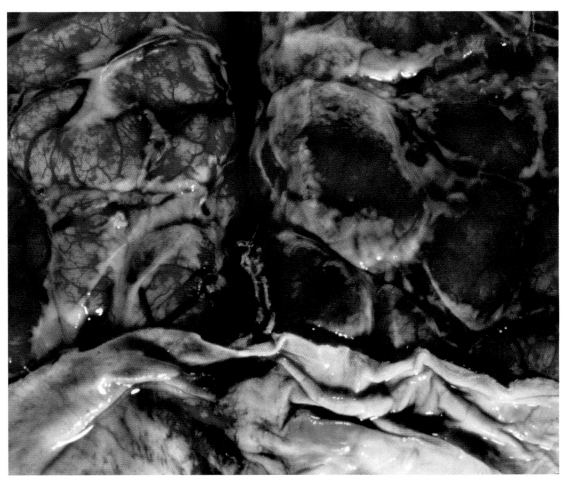

A magnified image of an influenza virus budding on the surface of an infected cell. (Reproduced by permission of CNRI/Science Photo Library, National Audubon Society Collection/Photo Researchers, Inc.)

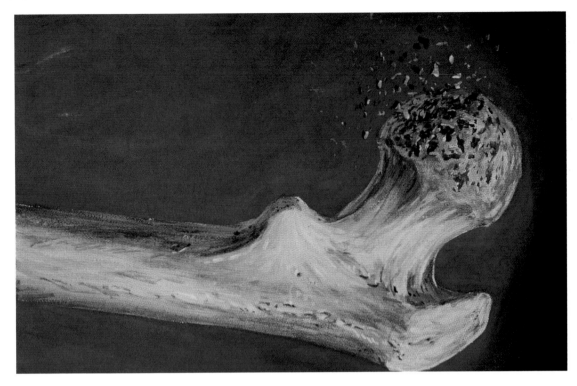

An illustration showing atrophy of a hip bone. (© 1993 Patrick McDonnel. Reproduced by permission of Custom Medical Stock Photo.)

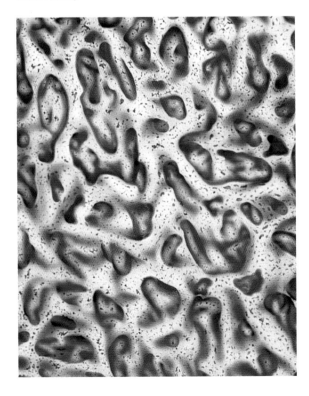

An illustration of osteoporosis bone matrix. (© 1997. Reproduced by permission of Custom Medical Stock Photo.)

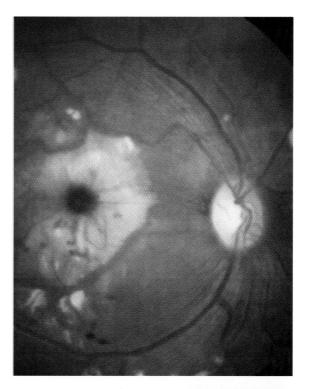

A view of the retina of a patient with systemic lupus erythematosus (SLE). The disease has caused extensive damage to the retina, seen as white patches around the macula (the dark spot at center-left). (© 1997 SPL, Sue Ford/Science Photo Library. Reproduced by permission of Custom Medical Stock Photo.)

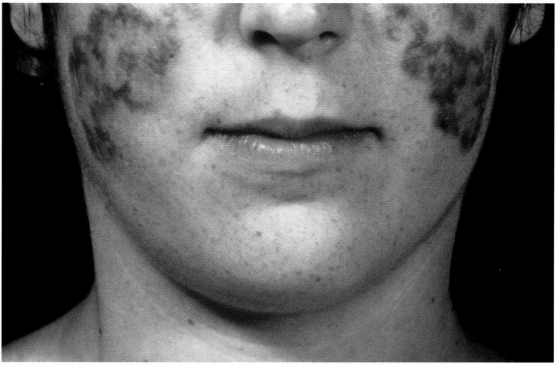

Lupus can cause skin rashes on any part of the body. One that often occurs on the face is called a butterfly rash. (© 1993 NMSB. Reproduced by permission of Custom Medical Stock Photo.)

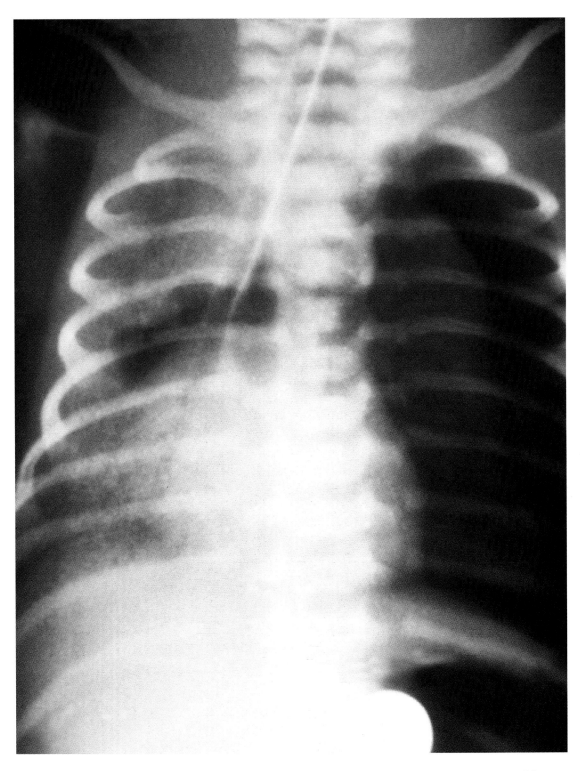

A chest x ray showing a collapsed right lung (the left side of the image). (© 1990. Reproduced by permission of Custom Medical Stock Photo.)

It also helps them develop skills for dealing with the special needs of a re-tarded child. Parents may also receive counseling to help them deal with feel-ings of anger or guilt.

PROGNOSIS

The prognosis for individuals with mild to moderate mental retardation is usually good. These individuals can often become self-sufficient to some degree. However, they may require some educational, community, social, fam-ily, and vocational support.

Lincoln Beard (back) and Forrest Beard (front), mentally retarded twin brothers, had their home converted into a group home where mentally retarded individuals can live in a community atmosphere with moderate supervision. (Reproduced by permission of AP/Wide World Photos)

The outlook is less promising for those with severe to profound retardation. These individuals tend to have a shortened life expectancy due to the medical problems that often accompany serious mental retardation.

PREVENTION

Many forms of mental retardation can be prevented. Pregnant women can avoid using alcohol, drugs, and tobacco. Infections they develop should be treated promptly. Good nutrition during pregnancy is always an important factor in providing the best possible environment for the fetus.

There are a variety of ways in which young children can be protected from mental retardation. For example, they should be vaccinated against infections that can lead to mental retardation. In addition, young children should see a medical professional on a regular basis. In this way, any decline in a child's health that could lead to mental retardation may be discovered.

FOR MORE INFORMATION

Books

Smith, Romayne, ed. *Children With Mental Retardation: A Parents' Guide.* Bethesda, MD: Woodbine House, 1993.

Organizations

American Association on Mental Retardation. 444 North Capitol Street NW, Suite 846, Washington, DC 20001-1512. (800) 424-3688. http://www.aamr.org.

The Arc of the United States (formerly, Association for Retarded Citizens of the United States). 500 East Border Street, Suite 300, Arlington, TX 76010. (817) 261-6003. http://www.thearc.org.

See also: Down's syndrome.

MULTIPLE SCLEROSIS

DEFINITION

Multiple sclerosis (MS; pronounced multiple skluh-RO-siss) is a chronic autoimmune disorder (see autoimmune disorders entry) that affects the nerves. "Chronic" means that it develops slowly over time; "autoimmune" means that the body's immune system becomes confused about some part of the body it is designed to protect. It attacks that part of the body as if it were a foreign invader. MS affects a person's ability to move, to feel, and to control his or her body functions.

DESCRIPTION

Nerve messages consist of electrical impulses that travel through the body by means of nerve cells. Nerve cells are also called neurons. Neurons are covered by a thin layer of tissue known as myelin (pronounced MY-uh-lin) that acts as an insulator. It prevents the electrical currents that pass through neurons from leaking away.

MS AFFECTS MORE THAN 250,000 PEOPLE IN THE UNITED STATES. MOST PEOPLE EXPERIENCE THEIR FIRST SYMPTOMS BETWEEN THE AGES OF TWENTY AND FORTY.

MS occurs when the myelin that surrounds neurons in the brain and spinal cord is destroyed. The loss of myelin causes electrical impulses to pass through neurons more slowly. Over time, scar tissue forms around the damaged myelin. This scar tissue, called plaque (pronounced PLAK), also reduces the neurons' ability to function normally.

Damage to myelin can cause a variety of symptoms. A person may lose the ability to use his or her senses, such as touch and vision. Loss of muscular control also occurs because movement of muscles is controlled by nerves. A person with MS may have problems with balance, strength, and coordination.

MS affects more than 250,000 people in the United States. Most people experience their first symptoms between the ages of twenty and forty. Symptoms rarely begin before the age of fifteen or after sixty. Women are twice as likely to get MS as men, especially in their early years. MS is more common among some ethnic groups than others. For example, the disease is more common in North America and northern Europe than in other parts of the world. MS is very rare among Asians, Indians of North and South America, and Eskimos.

CAUSES

Multiple sclerosis is an autoimmune disease in which the immune system begins to attack myelin. It "decides" that the myelin is a foreign

WORDS TO KNOW

Evoked potential test (EPT): A test that measures the brain's electrical response to certain kinds of stimulation, such as light in the eyes, sound in the ears, or touch on the skin.

Myelin: A layer of tissue that surrounds nerves and acts as an insulator.

Plaque: Patches of scar tissue that form in areas where myelin tissue has been destroyed.

Primary progressive: A form of multiple sclerosis in which the disease continually becomes worse without any major improvement.

Relapsing-remitting: A form of multiple sclerosis in which symptoms appear for at least twenty-four hours and then disappear for a period of time.

Secondary progressive: A form of multiple sclerosis in which a period of relapses and remissions is followed by another period in which the disease becomes progressively worse without improvement.

substance that threatens the body and must be destroyed. Researchers do not know why this happens.

As myelin is destroyed, neurons no longer function normally. Brain neurons cannot receive and process information from the outside world. Neurons in the brain and the spinal cord cannot send messages to other parts of the body. Normal muscular functions, such as standing, walking, lifting, and turning, become difficult or impossible.

The progress of MS seems to depend on the appearance of new plaques. These plaques slow down nerve messages and worsen the symptoms of the disease. Scientists do not understand how, where, and why plaques develop. For that reason, they cannot predict how the disease will progress in any one person over time.

Finding the reason for a body's autoimmune reaction to myelin is a major field of research. So far, no final answer has been found. Some possible factors leading to this condition are a person's heredity (his or her genes), environmental factors, viruses, or a combination of these factors.

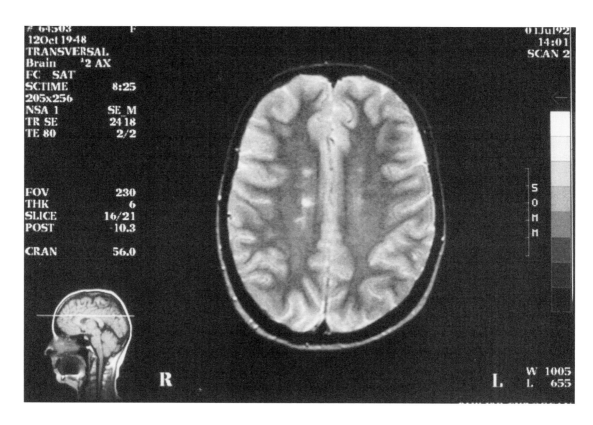

An MRI scan showing legions, which are often an indicator of MS, in the left lobe of the brain. (Reproduced by permission of Custom Medical Stock Photo)

The reason that heredity is considered a possible factor is that MS seems to run in some families. A person who has a family member with MS is more likely to develop the disease than someone whose family has no history of MS. In addition, the tendency of some ethnic groups to contract (get) the disease suggests a hereditary factor.

Support for environmental factors comes from data on migration. Migration is the process of moving from one part of the world to another part. Studies have been done on people who move from a low-risk part of the world (such as Asia) to a high-risk part (such as the United States). Young people who make such moves have a higher risk of developing MS than those of the same age who remained at home. Older people do not experience an increased risk. These data suggest that environmental conditions in the new location might be responsible for MS.

One possible environmental factor is viruses. There are some kinds of viruses that attack the body very slowly. HIV, the virus that causes AIDS (see AIDS entry), is one such virus. Some researchers think that a slow-acting virus may be responsible for MS. But no data supporting this theory have yet been produced.

SYMPTOMS

Multiple sclerosis can develop in one of three patterns. The most common pattern is called "relapsing-remitting." In this pattern, symptoms appear and then disappear. A person may feel fine for a while and then experience the symptoms of MS for a period of twenty-four hours or more. Then the symptoms disappear again for a span of time. That span may be as long as a year or more at the beginning of the disease. But the span grows shorter as the person becomes older. This pattern is especially common in younger people with MS.

"Primary progressive" is a second pattern. In this pattern, the disease simply gets worse over time. A person may have brief periods when the disease does not get worse, but these are rare. The primary progressive pattern is more common in older people.

The "secondary progressive" pattern is a combination of the first two patterns. A patient first goes through a period of relapsing and remitting. Eventually, however, the disease just continues to get worse, as in the primary progressive pattern.

Between 10 percent and 20 percent of MS patients have a benign form of MS. Benign means that the symptoms do not change very much throughout a person's life.

The actual symptoms of MS vary considerably from person to person. The reason for this is that plaques form in different places and at different times in different individuals. Some initial symptoms of the disease include:

• Muscle weakness, causing difficulty in walking
• Loss of coordination or balance
• Numbness, feelings of "pins and needles," or other abnormal sensations
• Problems with vision, including blurred or double vision

As the disease develops, other symptoms may appear. These include:

• Fatigue
• Muscle stiffness
• Tremors (shaking)
• Paralysis
• Pain
• Vertigo (dizziness, light-headedness)
• Difficulty with speech and/or swallowing
• Loss of bowel or bladder control
• Constipation
• Sexual problems
• Changes in one's ability to think clearly

Weakness in one or both legs is common. It is often the first symptom noticed by a person with MS. Excessive tightness of muscles is also common. It may actually cause more problems than muscular weakness.

Damage to myelin in the optical (eye) nerves can cause visual problems, such as blurred vision, changes in color vision, and even blindness. The condition may affect one or both eyes.

More than half of all people with MS have pain during the course of their disease. Many experience pain nearly all the time, often because of muscle spasticity (stiffness). The pain is often a sharp, stabbing pain, especially in the face, neck, or back. Numbness and weakness in the face are also common.

Some mental changes that can occur include loss of memory, depression, and personality changes. Some of these changes may result from damage to neurons. Others may be a side effect caused by the patient's despair about the disease. In less common cases, a person with MS may actually feel happier than usual.

The symptoms of MS can be affected by environmental conditions. Heat; increased body temperature; vigorous physical activity; or exposure to sun, hot baths, or showers can make symptoms worse.

DIAGNOSIS

Sometimes a doctor can make a reliable diagnosis of MS fairly easily and quickly. The distribution of symptoms is important since MS affects many different areas of the body over a period of time. The pattern of symptoms is also important. A case of relapsing-remitting MS can often be diagnosed because of the way the symptoms come and go.

Since the symptoms of MS are similar to those of other diseases, diagnosis can often be difficult and complicated. Many tests and extended observation may be necessary to decide what is causing the patient's symptoms.

The usual medical procedures used to make a diagnosis include a medical history, a standard neurological (nervous system) examination, and several laboratory tests. Among the tests most commonly used to confirm or rule out a diagnosis of MS are:

- Magnetic resonance imaging (MRI) can show plaques on the brain and spinal cord. But plaques are present with other disorders as well. For example, the plaques caused by MS are sometimes difficult to distinguish from those caused by strokes (see stroke entry) or the simple process of aging.
- A lumbar puncture (spinal tap) is a process in which cerebrospinal fluid (CSF) is removed from the patient's spine with a long, thin needle. The CSF is then studied. The presence of white blood cells and other substances may be a clue to the presence of MS.
- Evoked potential tests (EPT) are tests that measure how quickly an electrical current passes through neurons. Scientists know the normal rate at which currents pass. If they move more slowly than normal, plaques may be present. An EPT can be conducted in various ways. One method is to apply a small electrical charge to the skin. A light can also be shined into a person's eyes. Or a tone can be sounded near his or her ears.

The neurologist (nerve specialist) conducting these tests may decide the patient is in one of three categories: "definite MS," "probable MS," or "possible MS." These three categories represent decreasing confidence in the accuracy of the diagnosis.

TREATMENT

Treatment of MS takes two forms. First, although there are no drugs that will actually cure the disease, there are drugs that can slow down the course of MS. Second, a variety of treatments can be used to ease the symptoms of multiple sclerosis.

As of 1997, three drugs had been approved for use with multiple sclerosis: Avonex, Betaseron, and Copaxone. All three reduce the rate of relapses in the relapsing-remitting form of MS. Each has other benefits as well. Avonex may slow the progress of physical damage; Betaseron may reduce the severity of symptoms; and Copaxone may decrease disability. All three drugs are administered by injection.

Immunosuppressant drugs have also been used to treat severe relapses. These drugs act on the immune system directly, causing it to work less effectively. The drugs carry some risks, so a patient may have to be hospitalized during treatment.

MS causes a large variety of symptoms. For that reason, many different treatments may be necessary to relieve those symptoms. A person should be vaccinated against influenza (see influenza entry). The vaccination can help protect against respiratory (breathing) problems, thus reducing the symptoms of MS. Preventing complications from MS is also important. Such complications include pneumonia (see pneumonia entry), bed sores, injuries from falls, or urinary infections. These complications lead to death more often than does MS.

Physical therapy is important in treating MS. It helps the patient strengthen and retrain affected muscles, maintain range of motion to prevent muscle stiffening, learn to use assistive devices such as canes and walkers, and learn safer and more energy-efficient ways of moving and sitting.

A program of physical therapy usually includes exercise and stretching. These activities can be taught and practiced at home. Swimming is often recommended. It provides a way for a patient to get exercise without becoming overheated.

Treatment programs usually include occupational therapy as well. People with MS are taught how to deal with daily activities, such as dressing, feeding, and washing. The occupational therapist can make suggestions for arranging the home and work environment so that an MS patient can function more safely and efficiently.

An MS patient may need training in bowel and bladder control. Drugs are sometimes used to deal with these problems. They help the patient to empty his or her bowel and bladder on a more normal schedule.

Spasticity can be treated with drugs as well. Baclofen (pronounced BAK-lo-fen) and diazepam (pronounced di-AZE-uh-pam, trade name Valium) are given by mouth, while botulin toxin (Botox) is given by injection. These drugs can help relieve the pain caused by spasticity. Back pain can be treated with over-the-counter pain relievers, such as aspirin or acetaminophen (pronounced uh-see-tuh-MIN-uh-fuhn, trade name Tylenol), or with physical therapy.

Fatigue can be treated by having the patient plan and follow a regular daily routine. The routine should allow for frequent rest periods. Drugs such as amantadine (pronounced uh-MANT-uh-deen, trade name Symmetrel) and pemoline (pronounced PEM-uh-leen, trade name Cylert) can help improve alertness and lessen fatigue. Corticosteroids are used to treat visual problems. Other types of drugs can be used to treat seizures, vertigo, and tremor.

Alternative Treatment

A variety of alternative treatments have been recommended for multiple sclerosis. So far, there are few scientific data to support most of these claims. For example, bee venom has been suggested as a treatment for MS. But studies have not supported this claim. Marijuana has been recommended for the relief of certain symptoms of MS, including tremor, pain, and spasticity. But the drug has side effects of its own. It is not widely recommended in the United States for the treatment of MS.

Some practitioners suggest that high doses of vitamins, minerals, and other dietary supplements can help slow the progress of MS. Specific nutrients recommended include linoleic (pronounced lin-uh-LEE-ik) acids, selenium, vitamin E, and a diet low in saturated fats.

Lane Phalen, a multiple sclerosis sufferer, with her service dog. The dog helps her with daily activities that have become difficult because of MS. (Reproduced by permission of AP/Wide World Photos)

PROGNOSIS

The prognosis for MS differs markedly from person to person. Most people with the disease can continue walking and functioning at home and work for many years after their diagnosis. Some conditions that favor a promising diagnosis include being female, having the relapsing-remitting form of the disease, having the first symptoms at an early age, having long periods of remission between relapses, and having vision and touch symptoms rather than muscular problems.

Less than 5 percent of people with MS have a severe progressive form of the disease that leads to death within five years. At the other extreme, 10 percent to 20 percent have a benign (relatively harmless) form with very slow or no progression of symptoms. On average, MS shortens the lives of women with the disease by about six years and men by about eleven years. Suicide is a significant cause of death in people with MS, especially among younger patients.

Most people experience the severest disabilities of MS within five years of diagnosis. After that point, disabilities do not continue to worsen significantly. If no disabilities appear within the first five years, they are unlikely to occur at all.

PREVENTION

There is no known way to prevent multiple sclerosis. Until the cause of the disease is discovered, that will continue to be the case. The symptoms of the disease can be reduced, however, by good nutrition; adequate rest; avoidance of stress, heat, and extreme physical exercise; and good bladder hygiene.

FOR MORE INFORMATION

Books

Holland, Nancy T., Jock Murray, and Stephen Reingold. *Multiple Sclerosis: A Guide for the Newly Diagnosed.* New York: Demos Vermande, 1996.

Kalb, Rosalind C., ed. *Multiple Sclerosis: A Guide for Families.* New York: Demos Vermande, 1997.

Matthews, Bryan. *Multiple Sclerosis: The Facts.* New York: Oxford University Press, 1993.

Swank, R. L., and M. H. Pullen. *The Multiple Sclerosis Diet Book.* Garden City, NH: Doubleday, 1997.

Organizations

Multiple Sclerosis Association of America. 706 Haddonfield Road, Cherry Hill, NJ 08002-2652. (800) LEARN-MS; (609) 488-4500. http://www.msaa.com.

The National Multiple Sclerosis Society. 733 Third Avenue, New York, NY 10017. (800) FIGHT-MS. http://www.nmss.org.

MUMPS

DEFINITION

Mumps is a relatively mild viral infection of the salivary glands that usually occurs during childhood. Typically, mumps is characterized by a painful swelling of both cheeks. In some cases, the swelling may occur in only one cheek, or there may be no swelling at all. The word "mumps" comes from an old English word meaning lumps or bumps in the cheeks.

DESCRIPTION

Mumps is a very contagious (catching) infection. It spreads easily in densely populated areas, such as schools. At one time, mumps was very common in the United States. Prior to 1967, about 92 percent of all children had been exposed to mumps by the age of fifteen. Most children developed the disease between the ages of four and seven. Mumps epidemics reappeared in two- to five-year cycles. The greatest mumps epidemic in modern times occurred in 1941. There were about 250 cases of the disease for every 100,000 Americans.

This pattern began to change in 1968, when a mumps vaccine was released. The vaccine proved very effective in preventing the disease. By 1985, less than 3,000 cases of mumps were reported in the entire United States. That works out to less than 1 case per 100,000 people.

Only two years later, the news about mumps in the United States had taken a turn for the worse. The rate of infections had increased five times. The reason given for this increase was the failure to have all young children vaccinated against the disease. Many states became concerned about this trend. They passed laws requiring all children in kindergarten and first grade to have vaccinations against mumps. The success of these efforts became apparent in 1996. In that year, only 751 cases of mumps were reported nationwide, or about 1 case for every 5 million people.

WORDS TO KNOW

Encephalitis: Inflammation of the brain.

Meningitis: Inflammation of the tissue surrounding the brain and spinal cord.

CAUSES

The virus that causes mumps lives in a person's saliva. It is spread by coughing, sneezing, or other direct contact between people.

SYMPTOMS

Once a person is exposed to the virus, symptoms occur in fourteen to twenty-four days. Initial symptoms include chills, headache, loss of appetite, and a lack of energy. Less than twenty-four hours later, the salivary glands in the face begin to swell. The patient finds it painful to chew or swallow, especially acidic beverages like orange juice and lemonade. A fever as high as 104°F is also common.

The swelling reaches a maximum on about the second day. It usually disappears completely by the seventh day. Once a person has had mumps, he or she can never have the disease again.

The majority of cases of mumps disappear without complications. Complications are more likely to occur with adults who get the infection. In 15 percent of all cases, the mumps virus spreads to the brain. There, it causes an inflammation of brain tissue known as meningitis (pronounced meh-nen-JI-tiss; see meningitis entry). Symptoms of meningitis usually develop within four or five days after the first signs of mumps. These symptoms include a stiff neck, headache, vomiting, and a lack of energy. Meningitis is a very serious condition and must be treated very quickly.

The mumps virus can cause another disease of the brain known as encephalitis ("brain fever"; see encephalitis entry). The symptoms of mumps encephalitis include the inability to feel pain, seizures, and a high fever. Most patients recover from mumps encephalitis without complications. In about 1 percent of all cases, a person dies from mumps encephalitis. Those who survive may develop seizure disorders that can stay with a person throughout his or her life.

About a quarter of all adolescent boys who develop mumps also experience swelling of the scrotum (the sac that contains the testicles). This swelling is accompanied by severe pain, fever, nausea, and headache. These symptoms tend to disappear after five to seven days, although the testicles may remain tender for weeks.

DIAGNOSIS

Before the mumps vaccine was developed, diagnosing mumps was easy. Most doctors had seen many cases of mumps and recognized the characteristic swollen salivary glands as a sign of the disease. Today, the disease is so rare that it can easily be missed. A doctor may attribute the swelling to some other condition, such as a bacterial infection. To diagnose mumps, then, the doctor's primary goal is to rule out other possible explanations for swollen salivary glands. A simple test is available that tells whether the swelling is caused by mumps or by some other condition, such as poor oral (tooth-care) hygiene.

TREATMENT

There is no treatment for mumps. All that can be done is to allow the disease to run its course. However, steps can be taken to make the patient more comfortable. For example, acetaminophen (pronounced uh-see-tuh-

The greatest mumps epidemic in modern times occurred in 1941. There were about 250 cases of the disease for every 100,000 Americans. (Reproduced by permission of AP/Wide World Photos)

MIN-uh-fuhn, trade name Tylenol), or ibuprofen (pronounced i-byoo-PRO-fuhn, trade name Advil) can help relieve the pain due to swelling, headache, and fever. Aspirin should never be given to children who have mumps. Aspirin has been found to cause Reye's syndrome (see Reye's syndrome entry), a potentially fatal disease.

Because of difficulty swallowing, the most important challenge is to keep the patient fed and hydrated (given liquids). He or she should be provided with a soft diet, consisting of cooked cereals, mashed potatoes, broth-based soups, prepared baby foods, or foods put through a home food processor. Fruit juices should be avoided because they can irritate the salivary glands. Patients also should not be given dairy products because they may be difficult to digest.

In the event of complications, a doctor should be contacted at once. For example, there are treatments that can relieve the discomfort of swelling of the scrotum.

Alternative Treatment

Some patients find that acupressure (a Chinese therapy that involves applying pressure to certain points in the body) can help relieve the pain of swollen glands. They use their middle fingers to press gently on the area between the jawbone and the ear for two minutes while breathing deeply.

A number of homeopathic remedies have been recommended for various symptoms of mumps. These include belladonna for swelling and redness; wild hops for lack of energy, irritability, and thirst; and poke root for

GROWING VIRUSES

Until the 1940s, research on viruses progressed very slowly. A major problem was that no one knew how to grow viruses in the laboratory. By contrast, bacteria were easy to grow. Sometimes, all that was needed was to keep food open to the air. Bacteria grew quickly on the food.

An important breakthrough came when scientists discovered that viruses will grow in live chick embryos. Live chick embryos are easy to find—just crack open a fertilized egg! The problem was that bacteria also like to grow in chick embryos. By the 1940s, that problem could be solved as well.

Simply adding an antibiotic to the chick embryo killed the bacteria, but had no effect on the viruses.

Much of the work done on growing viruses was conducted by American bacteriologist John F. Enders (1897–1985) and his colleagues at Children's Hospital in Boston. With the technique they developed, Enders and his colleagues were able to grow the viruses that cause mumps, measles, poliomyelitis, chickenpox, and other diseases. They eventually developed vaccines for mumps and measles. Other researchers later used the same techniques to develop a vaccine for poliomyelitis.

swollen glands. Homeopathic remedies that do not have an effect on the patient should not be continued.

Several herbal remedies may be useful in helping the body recover from a mumps infection or helping to relieve the discomfort of the disease. These herbs include echinacea (pronounced ek-i-NAY-see-uh), cleavers, calendula (pronounced KUH-len-juh-luh), and poke root. Poke root can be toxic, so it should be used only under the close supervision of a trained practitioner.

Some herbal remedies are applied as packs placed directly on the swollen glands. These packs may be dipped in a solution of vinegar and cayenne or a solution made from cleavers or calendula mixed with vinegar and heated.

PROGNOSIS

The prognosis for mumps is usually excellent. Most patients recover completely from the disease with no aftereffects. In rare cases, a relapse (return of the disease) may occur after about two weeks. Complications occur rarely.

PREVENTION

Today, mumps is a preventable disease. A vaccine against the disease is usually given in combination with vaccines for measles (see measles entry) and rubella (see rubella entry). The vaccine is called the MMR vaccine. It is usually given in a single dose between the ages of twelve and fifteen months, four and six years, or eleven and twelve years. Anyone who is not certain whether he or she has had a vaccination should be vaccinated.

Vaccinations are also recommended for certain groups of people. For example, health-care workers should be vaccinated to protect them from infection by clients. People who travel to other parts of the world should consider a mumps vaccination. Although the disease has largely disappeared in the United States, it is still common in many other parts of the world.

On the other hand, there are some people who should not be vaccinated against mumps. For these people, the vaccine can be more dangerous than the disease it is intended to prevent. Among those who should not be vaccinated are the following:

- pregnant women
- anyone with an illness accompanied by a mild fever
- people who are allergic to eggs and/or egg products
- persons with conditions that have damaged their immune systems, such as those who are HIV-positive

FOR MORE INFORMATION

Books

Stoffman, Phyllis. *The Family Guide to Preventing and Treating 100 Infectious Diseases.* New York: John Wiley & Sons, 1995.

MUSCULAR DYSTROPHY

DEFINITION

Muscular dystrophy (MD) is the name for a group of disorders in which muscle size and strength gradually decrease over time. Nine different forms of the disorder have been discovered.

DESCRIPTION

The nine different forms of muscular dystrophy are usually distinguished by the part of the body they affect. They include the following:

- **Duchenne muscular dystrophy (DMD).** DMD primarily affects young boys. It causes weakness in the muscles that gets worse over time. The problem usually begins in the legs and then spreads to muscles in other parts of the body. It is the severest form of MD. DMD occurs in about 1 out of every 3,500 male births. About 8,000 boys and young men in the United States have the disorder. A milder form of the disorder occurs in a very few females.
- **Becker muscular dystrophy (BMD).** BMD affects older boys and young men. It is a milder form of MD than DMD, which occurs in about 1 in every 30,000 male births.
- **Emery-Dreifuss muscular dystrophy (EDMD).** EDMD is a very rare form of MD. It affects young boys exclusively. It causes contracture (permanent tightening) and weakness of the calf muscles and weakness in the shoulders and upper arms. It can also cause problems in the electrical signals that cause the heart to beat. Fewer than 300 cases of EDMD have been seen.
- **Limb-girdle muscular dystrophy (LGMD).** LGMD begins in later childhood or early adulthood. It affects both men and women. It causes weakness in the muscles around the hips and shoulders. LGMD has the greatest variety of symptoms of all forms of MD. In fact, researchers think it may actually consist of other forms of the disorder. Diagnosis of LGMD is difficult, and some patients with the disorder may have been diagnosed incorrectly in the past. The number of people with LGMD in the United States is probably a few thousand.

- **Facioscapulohumeral muscular dystrophy (FSH).** (pronounced FAY-shee-o-SKAP-yuh-lo-HYOOM-uh-ruhl) is also known as Landouzy-Dejerine disease. It begins in later childhood or early adulthood. It affects both men and women. FSH is characterized by weakness in the muscles of the face, shoulders, and upper arms. The hips and legs may also be affected. FSH occurs in about 1 out of every 2,000 people. About 13,000 people in the United States have the condition.
- **Myotonic dystrophy.** Myotonic (pronounced my-uh-TON-ik) dystrophy is also known as Steinert's disease. It affects both men and women. The disorder is usually seen first in the face, feet, and hands. It is characterized by an inability to relax the affected muscles. This condition is known as myotonia (pronounced my-uh-TO-nee-uh). Symptoms may first appear at any time between birth and adulthood. It is the most common form of MD. About 30,000 people in the United States have myotonic dystrophy.
- **Oculopharyngeal muscular dystrophy (OPMD).** Oculopharyngeal (pronounced OK-yuh-lo-fuh-RIN-jee-uhl) muscular dystrophy OPMD causes weakness in the eye muscles and throat. It affects adults of both sexes. It is most common among French Canadian families in Quebec and in Spanish American families in the southwestern United States.
- **Distal muscular dystrophy (DD).** DD begins in middle age or later. It causes weakness in the muscles of the feet and hands. It is most common in Sweden and rare in other parts of the world.
- **Congenital muscular dystrophy (CMD).** CMD appears at birth and progresses slowly thereafter. It causes a generalized weakness in muscles

---

WORDS TO KNOW

Becker muscular dystrophy (BMD): A type of muscular dystrophy that affects older boys and men and usually follows a milder course than DMD.

Contracture: A permanent shortening and tightening of a muscle or tendon causing a deformity.

Distal muscular dystrophy (DD): A form of muscular dystrophy that usually begins in middle age or later, causing weakness in the muscles of the feet and hands.

Duchenne muscular dystrophy (DMD): The severest form of muscular dystrophy, usually affecting young boys, beginning in the legs, and resulting in progressive muscle weakness.

Facioscapulohumeral muscular dystrophy (FSH): A form of muscular dystrophy that begins in late childhood to early adulthood; affects both men and women; and causes weakness in the muscles of the face, shoulders, and upper arms.

Limb-girdle muscular dystrophy (LGMD): A form of muscular dystrophy that begins in late childhood to early adulthood; affects both men and women; and causes weakness in the muscles around the hips and shoulders.

Myotonic dystrophy: A form of muscular dystrophy that affects both men and women and causes generalized weakness in the face, feet, and hands.

Oculopharyngeal muscular dystrophy (OPMD): A form of muscular dystrophy that affects adults of both sexes and causes weakness in the muscles of the eyes and throat.

throughout the body. One form of the disorder is called Fukuyama, for a district in Japan where it is relatively common. Fukuyama CMD also causes mental retardation.

CAUSES

All forms of muscular dystrophy are caused by wasting of muscle tissue. Muscle cells die, and muscles become weaker and unable to perform their normal functions. Researchers are still uncertain how this loss of muscle function takes place. They believe that cells may lose their ability to produce certain muscle proteins. Proteins are essential chemicals that occur in all cells and have many different functions. For example, they act as building blocks for cells and as enzymes. Enzymes are special kinds of proteins that control the rate at which chemical reactions take place in cells.

Researchers believe that some forms of MD occur because some muscle proteins are absent or present in smaller-than-average amounts. In such cases, muscle tissue becomes weak. Other muscle proteins may be needed to repair damage in muscle tissue. If those proteins are absent, muscles that are damaged cannot be repaired. In most cases, the connection between absent muscle proteins or reduced amounts of proteins and various forms of MD is simply not yet known.

ALL FORMS OF MUSCULAR DYSTROPHY ARE CAUSED BY WASTING OF MUSCLE TISSUE. RESEARCHERS ARE STILL UNCERTAIN HOW THIS LOSS OF MUSCLE TAKES PLACE.

What scientists do know is that MD is almost entirely a genetic disorder. A genetic disorder is a medical problem caused by defects in a person's genes. Genes are chemical units found within cells that carry essential information telling the cell what functions it should perform. Every person gets two sets of genes, one from each parent. Under most circumstances, the two sets of genes merge to produce a normal set of instructions. A cell follows those instructions to perform a normal set of functions.

Occasionally, a person inherits faulty genes from one or both of his or her parents. In such cases, the instructions provided to a cell can be incorrect and the cell is unable to perform its normal functions.

In the case of MD, a person may receive a single faulty gene from one parent or a pair of faulty genes, one from each parent. A single faulty gene may cause no problem at all. In that case, the person is said to be a carrier. A carrier can transmit the faulty gene to his or her own children. But it will not interfere with the person's own health.

In other cases, one faulty gene is all it takes to cause some form of MD. For example, DMD, FSH, OPMD, and some forms of LGMD and DD are thought to be caused by a single faulty gene. The faulty gene may make it impossible for muscle cells to function as they should. Muscle tissues weaken, and some form of muscular dystrophy results.

Other forms of MD require the presence of two faulty genes, one from each parent. CMD and some forms of LGMD and DD are thought to be caused by this mechanism. Again, the two faulty genes carry incorrect information to a cell and the cell does not function normally. It produces faulty muscle protein, an insufficient amount of the protein, or no protein at all. Muscle tissue weakens and dies, and MD results.

SYMPTOMS

All forms of MD have one characteristic in common—muscular weakness. Other symptoms differ, however, depending on the type of MD involved.

DMD Symptoms

The first symptoms of DMD appear during preschool years. The disorder affects the legs first. A boy has trouble walking and maintaining balance. In most cases, he begins walking three to six months later than average. As his calf muscles begin to weaken, he may change the way he walks. He places his legs farther apart in order to maintain balance. Walking this way produces a waddling effect that is characteristic of DMD.

Contractures usually begin at about the age of five or six. They affect the calf muscles most severely, pulling the foot down and back. This forces a boy to walk on his tiptoes. Balance becomes more of a problem. As a result, falls and broken bones become common at this age. By the age of nine or ten, a boy with DMD might not be able to climb stairs or stand by himself. Most DMD patients have to use a wheelchair by the age of twelve.

Muscles in other parts of the body are also weakened. When muscles in the upper body are affected, scoliosis (see scoliosis entry), or curvature of the spine, may result. The most serious problem, however, affects the muscles of the diaphragm. The diaphragm provides the in-and-out force that allows a person to breathe and to cough. As the diaphragm weakens, breathing becomes more difficult and patients will have less energy and stamina. They also become more subject to infection because they cannot cough up infectious agents that get into their lungs. Young men with DMD can live into their twenties provided they have mechanical aids to help with their breathing and good respiratory (breathing system) hygiene.

FAULTY GENES AND MD

Sometimes faulty genes occur on the Y chromosome but not the X chromosome. Chromosomes are structures in cells that contain many genes. Women have two X chromosomes and no Y chromosomes. Men have one X chromosome and one Y chromosome. Faulty genes that occur in Y chromosomes are only present in men. This explains why some forms of muscular dystrophy affect men only. Men inherit those faulty genes, but women do not.

About a third of the boys with DMD also have learning disorders. These disorders can include problems with learning by ear and trouble paying attention to some tasks. Specialized educational problems can help compensate for these disorders.

BMD Symptoms

The symptoms of BMD usually appear in late childhood to early adulthood. They are similar to those of DMD, but they are usually less severe. They may also develop at a different rate and in a different pattern. For example, young men with BMD can often walk on their own into their twenties or early thirties. Scoliosis may also develop, but it is less severe and develops more slowly. One symptom that is more serious in BMD than DMD involves heart problems. These problems include irregular heartbeats and congestive heart failure. Symptoms related to heart problems include fatigue, shortness of breath, chest pain, and dizziness. Respiratory problems may also develop, requiring the use of a mechanical device to help the patient breathe.

EDMD Symptoms

EDMD usually begins in early childhood. The first symptom is likely to be contractures, which is a permanent shortening of a muscle. Muscle weakness then appears in the shoulders, upper arms, and calves. Most men with EDMD survive into middle age. As with BMD, heart problems may develop and can cause death.

LGMD Symptoms

At least two forms of LGMD occur. One develops during childhood and the other in the teens or twenties. The major symptom is weakening of muscles in the center of the body. Contractures may occur, and most people lose the ability to walk about twenty years after their disorder is diagnosed. In some people, respiratory problems may require the use of a mechanical device to assist with breathing.

FSH Symptoms

FSH varies in its severity and age of onset. Symptoms can begin anywhere from childhood to the early twenties. Symptoms tend to be more severe when the disorder appears earlier. The condition mostly affects muscles of the face, shoulders, and upper arms, although hips and legs may also be affected. Children with FSH often develop partial or complete deafness.

Symptoms of Myotonic Dystrophy

Symptoms of myotonic dystrophy include facial weakness, a slack (loose) jaw, drooping eyelids, and muscle wasting in the forearms and calves. A person with this dystrophy has difficulty letting go of an object, especially if it's cold. Myotonic dystrophy affects heart muscles, causing irregular heartbeats, and the muscles of the digestive system, leading to digestion problems and constipation.

Myotonic dystrophy can also affect other body systems. It can cause cataracts (see cataracts entry), destruction of the retina, mental retardation (see mental retardation entry), skin disorders (see skin disorders entry), wasting of the testicles, sleep problems (see insomnia entry), and diabetes-like problems (see diabetes mellitus entry). Most people with this type of dystrophy are severely disabled within twenty years of first diagnosis. They usually do not require a wheelchair, however.

Symptoms of OPMD

OPMD usually begins when a person has reached his or her thirties or forties. The disorder affects muscles controlling the eyes and throat. Symptoms include drooping eyelids and difficulty swallowing. Muscle weakness later spreads to the face, neck, and sometimes the upper limbs. Difficulty in swallowing can result in problems of the upper respiratory system. Among the most serious of these problems is pneumonia (see pneumonia entry).

Symptoms of DD

DD usually begins in the twenties or thirties. It first appears as a weakness in the hands, forearms, and lower legs. One of the first symptoms may be difficulty with fine movements, such as typing or fastening buttons. Symptoms usually progress slowly. The disorder seldom affects a person's normal life span.

Symptoms of CMD

CMD is marked by severe muscle weakness from birth. Infants with the disorder cannot control their muscles and tend to flop around. Nonetheless, children with CMD may learn to walk, with or without a supporting device, such as crutches. Many live into young adulthood and even beyond. Fukuyama CMD is a far more serious disorder, however. Children with this condition seldom learn to walk and suffer severe mental retardation. They generally die in childhood.

DIAGNOSIS

Diagnosis begins with a medical history and a complete physical examination. A medical history is important to find out if dystrophy has occurred in other family members. Since the disorder is hereditary, family patterns are helpful in diagnosing the condition. A physical examination is necessary to rule out conditions with similar symptoms.

A number of laboratory tests are available for diagnosing MD. These tests include:

- Blood levels of creatine kinase (CK; pronounced KREE-uh-teen KIE-nase). CK is an enzyme present in muscle tissue. Its production increases when muscle tissue is damaged.
- Muscle biopsy. A biopsy is a procedure by which a small sample of tissue is removed with a needle. The sample can then be studied under a microscope. Changes in muscle tissue can be observed, indicating the presence of a dystrophy.
- Electromyogram (EMG; pronounced e-LEK-tro-my-o-gram). An EMG is an electrical test to see how well muscles are functioning. If muscles do not respond normally to the test, a dystrophy may be present.
- Genetic tests. It is now possible to examine the genes present in a person's cells and identify genes that are faulty.
- Other tests for specific forms of MD. Specific tests can be conducted for certain types of MD. For example, a hearing test can be used to help diagnose FSH in children.

Most doctors with experience in dealing with MD can diagnose the disorder quite easily. In some cases, however, MD can be confused with other diseases that have similar symptoms. For example, the disorder known as myasthenia gravis (pronounced MY-uhs-THEE-nee-uh GRA-vuhs) affects the site where nerves and muscles come together. Its symptoms are somewhat similar to those of some forms of MD.

TREATMENT

There are currently no cures for any form of muscular dystrophy. A few drugs have been found that slow the progress of some forms of MD. For example, prednisone (pronounced PRED-nih-zone), a corticosteroid (pronounced kor-tih-ko-STIHR-oid), slows the progress of DMD. Generally speaking, however, drugs have a limited and uncertain value in the treatment of MD.

The primary goal of treatment programs for MD is to prevent complications. The major complications are decreased ability to move on one's own, contractures, scoliosis, heart defects, and respiratory problems.

Physical Therapy

Regular stretching exercises help prevent or delay contractures. Braces may be used to help support ankles, feet, legs, and other body parts with weakened muscles. Patients can sometimes be taught to use another set of muscles in place of muscles damaged by MD. A program of regular, light exercise can help keep muscles in good condition.

Surgery

Surgery may be necessary to correct some severe symptoms of MD. Contractures can be treated, for example, by cutting the damaged muscle. The muscle is then held in place until it grows back normally. In FSH, the shoulder blade can be braced to compensate for muscle weakness. For a person with OPMD, eyelids can be lifted by a surgical procedure to correct for drooping eyelids. Scoliosis can sometimes be corrected by back surgery. In this surgery, the vertebrae that make up the spine are fused (fixed) together. Steel rods are then inserted and attached to the vertebrae to keep the spine in a straight, stiff position.

Occupational Therapy

The purpose of occupational therapy is to help patients find ways of making up for their loss of strength and dexterity. Strategies may include changes in the home environment, learning to use special utensils and dressing aids, and use of a wheelchair and communication devices, such as hearing aids.

Nutrition

Good nutrition helps promote general health in all forms of MD. No special diet is needed or has been shown to relieve any of its symptoms, however.

Cardiac Care

EDMD and BMD may require certain kinds of treatment for heart problems. For example, drugs such as nifedipine (pronounced nie-FED-uh-peen) help maintain a regular heartbeat. An artificial pacemaker may also need to be installed in patients with an irregular heartbeat.

Respiratory Care

Weakness in diaphragm muscles can be a very serious condition that may result in a person losing the ability to breathe on his or her own. In such cases, a mechanical device may be needed to help the patient breathe. For example, air may be administered through a face mask or mouthpiece. Or a tracheotomy (pronounced TRAY-kee-OT-uh-mee) may be necessary. In a tracheotomy, a tube is inserted through a hole cut in the throat. Air can then be provided directly to the person's respiratory system.

Good lung hygiene is always necessary. Without proper care, infections of the lungs are common. Such infections can easily lead to pneumonia and even death. Patients with MD may also need to learn techniques for coughing. The normal cough reaction is usually difficult because of damaged muscles. But coughing is necessary to expel foreign particles that can cause disease and infection.

Experimental Treatments

Two experimental procedures may hold some promise for treating MD. One of these procedures is called myoblast transfer. In this procedure, millions of immature muscle cells are injected into a patient's damaged muscle. The goal of the procedure is to provide the person's body with normal, healthy cells that may be able to function in place of damaged ones. Thus far, there seems to be no evidence that this procedure is successful, although research continues in the hope of success in the future.

The second procedure is gene therapy. In gene therapy, a person with MD is injected with artificially produced genes that are correct copies of the faulty genes in their body. The hope is that the correct genes will function in cells the way the faulty genes are supposed to but don't. Gene therapy is a very difficult task complicated with many side effects. However, many researchers believe that it may be the most likely way of curing MD.

PROGNOSIS

The expected lifetime for a male with DMD has increased significantly in the past two decades. Most young men will now live into their early or mid-twenties. The main cause of death is respiratory infection.

Prognosis for other forms of MD is highly variable. It depends very much on the age at which symptoms first appear and how severe those symptoms are. People with BMD, EDMD, and myotonic dystrophy may have normal life spans. The critical issue for people with these disorders is attention to and care for heart problems that may develop.

PREVENTION

There is no way to prevent any form of MD. Some forms of the disorder can now be detected by genetic tests. Parents can have their unborn children tested for these forms of muscular dystrophy. They can then use that information for family planning purposes.

FOR MORE INFORMATION

Books

Bergman, Thomas. *Precious Time: Children Living With Muscular Dystrophy (Don't Turn Away)*. Milwaukee, WI: Gareth Stevens, 1996.

Emery, Alan. *Muscular Dystrophy: The Facts*. Oxford Medical Publication, 1994.

Organizations

The Muscular Dystrophy Association. 3300 East Sunrise Drive, Tucson, AZ 85718. (520) 529–2000; (800) 572–1717. http://www.mdausa.org.

OBESITY

DEFINITION

Obesity is an abnormal accumulation of body fat, usually 20 percent or more over an individual's ideal body weight. Obesity is associated with an increased risk of illness, disability, and death.

DESCRIPTION

Medical researchers have developed charts showing a person's ideal body weight. Ideal body weight means the weight a person should be in order to maintain good health. Ideal body weight depends primarily on three factors: gender, age, and height.

A person is said to be obese if his or her body weight is at least 20 percent more than his or her ideal weight. A range of 20 percent to 40 percent overweight is regarded as mild obesity; 40 percent to 100 percent overweight is regarded as moderate obesity; and more than 100 percent overweight is regarded as severe obesity. Severe obesity is also called morbid obesity. The term "morbid" is used for conditions that can lead to death. A person more than 100 percent overweight is regarded to have such serious health problems that his or her life is threatened.

Obesity can result in many serious, and potentially deadly, health problems. These problems include hypertension (high blood pressure;

WORDS TO KNOW

Appetite suppressant: Drugs that decrease feelings of hunger and control appetite.

Ideal weight: Weight corresponding to the appropriate, healthy rate for individuals of a specific height, gender, and age.

see hypertension entry), Type II diabetes mellitus (see diabetes mellitus entry), coronary (heart) disease, infertility, and a higher risk for certain forms of cancer (see cancer entry), such as those that affect the colon, prostate, endometrium, and possibly breasts.

According to some estimates, about one-quarter of the U.S. population can be considered obese. Four million of these people may be classified as morbidly obese. About three hundred thousand deaths each year can be blamed on obesity. Public-health leaders point out that obesity is the second leading cause of preventable deaths (after smoking) in the United States.

CAUSES

Part of the food we eat is "burned" to make energy. We use this energy to move, breathe, and carry out all our normal daily activities. The amount of energy present in food is measured in calories. If a person takes in more calories than his or her body burns up, the extra calories are stored in the form of fat.

There are other reasons why an individual's body might retain fat. Some people have a larger appetite than others. Their bodies seem to expect them to eat more often. For others, their bodies do not efficiently convert food to energy. They are more likely to convert the food they eat to fat.

Scientists now think that heredity is an important factor in obesity. That is, some people may inherit from their parents a genetic predisposition to gain weight. A genetic predisposition is a natural tendency over which a person has some, but not complete, control.

This theory has been supported by studies of adopted children. These children tend to have weight patterns more like those of their natural parents than those of their adoptive parents. This finding suggests that the children inherited from their natural parents the tendency to eat normally or excessively.

Even if people do inherit a tendency toward obesity, they do not necessarily have to become overweight. First, they can choose a diet that will reduce the risk of gaining weight. Some types of food, such as carbohydrates, are turned into energy more quickly than other types of foods, such as fats. A beneficial diet high in carbohydrates would consist of cereals, breads, fruits, and vegetables.

Second, a person can choose a lifestyle that will help burn up excess calories. A quiet lifestyle spent watching television will not burn up many calories compared with one that includes jogging, swimming, walking, or other forms of exercise.

Obesity can be caused by other factors as well. For example, a person may feel depressed (see depressive disorders entry) or have a low self-image.

In response to those feelings, the person may eat more than his or her body really needs. The excess calories are converted to body fat.

The stage at which a person first becomes obese can affect his or her ability to lose weight. In childhood, excess calories are converted into new fat cells. Those fat cells remain in the child's body throughout life. In adulthood, excess calories simply cause existing fat cells to get larger. What this means is that obesity in childhood is especially serious. In some studies, people who became obese as children had up to five times as many fat cells as those who became obese as adults.

Obesity can also be caused by certain medical conditions. For example, hypothyroidism (pronounced HI-po-THIE-roi-DIZ-uhm) is a condition in which the thyroid gland does not function normally. The thyroid gland is responsible for the body's general level of activity. In hypothyroidism, the body's overall level of activity is reduced, causing fewer calories to be burned. As a result, the body tends to gain weight.

Consumption of certain drugs can also result in obesity. Steroids and antidepressants are examples of such drugs.

SYMPTOMS

The major symptoms of obesity are excessive weight gain and the presence of large amounts of fatty tissue. Obesity can also give rise to several other conditions, including:

- Arthritis (see arthritis entry) and other problems with bones and muscles, such as lower back pain
- Heartburn
- High cholesterol levels
- High blood pressure
- Menstrual problems
- Shortness of breath
- Skin disorders

DIAGNOSIS

Diagnosis of obesity is made by comparing the patient's weight with ideal weight charts. A direct measure of body fat can also be made with an instrument known as calipers. Calipers are a scissor-shaped device used to measure the thickness of a person's flesh at the back of the upper arm. This measurement can be used to tell whether a person has an excess of fatty tissue. Women whose body weight consists of more than 30 percent fatty tissue are regarded as obese. Men with 25 percent fatty tissue in their body weight are considered to be obese.

Doctors may also note the way in which a person's body fat is distributed. Some patterns of distribution are associated with certain complications of obesity. For example, a person who is "apple-shaped" has a higher risk of cancer, heart disease, and diabetes than someone who is "pear-shaped." An "apple-shaped" person is one whose weight is concentrated around the waist and abdomen. A "pear-shaped" person is one whose extra weight tends to be around the hips and thighs.

TREATMENT

Treatment of obesity depends on two factors: how overweight is a person and how good is his or her general health. The most important point is that to be successful, any treatment must effect lifelong, not short-term, changes. Many people try "yo-yo" dieting. Yo-yo dieting is a pattern in which a person tries some kind of diet for a few weeks or a few months and then quits the diet. Later on, the person tries the same diet again or a new one.

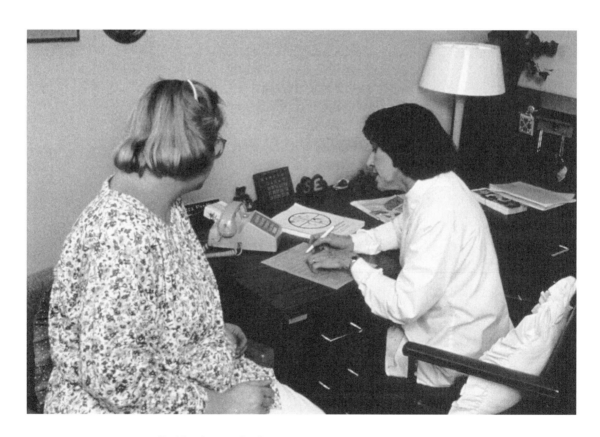

Nutritional counseling is sometimes recommended to help people lose weight. (© 1992 SIU Biomed Comm. Reproduced by permission of Custom Medical Stock Photo.)

As a result, the person is constantly losing weight and then regaining it. This pattern can be very dangerous. A person who practices yo-yo dieting is more likely to develop fatal health problems than someone who lost the weight all at once and kept it off or someone who never lost the weight at all.

Effective treatment for obesity depends on a few general issues, such as:

- What and how much a person eats. Patients are often asked to keep a food diary listing the foods they eat each day. Then they can analyze their diet to determine its nutritional value and the fat content of foods. The patient may be encouraged to change his or her grocery-shopping habits. For example, buying only the items on a shopping list prevents a person from buying other foods on impulse. Patients can also be taught to eat smaller, more frequent meals and to slow down the rate at which they eat during meals.
- How a person responds to food. Patients can be taught that eating can reflect psychological issues. For example, a person under stress may binge— that is, eat large amounts of food at once. With this understanding, a person may be able to find other ways of dealing with emotional issues besides eating.
- How they spend their time. Many obese people engage in little or no exercise. By making exercise a regular part of their lives, they may be able to lose weight and to keep it off. A variety of exercises can be tried so that the patient does not become bored with only one kind of activity.

For most individuals who are mildly obese, changes of this kind can be made with or without consulting a physician. Other mildly obese people may seek the help of a commercial weight-loss program, such as Weight Watchers. The success of such programs is difficult to measure, however. The programs themselves vary from the highly reputable to the less promising. Also, people tend to drop out of such programs quickly, so it is difficult to judge how effective any one program might be in helping a person lose weight.

Generally speaking, people should be cautious of programs that offer quick and easy results. Losing weight usually requires significant lifestyle changes, including diet and amount of exercise.

People who are moderately obese may require a higher level of professional help. A common approach is to recommend a balanced diet of no more than 1,500 calories per day. Less commonly, a doctor may recommend a very-low-calorie liquid protein diet. A diet of this kind provides no more than 700 calories a day and may be continued for up to three months. This kind of diet should not be confused with commercial liquid protein diets or commercial weight-loss shakes and drinks. Doctors design these diets for the specific needs of each individual patient.

Doctors may also recommend counseling for obese patients. Counseling sometimes helps people deal with psychological issues that lead to their weight-gain problems.

Dietary and lifestyle changes are useful with severely obese patients. But such patients may need even more aggressive treatment. For example, surgery may be performed to decrease the size of a person's stomach or small intestine. The purpose of this kind of surgery is to reduce the volume of food a person can eat.

Other forms of obesity surgery are sometimes performed. Liposuction, for example, is a procedure in which fat is removed from beneath the skin. Liposuction is of little or no value in solving a person's obesity problems. It may change his or her physical appearance, but it does not solve any of the underlying problems that lead to obesity in the first place.

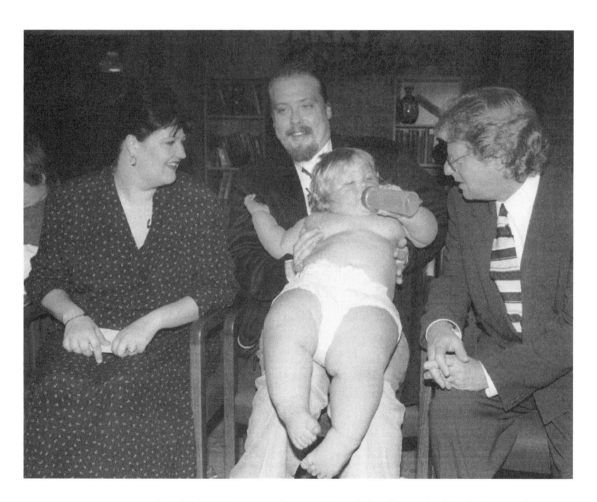

Zack Stenkert at age seventeen months weighing 70 pounds. Obesity is generally measured as 20 percent or more over an individual's ideal body weight. (Reproduced by permission of AP/Wide World Photos)

Appetite-suppressant drugs are sometimes prescribed to aid in weight loss. These drugs work by increasing the level of certain chemicals that occur naturally in the brain, making a person feel full. Appetite suppressants can work on a short-term basis. That is, people are likely to lose weight while they are taking the drugs. But the drugs do not solve the basic problems that lead to obesity. When a person stops taking the drugs, his or her appetite returns. The person once again begins eating too much, and the weight returns.

Appetite suppressants are also of some concern because they may have harmful side effects and long-term effects that are not well understood. In November 1997, for example, the U.S. Food and Drug Administration removed a group of appetite-suppressant drugs from the market because they could cause potentially fatal heart defects.

The only weight-loss drug available without a prescription is phenyl-propanolamine (pronounced FEN-uhl-PRO-puh-NOL-uh-meen, trade names Acutrim, Dexatrim). This drug has been found to increase weight loss by a factor of about 5 percent. The problem is that the weight tends to return as soon as the drug is discontinued.

Some of the side effects that may accompany the use of weight-loss drugs include:

- Constipation
- Dry mouth
- Headache
- Irritability
- Nausea
- Nervousness
- Sweating

Alternative Treatment

Some alternative forms of treatment for obesity have problems similar to those of drugs. For example, the Chinese herb ephedra has been recommended in a weight-loss program that also includes a low-fat diet and exercise. The herb does help a person lose weight on a short-term basis. But the weight tends to return when use of the herb is discontinued. In addition, large amounts of ephedra can produce a number of side effects, such as anxiety, irregular heartbeat, heart attack, high blood pressure, insomnia, irritability, nervousness, seizures, stroke, and even death.

Diuretic herbs have also been suggested for the treatment of obesity. A diuretic is a substance that increases the rate of urine output. As a person produces more urine, his or her weight decreases. However, once the herb is discontinued, urine production returns to normal, as does obesity.

Other natural remedies that have been suggested for weight loss include:

- Red peppers and mustard, because they increase a person's metabolic rate (the rate at which food is digested). They also make a person thirsty, so he or she is more likely to drink water (which contains no calories) than to eat food.
- Walnuts, because they increase the level of brain chemicals that tell a person he or she is no longer hungry.
- Dandelion, because it increases the metabolic rate and decreases desire for sugary foods.

Acupressure and acupuncture are also said to decrease the desire for food. Acupuncture is a Chinese therapy that uses fine needles to pierce the body; acupressure involves applying pressure to certain points in the body. Mental techniques such as visualization and meditation may create a better self-image and decrease the need to overeat. Mental concentration, yoga, and similar techniques may provide similar benefits. In many cases, support groups can help a person deal with the problems that led to his or her obesity.

PROGNOSIS

Short-term diet programs are seldom successful. Studies show that 85 percent of dieters who do not exercise on a regular basis regain their lost weight within two years. Yo-yo dieting encourages the body to store fat and may increase the risk of heart problems. The only certain way to conquer obesity is to make fundamental changes in eating and exercise habits.

STUDIES SHOW THAT 85 PERCENT OF DIETERS WHO DO NOT EXERCISE ON A REGULAR BASIS REGAIN THEIR LOST WEIGHT WITHIN TWO YEARS.

PREVENTION

The best way to prevent obesity is to avoid a high intake of fats. The National Cholesterol Education Program suggests that no more than 30 percent of the calories people eat should come from fats. A good way to monitor one's diet is to keep a detailed food diary. That way, one will know exactly how many calories are consumed in a day and where those calories come from.

A program of vigorous exercise is also very important. Activity is the only way that calories are used up. The more active a person is, the less likely that calories will be converted into fat.

Finally, children should learn early in their lives the value of a healthful diet and exercise. By controlling their intake of calories and planning activities that will burn them up, the problems of obesity can usually be avoided.

FOR MORE INFORMATION

Books

Gottlieb, Bill, ed. *New Choices in Natural Healing*. Emmaus, PA: Rodale Press, 1995.

Harris, Dan R., ed. *Diet and Nutrition Sourcebook*. Detroit: Omnigraphics, 1996.

Slupik, Ramona I., ed. *American Medical Association Complete Guide to Women's Health*. New York: Random House, 1996.

Organizations

HFC Nutrition Research Foundation, Inc. P.O. Box 22124, Lexington, KY 40522. (606) 276-3119.

National Institute of Diabetes and Digestive and Kidney Diseases of the National Institutes of Health. 2 Information Way, Bethesda, MD 20892-3570. http://www.niddk.nih.gov.

National Obesity Research Foundation. Temple University, Weiss Hall 867, Philadelphia, PA 19122.

The Weight-Control Information Network. 1 Win Way, Bethesda, MD 20896-3665. (301) 951-1120.

OBSESSIVE-COMPULSIVE DISORDER

DEFINITION

Obsessive-compulsive disorder (OCD) is a type of anxiety disorder. A person with an anxiety disorder worries excessively about the circumstances of his or her life over a long period of time. OCD is characterized by distressing thoughts that never seem to go away. These thoughts are often accompanied by images that are powerful, unusual, frightening, or absurd.

A person with OCD deals with these thoughts and feelings with ritualized actions. A ritualized action is a behavior that is performed again and again in exactly the same way. Patients believe that these actions will protect them from the terrible thoughts in their minds. Ritualized actions are often unusual and meaningless. They are also called compulsions or compulsive behaviors.

OCD is sometimes known as the "disease of doubt." The patient often knows that his or her obsessive thoughts and ritualized actions are not rational (make no logical sense). Yet he or she may still worry that the fears may be true.

DESCRIPTION

About one out of every forty people will experience obsessive-compulsive disorder at some time in their lives. It occurs with equal frequency among men and women, all ages, and all ethnic groups. Many people with the disorder try to hide their condition from other people. Yet they are unable to avoid acting out their compulsions.

Most people with OCD have both obsessions and compulsions. Some people may have only obsessions or only compulsions. The extent to which OCD affects a person's daily life varies. Some people are barely bothered. Others are terribly troubled by their obsessions. They may spend a large part of the day carrying out their compulsive behaviors.

An obsession is an irrational thought that occurs again and again. As an example, a person might think, "My hands are dirty, and I must wash them again." The person's hands may be (and probably are) totally clean. Yet the person cannot get the thought out of his or her mind that the hands are still dirty.

Some typical obsessions include:

- Fear of dirt, germs, or contamination
- A desire to perform violence on other people
- A feeling of responsibility for other people's safety
- Fear of hitting a pedestrian with a car
- Excessive religious feelings
- Intense sexual thoughts

A compulsion is a particular behavior that is performed repeatedly to protect against an obsession. Some common compulsions are excessive washing (especially hand washing or bathing); housecleaning; and touching, counting, arranging, or hoarding objects. The patient may feel better while performing these actions. But that sense of satisfaction does not last long. Soon, the person will feel the need to do the action again.

For a person with OCD, a compulsive behavior is a form of protection. He or she feels that something terrible will happen if the be-

WORDS TO KNOW

Anxiety disorder: An experience of prolonged, excessive worry about the circumstances of one's life.

Cognitive-behavioral therapy: A form of psychological counseling in which patients are helped to understand the nature of their disorder and reshape their environment to help them function better.

Compulsion: A ritualistic behavior that is repeated again and again.

Neurotransmitter: A chemical that occurs in the brain and that helps electrical signals travel from one nerve cell to another.

Obsession: A troubling thought that occurs again and again and causes severe distress in a person.

An obsessive fear of dirt and germs can lead to compulsive handwashing. (© Eric Nelson.
Reproduced by permission of Custom Medical Stock Photo.)

havior is not repeated. The behavior may relieve stress for a short time, but
it does not bring any kind of pleasure to the patient.

OCD is sometimes related to other emotional disorders. For example,
some people feel a constant urge to pull hair out of their bodies. Others are
constantly afraid of catching some terrible disease. Still others worry that

there is something wrong with the way their bodies look. OCD is often linked with depression (see depressive disorders entry) and other anxiety disorders.

CAUSES

The cause of obsessive-compulsive disorder has not yet been found. Many researchers believe that it may be inherited. If one person in a family has OCD, there is a 25 percent chance that another family member will also have the condition. Stress and other psychological factors may also contribute to the development of OCD.

One popular theory is that OCD is caused by low levels of seratonin (pronounced sihr-uh-TOE-nun), a neurotransmitter. Neurotransmitters are chemicals that occur in the brain. They are responsible for delivering electrical signals from one nerve cell to another and help control many of the mental activities that occur in the brain.

Some researchers think that OCD develops when the brain produces too much or too little of some particular neurotransmitter. In such a case, nerve messages cannot travel smoothly from one part of the brain to another. They may begin to recycle—that is, to travel again and again across the same set of nerves. This constant repetition of nerve messages might be responsible for the repetitive behavior characteristic of compulsions.

Another theory is that OCD may be related to childhood episodes of strep throat (see strep throat entry), a bacterial infection. In some children, strep throat antibodies attack a certain part of the brain. Antibodies are chemicals produced by the immune system. Their job is to fight off infections. But antibodies can sometimes cause damage to the body itself. Researchers think that damage to the brain caused by strep throat antibodies may lead to obsessions and compulsions such as fear of germs and excessive hand washing. Some children with OCD have benefited from treatment with antibiotics.

SYMPTOMS

While some children may experience OCD, symptoms usually begin when a person reaches adolescence. While everyone has a tendency to double check to make sure that the doors are locked or the stove is turned off when leaving the house, the compulsions of OCD sufferers are so great that they may interfere with daily life. Individuals with the disorder have been known to wash their hands for hours at a time or to rearrange and clean their household several times throughout a day. They usually recognize that their behavior is irrational, but they have no control over their actions.

DIAGNOSIS

Psychiatrists diagnose obsessive-compulsive disorder based on the described symptoms. No blood tests or other kinds of laboratory tests are available for diagnosing OCD. Many people with the condition are never diagnosed or are diagnosed only after many years. The delay in diagnosis is due to the shame that many patients feel about their condition. They become skillful at hiding their symptoms from other people.

TREATMENT

Two forms of treatment are used with obsessive-compulsive behavior: drugs and cognitive-behavioral therapy. The drugs used with OCD are designed to alter the amount of neurotransmitters in the brain. They include fluoxetine (pronounced floo-AHK-suh-teen, trade name Prozac), paroxetine (pronounced par-AHK-suh-teen, trade name Paxil), and sertraline (pronounced SIR-truh-leen, trade name Zoloft). An older drug that is sometimes used is clomipramine (pronounced KLO-mip-ruh-meen, trade name Anafranil). However, Clomipramine has more side effects than the newer drugs listed.

Cognitive-behavioral therapy is a form of counseling conducted by trained medical professionals. The goal is to help patients understand the basis of their disorder. They are encouraged to accept the fact that they have fears and obsessive thoughts. Then they are helped to find ways to tolerate the conditions that cause their anxiety and avoid performing the ritualistic activities of their compulsions. Patients sometimes find it helpful to think about other things by taking up a hobby or finding activities of interest.

Some patients do not benefit from drugs or cognitive-behavioral therapy. Brain surgery is the treatment of last resort with these patients. Surgery involves removing the small part of the brain that controls compulsive behavior. The surgery is successful in about a third of all cases. It may have very serious side effects, however, including seizures, personality changes, and loss of some mental functions.

Alternative Treatment

St. John's wort is sometimes recommended as a treatment for OCD. St. John's wort is an herb that has long been used to treat anxiety and depression. Some practitioners believe that the herb has the same effect on neurotransmitters as the conventional drugs described. Research suggests that a very small fraction of people with OCD may benefit from the use of St.-John's-wort.

Some people believe that homeopathic treatments can help people with OCD. They try to rebalance a patient's mental, emotional, and physical well-being, allowing compulsive behaviors to disappear over time.

Chloe Ruth, age fourteen, takes medication for her anxiety and obsessive-compulsive disorder. Obsessive-compulsive disorder occurs with equal frequency among men and women, all age groups, and all ethnic groups. (Reproduced by permission of AP/Wide World Photos)

PROGNOSIS

The prognosis for obsessive-compulsive disorder varies widely among patients. If left untreated, the condition can last for decades. People go through periods when symptoms alternate between mild and severe. The symptoms usually get worse with age.

Treatment with drugs and cognitive-behavioral therapy can be very helpful. Some people recover from the disorder completely. They may need to stay on some type of treatment program for many years, however, or even for life. About 20 percent of all OCD patients do not respond to any form of treatment. These individuals may require hospitalization.

Many people with OCD can eventually live happy and productive lives. They find success in nearly every career field, from doctors and lawyers to businesspeople and entertainers. Keeping the condition under control can be very difficult, however. It may require a considerable emotional effort and a serious financial investment.

PREVENTION

There are no known ways to prevent obsessive-compulsive disorder.

FOR MORE INFORMATION

Books

Dumont, Raeann. *The Sky Is Falling: Understanding and Coping with Phobias, Panic, and Obsessive-Compulsive Disorder.* New York: W. W. Norton & Company, 1996.

Foa, E., and R. Wilson. *Stop Obsessing! How to Overcome Your Obsessions and Compulsion.* New York: Bantam Books, 1991.

Schwartz, Jeffrey. *Free Yourself from Obsessive-Compulsive Behavior: A Four-Step Self-Treatment Method to Change Your Brain Chemistry.* New York: Harper-Collins, 1996.

Swedo, S. E., and H. L. Leonard. *It's Not All in Your Head.* New York: Harper-Collins, 1996.

Organizations

Anxiety Disorders Association of America. 11900 Parklawn Drive, Suite 100, Rockville, MD 20852. (301) 231-9350. http://www.adaa.org.

National Alliance for the Mentally Ill. 200 N. Glebe Road, #1015, Arlington, VA 22203-3728. (800) 950-NAMI. http://www.nami.org.

National Mental Health Association. 1021 Prince Street, Alexandria, VA 22314-2971. (800) 969-NMHA. http://www.nmha.org.

Obsessive-Compulsive Anonymous. PO Box 215, New Hyde Park, NY 11040. (516) 739-0662. http://members.aol.com/west24th.

OSTEOPOROSIS

DEFINITION

The word "osteoporosis" literally means "porous bones." Osteoporosis (pronounced OSS-tee-o-puh-RO-sis) occurs when bones begin to lose some of their essential elements. The most important of these elements is calcium. Over time, bone mass decreases. As a result, bones lose their strength, become fragile, and break easily. In extreme cases, even a sneeze or a sudden movement may be enough to break a bone.

DESCRIPTION

Osteoporosis is a serious health problem. About 28 million people in the United States have the condition. It is responsible for about 1.5 million fractures (broken bones) each year. The most common locations where breaks occur are the hip, spine, and wrist. Hip and spine injuries are the most serious. They often require hospitalization and major surgery. They may also lead to other serious consequences, including permanent disability and death.

To understand osteoporosis, it is helpful to understand how bones form. Bone is living tissue that is constantly renewed in a two-stage process. The first stage is formation. During formation, new bone tissue is built up from nutrients present in the bloodstream. The second stage is resorption. In this

WORDS TO KNOW

Alendronate: A drug used to treat osteoporosis in women who have passed through menopause.

Calcitonin: A drug used to treat osteoporosis in women who have passed through menopause.

Calcium: An essential mineral with many important functions in the body, one of which is in the formation of bone.

Computed tomography (CT) scan: A diagnostic technique in which a specific region of the body is X-rayed from many angles. A computer then combines the various X-ray photographs.

Computerized axial tomography (CAT) scan: Another name for a computed tomography (CT) scan.

Densitometry: A technique for measuring the density of bone by taking photographs with low-energy X rays from a variety of angles around the bone.

Estrogen: A female hormone with many functions in the body, one of which is to keep bones strong.

Hormone replacement therapy (HRT): A method of treating osteoporosis by giving supplementary doses of estrogen and/or other female hormones.

Menopause: The period in a woman's life when she stops menstruating.

Protein: A type of chemical compound with many essential functions in the body, one of which is to build bones.

Resorption: The process by which the elements of bone are removed from bone and returned to the body.

stage, bone cells break down. The elements of which are returned to the blood and other body fluids.

For about the first thirty years of life, bone formation takes place faster than resorption. Bones grow to be larger and stronger during this period. After middle age, resorption takes place faster and bones become smaller and weaker.

Osteoporosis is a continuation of this process. The balance between resorption and formation becomes very one-sided. Almost no new bone is formed, but bone continues to be removed. When bones are made smaller and weaker by this mechanism, the process is called primary osteoporosis.

Osteoporosis can also occur in another way. Some drugs and diseases can increase the rate at which resorption occurs. The end result is the same: bones become smaller and weaker. In this case, however, the process is called secondary osteoporosis.

Osteoporosis occurs most commonly in older people. It affects nearly half of all men and women over the age of seventy-five. Women are five times more likely than men to develop the condition. They have smaller, weaker bones to begin with, so resorption of bone material in women's bodies has a greater effect than in men's bodies.

Another important factor in osteoporosis is menopause. Menopause is the period in a woman's life when she stops menstruating. During this period, she also stops producing the hormone estrogen. Estrogen helps prevent the resorption of bone. As levels of estrogen fall in a woman's body, she is at greater risk for osteoporosis.

CAUSES

As outlined, osteoporosis is caused when the rate of bone resorption becomes greater than the rate of bone formation. This process is a normal part of aging. There are certain factors, however, that increase a person's risk for osteoporosis. These factors include:

- **Gender.** Women are more likely to have osteoporosis than men. Women commonly lose 30 percent to 50 percent of their bone mass over their lifetimes. Men lose about 20 percent to 35 percent of their bone mass.
- **Race.** Caucasian and Asian women are at somewhat higher risk for osteoporosis than are African American and Hispanic women.
- **Body structure.** Individuals with smaller, thinner bones are at higher risk for osteoporosis.
- **Early menopause.** Women who go through menopause earlier start losing bone mass earlier. Early menopause may be caused by a number of factors, such as heredity, surgery, vigorous exercise, anorexia (see anorexia nervosa entry), and bulimia (see bulimia nervosa entry).

- **Lifestyle.** Alcohol consumption and tobacco use are thought to increase risk for osteoporosis. Lack of exercise may have the same effect.
- **Diet.** Two important nutrients needed for bone formation are protein and calcium. A diet low in either of these nutrients may lead to osteoporosis.

SYMPTOMS

Osteoporosis is sometimes called the "silent disease." The term reflects the fact that the condition usually has no symptoms. People often don't know they have the disorder until they break a bone during some minor accident.

As osteoporosis develops, changes in body structure may occur. A person may actually grow shorter. This change occurs when vertebrae (bones in

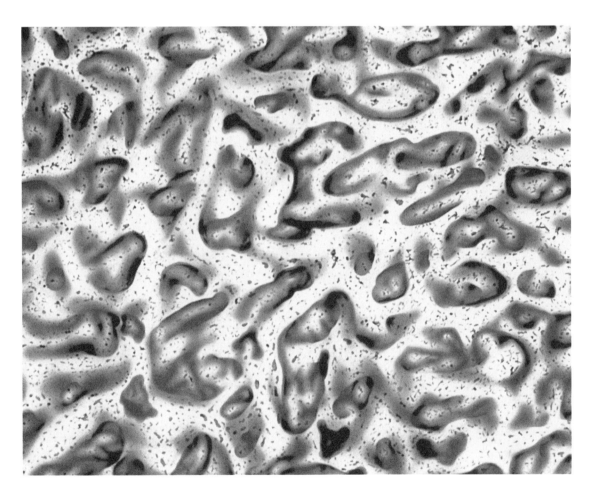

Illustration of osteoporosis bone matrix. (© 1997. Reproduced by permission of Custom Medical Stock Photo.)

the spine) deteriorate and collapse. Loss of vertebrae mass can also result in the condition known as "dowager's hump" or "widow's hump." This condition is characterized by the hunchbacked appearance often seen in older women.

DIAGNOSIS

The only way to diagnose osteoporosis with certainty is with X rays. Ordinary X-ray techniques, like those used for chest X rays, are usually not very helpful. They do not show bone loss until the disease has progressed and extensive damage has occurred.

Computed tomography (CT) scans may be more helpful. In a CT scan, a specific region of the body is X-rayed from many angles. A computer then combines the various X-ray photographs. CT scans are not the best choice for diagnosing osteoporosis, however, because they require relatively high levels of radiation. Another common name for a CT scan is a computerized axial tomography (CAT) scan.

A better method for diagnosing osteoporosis is densitometry (pronounced DEN-si-TOM-i-tree). Densitometry is also a technique for X-raying bones. However, the amount of radiation used is very low. The X rays are taken from different angles and can show how much bone has been lost.

Some doctors recommend that people be tested on a regular basis for bone loss. For women, those tests should begin after menopause. For men, they should begin after the age of sixty-five. Such tests are important since there are seldom other signs of osteoporosis.

TREATMENT

Treatment depends on the form of osteoporosis a patient has. If a patient has secondary osteoporosis, treatment is aimed at curing the disease that has caused osteoporosis. In the case of primary osteoporosis, medications are used to adjust the balance between bone resorption and bone formation. Treatment may also be necessary for bone fractures resulting from osteoporosis. The most common treatment for such fractures is surgery.

Drugs

For women who have gone through menopause, the first line of treatment may be hormone replacement therapy (HRT). In hormone replacement therapy, a woman is given the estrogen that her body no longer produces on its own. The estrogen can be given orally (by mouth) or by injection. Many women choose HRT for other reasons as well. It helps ease the symptoms of menopause. It can also protect against heart disease, the number-one killer of women in the United States. HRT does have some harmful side effects, however. For example, it may increase a woman's risk for breast cancer (see breast cancer entry).

Other medications can be used to treat osteoporosis. These medications reduce the rate of bone resorption and/or increase the rate of bone formation. The two most common drugs used for these purposes are alendronate and calcitonin. These drugs may be given by injection or in the form of nose sprays.

Surgery

In advanced stages of osteoporosis, major fractures are common. In such cases, surgery may be required to repair the fracture. One of the most common procedures is hip replacement surgery. Hip replacement surgery is used to repair a broken hip. The original hip is removed and replaced with an artificial metal and/or plastic hip. Hip replacement surgery is usually quite successful. Patients can often re-

> TO A SIGNIFICANT EXTENT, OSTEOPOROSIS IS A PREVENTABLE DISEASE. PEOPLE CAN TAKE A NUMBER OF STEPS TO BUILD STRONG BONES, INCLUDING EATING CALCIUM RICH FOODS AND EXERCISING REGULARLY.

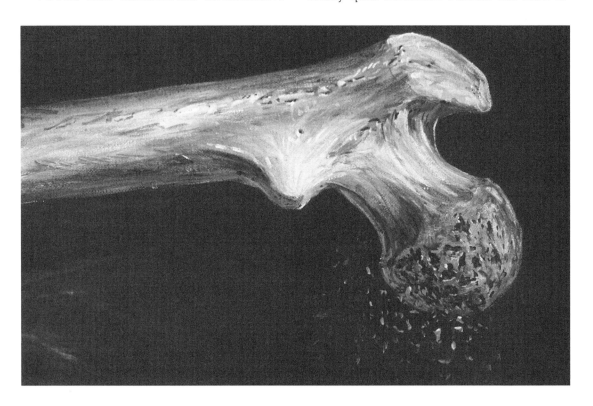

Illustration showing atrophy of a hip bone. (© 1993 Patrick McDonnel. Reproduced by permission of Custom Medical Stock Photo.)

turn to a relatively normal life. However, the surgery carries some serious risks. The death rate following such surgery may be 5 percent to 20 percent greater than for others of the same age group who have not had surgery.

Alternative Treatment

The primary approach for most alternative practitioners is the same as it is in traditional medicine. The goal is to make sure that individuals receive the nutrients they need to build strong bones in their daily diet. This means a diet rich in calcium and protein, including foods such as dairy products, dark-green leafy vegetables, sardines, salmon, and almonds. Nutritional supplements such as vitamin D, calcium, and magnesium may also be recommended.

Herbalists and Chinese medicine practitioners believe that certain herbs can slow the rate of bone loss. Among the products they recommend are horsetail, oat straw, alfalfa, licorice, marsh mallow, yellow dock, and Asian ginseng. Homeopathic practitioners recommend minerals such as *Calcarea carbonica* or silica. A substitute for HRT is to obtain hormones from natural sources, such as soybeans and wild yams.

PROGNOSIS

There is no cure for osteoporosis. However, it can be controlled quite well once it has been diagnosed. Medications, nutritional supplements, and a diet rich in calcium and protein can help slow the progress of the disorder.

PREVENTION

To a significant extent, osteoporosis is a preventable disease. People can take a number of steps beginning early in life to build strong bones. By continuing those practices as they grow older, they can reduce the rate of bone loss. Some of these steps include:

- Get calcium in foods. Foods rich in calcium include milk, cheese, yogurt, and other dairy products; green leafy vegetables; tofu; shellfish; Brazil nuts; sardines; and almonds.
- Take calcium supplements. A person can be certain of getting enough calcium by taking supplements in the form of pills.
- Get enough vitamin D. Vitamin D helps the body absorb calcium. The easiest way to get vitamin D is from sunshine. A fifteen-minute walk each day usually provides all the vitamin D one needs. Foods rich in vitamin D include liver, fish oil, and milk fortified with vitamin D.
- Avoid or limit smoking and the use of alcohol. Both smoking and alcohol use seem to increase the rate of bone loss. By limiting both activities, the risk of osteoporosis may be reduced.

• Exercise. Regular exercise builds strong bones. The forms of exercise likely to be most effective include aerobics, dancing, jogging, stair climbing, tennis, walking, and lifting weights. Experts recommend twenty to thirty minutes of exercise three to four times a week.

FOR MORE INFORMATION

Books

Brown, Susan E. *Better Bones, Better Body: A Comprehensive Self-Help Program for Preventing, Halting, and Overcoming Osteoporosis.* New Canaan, CT: Keats Publishing, 1996.

Notelovits, Morris, with Marsha Ware and Diana Tonnessen. *Stand Tall! Every Woman's Guide to Preventing and Treating Osteoporosis,* 2nd ed. Gainesville, FL: Triad Publishing Co., 1998.

Periodicals

Bilger, Burkhard. "Bone Medicine." *Health Magazine* (May–June 1996): pp. 125–28.

Braun, Wendy. "Do Your Bones Pass the Test?" *Saturday Evening Post* (March–April 1997): pp. 18–22+.

Organizations

Arthritis Foundation. 1330 West Peachtree Street, Atlanta, GA 30309. (404) 872–7100. http://www.arthritis.org.

National Institutes of Health. Osteoporosis and Related Bone Diseases: National Resource Center. 1232 22nd St. NW, Suite 500, Washington, DC 20037-1292. (800) 624-BONE. http://www.osteo.org.

National Osteoporosis Foundation. 1232 22nd Street NW, Washington, DC 20037-1292. (202) 223-2226. http://www.nof.org.

PANIC DISORDER

DEFINITION

Panic disorder is a condition in which a person feels sudden overwhelming fright, usually without any reasonable cause. A panic attack is generally accompanied by physical symptoms, such as a pounding heart, sweating, and rapid breathing. A person with panic disorder may have repeated panic attacks and feel constant fear as to when the next attack will occur.

DESCRIPTION

Most people experience moments of anxiety. They worry about money, their job, the future, or some other issue. But panic disorder is far more serious. It is a chronic (long-lasting), crippling condition that can have a devastating impact on a person's family, work, and social life. Panic disorder is thought to affect about one in every sixty Americans.

The first panic attack can strike a person anywhere. Suddenly, for no good reason, the person has a sense of impending doom. His or her palms begin to sweat, and the heart begins to beat wildly.

Panic attacks usually last only a few seconds or minutes. But they are terrifying. People who

WORDS TO KNOW

Agoraphobia: A fear of open spaces.

Anxiety: Feeling troubled, uneasy, or worried.

Cognitive-behavioral therapy: A form of counseling designed to help patients change the way they think about their problems and change the way they respond to those problems.

Neurotransmitters: Chemicals that help carry messages between nerve cells in the brain.

Serotonin: An important neurotransmitter in the brain.

have experienced a panic attack begin to wonder and worry about when the next attack will occur. They will start to avoid situations that might trigger an attack. In extreme cases, patients may become so frightened that they refuse to leave their homes. This condition is known as agoraphobia (pronounced AG-uh-ruh-FO-bee-uh) .

People who have untreated panic disorder are likely to have problems holding a job. They may become depressed, begin to abuse drugs, and even commit suicide.

CAUSES

The cause of panic disorder is not known. Some authorities believe that the condition is inherited. They think that patients may have unusually sensitive nervous systems that respond inappropriately to events and surroundings.

Panic disorder is a condition in which a person feels sudden overwhelming fright, usually without any reasonable cause. (© 1999 T. Jacobs. Reproduced by permission of Custom Medical Stock Photo.)

SYMPTOMS

People with panic disorder usually have their first attack in their twenties. Specialists define a panic attack as an event with any four of the following symptoms:

- Pounding, skipping, or fluttering heartbeat
- Shortness of breath or a sense of being smothered
- Dizziness or light-headedness
- Nausea or stomach problems
- Chest pains or pressure on the chest
- Choking sensation or a "lump in the throat"
- Chills or hot flashes
- Sweating
- Fear of dying
- Feelings of unreality
- Feelings of tingling or numbness
- Shaking and trembling
- Fear of losing control or going crazy

DIAGNOSIS

The first step in diagnosing panic disorder is to rule out physical disorders. Some of the symptoms described also occur with medical conditions, such as heart problems. A doctor must first confirm that the patient does not have some type of medical condition that produces these symptoms.

Once physical causes are eliminated, the patient should be seen by a mental health professional. He or she will take a personal history to learn more about the nature of the panic attacks and the patient's feelings about those attacks. They will also assess the way in which the panic attacks affect the patient's daily life.

TREATMENT

As with most mental disorders, panic disorder is treated with a combination of medication and counseling. Many experts believe that panic attacks are caused by an imbalance of neurotransmitters. Neurotransmitters are chemicals that help carry messages between nerve cells in the brain. An excess or shortage of neurotransmitters can cause a wide variety of mental disorders.

Medications prescribed for panic disorder are designed to restore the proper balance of neurotransmitters. For example, a group of drugs called

Most people experience moments of anxiety. But panic disorder is far more serious. It is a chronic, crippling condition that can have a devastating impact on a person's family, work, and social life. (© 1993 Andrew Bezear, Reed Business Publishing, Science Photo Library. Reproduced by permission of Custom Medical Stock Photo.)

selective serotonin reuptake inhibitors (SSRIs) control the action of serotonin (pronounced sihr-uh-TOE-nun). Serotonin is one of the most important neurotransmitters in the brain.

Other medications are designed to calm patients down. These medications are called antidepressants. They can often help relieve the worst symptoms of panic disorder.

One of the most effective forms of counseling is called cognitive-behavioral therapy. The purpose of cognitive-behavioral therapy is to help patients understand the nature of their disorder. Patients are taught to recognize the symptoms of an oncoming panic attack and to learn how to respond to the attack in a reasonable way. They learn breathing exercises that help them to calm down and control the physical symptoms of panic.

A COMBINATION OF MEDICATION AND COGNITIVE-BEHAVIORAL THERAPY CAN REDUCE SYMPTOMS IN UP TO 90 PERCENT OF PATIENTS WITH PANIC DISORDER.

Patients can also make changes in their lifestyle to reduce the risk of panic attacks. These changes include eliminating caffeine and alcohol from their diets and avoiding certain legal and illegal drugs, such as marijuana, cocaine, and amphetamines.

Alternative Treatment

Some forms of relaxation therapy may help relieve the symptoms of panic disorder. Yoga, biofeedback training, and hypnotherapy may help patients achieve a more balanced outlook on life. Some practitioners recommend certain herbs to strengthen the nervous system. These herbs include lemon balm, oat straw, passion flower, and skullcap. Hydrotherapy (water therapy) may also help patients relax. The recommended treatment is hot Epsom-salt baths with oil of lavender.

PROGNOSIS

Panic disorder rarely improves without treatment. However, a combination of medication and cognitive-behavioral therapy can reduce symptoms in up to 90 percent of patients. Unfortunately, many people with panic disorder are never diagnosed with the condition and may struggle with their symptoms for years. The disorder may become so bad that they can no longer hold a job or hold on to friends.

PREVENTION

There is no way to prevent an initial panic attack. Future attacks can be prevented or made less severe by a combination of drugs and cognitive-behavioral therapy.

FOR MORE INFORMATION

Books

Bassett, Lucinda. *From Panic to Power: Proven Techniques to Calm Your Anxieties, Conquer your Fears and Put You in Control of Your Life.* New York: HarperCollins, 1995.

Bemis, Judith, and Amr Barrada. *Embracing the Fear: Learning to Manage Anxiety and Panic Attacks.* Center City, MN: Hazelden, 1994.

Peurifoy, Reneau Z. *Phobias and Panic: A Step by Step Program for Regaining Control of Your Life.* New York: Warner Books, 1996.

Sheehan, Elaine. *Phobias and Panic Attacks: Your Questions Answered.* New York: Element, 1996.

Wilson, Robert R. *Don't Panic: Taking Control of Anxiety Attacks.* New York: HarperCollins, 1996.

Zuercher-White, Elke. *An End to Panic: Breakthrough Techniques for Overcoming Panic Disorder.* Oakland, CA: New Harbinger Publications, 1995.

Periodicals

Kram, Mark, and Melissa Meyers Gotthardt. "Night of the Living Dread." *Men's Health* (April 1997): pp. 68–70.

Organizations

Anxiety Disorders Association of America. 11900 Parklawn Drive, Suite 100, Rockville, MD 20852. (301) 231-9350. http://www.adaa.org.

National Alliance for the Mentally Ill. 200 N. Glebe Road, #1015, Arlington, VA 22203-3728. (800) 950-NAMI. http://www.nami.org.

National Institute of Mental Health. Panic Campaign. Rm. 15C-05, 5600 Fishers Lane, Rockville, MD 20857. (800) 64-PANIC. http://www.nimh.nih.gov.

National Mental Health Association. 1021 Prince Street, Alexandria, VA 22314-2971. (800) 969-NMHA. http://www.nmha.org.

Web sites

The Anxiety and Panic Internet Resources (tAPir). [Online] http://www.algy.com/anxiety (accessed on October 30, 1999).

The Anxiety Network International Homepage. [Online] http://www.anxietynetwork.com (accessed on October 30, 1999).

"Panic Disorder." *Internet Mental Health.* [Online] http://www.mentalhealth.com (accessed on October 30, 1999).

PARKINSON'S DISEASE

DEFINITION

Parkinson's disease (PD) is a chronic, progressive disorder of the nervous system. A chronic disorder continues for long periods of time, usually many years. Parkinson's disease affects a person's muscular coordination. Symptoms of PD include tremor (shaking), rigidity in some muscles, slow movements, and problems with maintaining normal posture. The disease is caused by the death of cells in one of the movement control centers of the brain. These nerve cells control body movement.

DESCRIPTION

Parkinson's disease affects about five hundred thousand people in the United States. It occurs with equal frequency in men and women. About fifty thousand new cases appear each year. The disease usually develops when a person is in his or her late fifties or early sixties. It develops gradually over a matter of months and years. A PD patient slowly loses control over the muscles that control movement. About 15 percent of people between the ages of sixty-five and seventy-four show some signs of PD. The rate among those in the age group between seventy-five and eighty-four is about 30 percent.

> PARKINSON'S DISEASE DEVELOPS GRADUALLY OVER A MATTER OF MONTHS AND YEARS. A PD PATIENT SLOWLY LOSES CONTROL OVER THE MUSCLES THAT CONTROL MOVEMENT.

CAUSES

The immediate cause of Parkinson's disease is the destruction of brain cells in a part of the brain known as the substantia nigra (SN). The substantia nigra controls many types of muscular movement by releasing a neurotransmitter called dopamine. A neurotransmitter is a chemical that transports electrical signals between brain cells. Dopamine is needed to carry nerve messages from one brain cell to another.

When brain cells die in the substantia nigra it doesn't release enough dopamine. Without dopamine, signals cannot travel from SN brain cells to cells in other parts of the brain. The "in-

WORDS TO KNOW

Chronic: Recurring frequently or lasting a long time.

Dopamine: A neurotransmitter that helps send signals that control movement.

Neurotransmitter: A chemical that helps transmit electrical signals from one brain cell to another.

Substantia nigra: A region of the brain that controls movement.

structions" that brain cells need to move muscles do not reach their targets. Eventually, walking, writing, reaching for objects, and other basic movements do not occur correctly. Muscular movement becomes weaker and more erratic.

Researchers have not yet discovered the basic cause of Parkinson's disease. They do not know why SN brain cells lose the ability to produce dopamine. Some scientists think that the disease is hereditary. They believe that PD can be passed down from generation to generation. Other researchers think that environmental factors may be to blame. They suspect that certain chemicals in the world around us get into the human body and damage SN brain cells.

So far, a few chemicals have been found that cause the symptoms of PD. One chemical known to cause symptoms of PD is called MPTP. MPTP is sometimes found as an impurity in illegal drugs. A person who accidentally ingests (eats) MPTP begins to show signs of PD within hours. These symptoms become permanent.

SYMPTOMS

The symptoms by which PD can be identified include:

- Tremor (shaking), usually beginning in the hands. The classic tremor associated with PD is called "pill-rolling tremor." The movement is like rolling a pill between the thumb and forefinger. The movement occurs about three times per second.
- Slowing down of movements. A person may slow down or even stop in the middle of familiar movements, such as walking, eating, or shaving.
- Muscle rigidity (stiffness). A PD patient's movements may be jerky rather than smooth.

JAMES PARKINSON

"Shaking palsy" was a disease well known to physicians for hundreds of years. Patients with the disorder gradually became worse over a period of years. They slowly lost control over their limbs, and eventually lost the ability to dress and care for themselves.

The first scientific description of this disease was written in 1817 by Dr. James Parkinson (1755–1824). Parkinson was a man of many interests. Not only did he describe the nature of "shaking palsy," but he also provided the first ex-

planation of appendicitis. Parkinson was also interested in the study of geology and paleontology (fossils), and was a social reformer. He fought for reform of the English parliamentary system and for better treatment of mental patients.

Parkinson also went one step beyond describing "shaking palsy." He conducted an autopsy on a patient who died of the condition. He found a swelling of the medulla, a part of the brain, which he said might be the cause of the disorder. For his research on this disease, "shaky palsy" was eventually renamed Parkinson's disease in his honor.

Former world champion boxer Muhammad Ali now suffers from Parkinson's disease. (Reproduced by permission of AP/Wide World Photos)

- Problems with posture and balance. A person may change the way he or she walks to keep from falling over.
- "Masked face." This condition gets its name from the fact that the patient seems to have no facial expression. He or she may even have a greatly reduced rate of eye blinking.

Parkinson's disease may also be accompanied by one or more other symptoms, including:

- Depression
- Changes in the way a person speaks
- Sleep problems, including restlessness and nightmares
- Emotional changes, including increased fear, irritability, and feelings of insecurity
- Incontinence (loss of bladder control)
- Constipation
- Changes in handwriting
- Dementia (increased problems with mental functions)

DIAGNOSIS

There are no laboratory tests for the diagnosis of Parkinson's disease. The condition is fairly easy to diagnose based on the presence of the characteristic symptoms listed above. A person suspected of having PD will have a complete neurological (nervous system) examination. Tests may be conducted to rule out other conditions with similar symptoms. PD can also be diagnosed after a person has died. Characteristic structures in the brain are taken as proof of the disease.

TREATMENT

There is no cure for Parkinson's disease. One drug, selegiline (trade name Eldepryl) may slow the destruction of SN brain cells. However, there are a number of treatments for the symptoms of PD.

Exercise, Nutrition, and Physical Therapy

Regular, moderate exercise can improve motor (muscular) control. It improves a person's circulation and appetite and frees up stiff muscles. A physical therapist can help a patient design an exercise program for his or her special needs.

Good nutrition is also important. PD patients often lose interest in food. They may simply lose their appetite, or they may have nausea from drugs they are taking for treatment. Also, as their bodies begin to move more slowly, they may become irritated by how long it takes to eat. Food may digest slowly as well, causing the person to feel full much of the day.

These problems can be partially solved by including more fiber in a person's diet. Soft foods also go down more easily and are digested more quickly. Certain types of drugs can also increase the movement of food through the digestive system.

There is currently no evidence that vitamins, minerals, or other nutritional supplements have any effect on the symptoms of PD.

Drugs

Researchers have discovered a number of drugs that can help relieve the symptoms of Parkinson's disease. The effectiveness of the drugs depends on many factors. These factors include the patient's body chemistry, the rate at which the disease is progressing, and the length of time the drug has been used. Each PD drug also has side effects. In some cases, those side effects may limit the use of a drug by some patients.

There are presently five classes of drugs used to treat Parkinson's disease.

DRUGS THAT REPLACE DOPAMINE. The symptoms of the disease develop because SN brain cells do not produce enough dopamine. One solution, then, would be to give dopamine to the brain.

The problem with this solution is that the body's blood-brain barrier (BBB) gets in the way. It stops certain toxins and chemicals from entering the brain. In most places in the body substances can pass easily in and out of the blood vessels. This is how the cells of the body get the things they need to function properly. In the BBB, the walls of the blood vessels are much less permeable (open to penetration). The blood-brain barrier is very important because it protects the brain from harmful chemicals and helps maintain a safe, stable environment for sensitive brain tissues. But sometimes helpful chemicals are also kept from entering the brain.

The BBB doesn't allow neurotransmitters or hormones from elsewhere in the body to enter the brain. Dopamine, the chemical needed by Parkinson's patients, is a neurotransmitter. This is a problem for doctors. A person cannot be treated for Parkinson's by being given a pill or an injection of dopamine. The chemical in the pill or injection cannot get through the blood-brain barrier into the brain.

One solution is to "fool" the blood-brain barrier. A patient can be given a drug that looks to the blood-brain barrier like a material it should let through. Researchers have had some success attaching medicines to elements that can pass through the BBB.

In the case of Parkinson's doctors found that they could inject the body with levodopa or L-dopa, a substance that the BBB lets pass into the brain and then turns into dopamine. L-dopa treatments often work for five years or longer. Then the drug begins to lose its effectiveness. It may also begin to produce side effects that are as bad as the symptoms of PD itself.

ENZYME INHIBITORS. Dopamine does not stay in the brain forever. Instead, it is attacked by other chemicals that break it down into other substances. These chemicals are known as enzymes.

Another way to relieve the symptoms of PD, then, is to prevent enzymes from acting on dopamine—that is, to inhibit them from breaking it down. If the enzymes are inhibited, more dopamine will remain in the brain. The drugs given to PD patients often contain L-dopa and one or more enzyme inhibitors.

DOPAMINE AGONISTS. A dopamine agonist is a drug that acts in the brain in much the same way that dopamine does. Patients with Parkinson's disease can take dopamine agonists to make up for missing dopamine. Like other drugs used to treat PD, dopamine agonists can have serious side effects, including confusion and hallucinations at higher doses.

ANTICHOLINERGIC DRUGS. Dopamine is only one of many neurotransmitters in the brain. Brain function depends on a balance of all neurotransmitters. This balance changes as the amount of dopamine decreases. One way to restore this balance is with anticholinergic drugs. These drugs reduce the

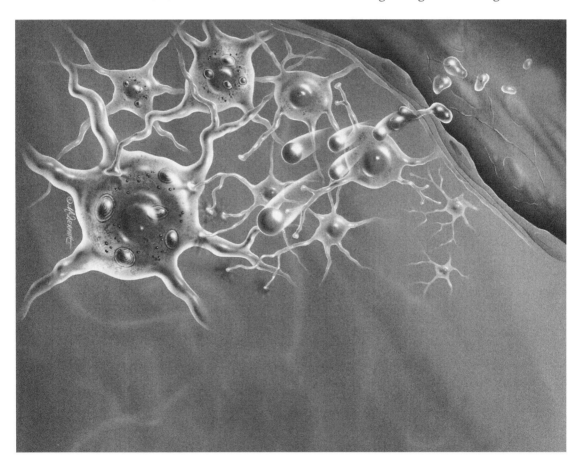

Illustration of Parkinson's disease at the cellular level. Parkinson's is caused by a disturbance in dopamine balance in the brain. (© 1996 Teri J. McDermott. Reproduced by permission of Custom Medical Stock Photo.)

amount of other neurotransmitters in the brain. They help maintain the correct balance of all neurotransmitters.

DRUGS WHOSE MODE OF ACTION IS UNCERTAIN. Sometimes drugs will work with PD patients, but researchers don't know why. The drug known as amantadine (pronounced uh-MANT-uh-deen, trade name Symmetrel) is an example. Amantadine is used to treat the symptoms of a variety of mental disorders. No one knows exactly how the drug relieves these symptoms, but it does, at least to a modest degree.

Surgery

Some symptoms of Parkinson's disease occur because one part of the brain receives too much stimulation or another part receives too little. These problems can sometimes be helped by surgery. In one surgical procedure, a long thin needle is inserted into a certain part of the brain. The cells in that part of the brain are then killed with heat or electricity. This procedure prevents that region of the brain from becoming overactive.

A similar procedure can be used to make another part of the brain more active. A needle is inserted into the correct region of the brain. A mild electric current is then sent into the brain through the needle. The electric current may cause that region of the brain to become more active.

Surgery is used when patients do not respond to drugs or when drugs no longer work. Surgical procedures are often effective in helping people recover some of their normal muscular movement.

A third surgical procedure involves transplanting SN cells from the brain of a fetus. The brain cells in a fetus are in an early stage of development. When implanted into the brain of a PD patient, they sometimes take over the job of making dopamine. They begin to function in place of the patient's own SN cells that have lost the ability to produce dopamine. This procedure is still in an experimental stage.

Alternative Treatment

Alternative treatments have limited promise for treating Parkinson's disease. Acupuncture, massage, and yoga may help relieve some symptoms of the disease by loosening tight muscles. Some alternative practitioners recommend the use of herbs and nutritional supplements, such as vitamins A, B, C, E, and the minerals calcium, selenium, and zinc. These supplements can sometimes have harmful side effects when used with drugs, however.

PROGNOSIS

There is no cure for Parkinson's disease. Drugs may help relieve symptoms for a few or many years. Those symptoms eventually get worse, however. Drug therapy becomes less successful. During the late stages of the disease, psychiatric symptoms become most troubling. These symptoms include problems with sleeping, increasing dementia, hallucinations, and loss of contact with reality.

PREVENTION

There is no known way to prevent Parkinson's disease.

FOR MORE INFORMATION

Books

Atwood, Glenna Wotton. *Living Well With Parkinson's.* New York: John Wiley & Sons, 1991.

Biziere, Kathleen, and Matthias Kurth. *Living with Parkinson's Disease.* New York: Demos Vermande, 1997.

Hauser, Robert, and Theresa Zesiewica. *Parkinson's Disease : Questions and Answers,* 2nd edition. Chicago: Merit Publishing International, 1998.

Williams, Frank L. *Parkinson's Disease : The Complete Guide for Patients and Caregivers.* New York: Fireside, 1993.

Organizations

National Parkinson Foundation. 1501 NW Ninth Ave., Bob Hope Road, Miami, FL 33136. http://www.parkinson.org.

Parkinson's Disease Foundation. 710 West 168th St., New York, NY 10032. (800) 457–6676. http://www.apdaparkinson.com.

Worldwide Education and Awareness for movement Disorders. Mt. Sinai Medical Center, 1 Gustave Levy Place, New York, NY 10029. (800) 437–MOV2. http://www.wemove.org.

Web sites

About Parkinson's Disease. [Online] http://www.parkinsonsinfo.com/about_parkinsons/ (accessed on October 27, 1999).

"Ask NOAH About: Parkinson's Disease." *NOAH: New York Online Access to Health.* [Online] http://www.noah.cuny.edu/neuro/parkin.html (accessed on October 27, 1999).

AWAKENINGS. [Online] http://www.parkinsondisease.com (accessed on October 27, 1999).

"Parkinson's Disease." *Health-Center.com* [Online] http://www.healthguide.com/english/brain/pd/default.htm (accessed on October 27, 1999).

The Parkinson's Web. [Online] http://pdweb.mgh.harvard.edu (accessed on October 28, 1999).

PERIODONTAL DISEASE

DEFINITION

Periodontal disease affects the tissues that support and anchor the teeth. Left untreated, periodontal disease results in destruction of the gums, parts of the jawbone, and portions of the tooth root.

DESCRIPTION

In a healthy person, teeth are held in place by a combination of soft tissue and bone. The soft tissue is known as the gums. Periodontal disease can attack any part of the gums or bone. The most common forms of periodontal disease are gingivitis, periodontitis, and trench mouth.

Gingivitis

The gingiva is the outermost part of the gums. Gingivitis is an inflammation of the gingiva. The gingiva becomes red and loses its normal shape. Bleeding occurs easily, during toothbrushing, for example. Gingivitis may be present for many years without becoming a serious medical problem. In some cases, however, it may become more severe. It may become very painful and lead to loss of tissue between the teeth. Poor oral (mouth) hygiene, fatigue, a poor diet, and stress may all lead to gingivitis.

Periodontitis

Periodontitis is a more serious form of gingivitis. Periodontitis is also called pyorrhea. Plaque and tartar sometimes form on the outer surfaces of teeth. Plaque and tartar are thin films of food particles and saliva. They provide a home for bacteria that cause tooth decay.

The decay caused by these bacteria sometimes extends down into the gums. There may be damage to the bone structure that holds teeth in place. The teeth become loose and may fall out. Periodontitis in adults is the most serious form of periodontal disease. It is the main cause of tooth loss in adults.

Periodontitis also occurs in children, but it is much less common than in adults. If not treated, periodontitis in children can become chronic. That is, it does not get better but is always present as a health problem. In some cases, it may become much worse in adulthood, leading to tooth loss.

> **WORDS TO KNOW**
>
> **Gingiva:** The outer layer of the gums.
>
> **Plaque:** A thin layer of food and saliva that forms on the surface of teeth.
>
> **Tartar:** Plaque that has become hardened and attached to the tooth surface.

Trench Mouth

Gingivitis can also lead to a condition known as trench mouth. The most common cause of trench mouth is poor oral hygiene. Stress, a poor diet, and lack of sleep may also be factors.

CAUSES

How bacteria in the periodontal pocket cause tissue destruction is not fully understood. Researchers to know that bacteria that live in plaque and tartar produce acids when they digest foods. These acids can destroy tooth enamel and bone. The bacteria also produce toxins (poisons) that can kill cells in gum tissue. Finally, when the body's immune system attacks the bacteria, some gum tissue is destroyed at the same time.

The most basic cause of periodontal disease is poor oral hygiene. Regular toothbrushing and flossing remove most of the plaque and tartar on which bacteria live. They can greatly reduce the risk for any form of periodontal disease. Regular dental checkups are also important. Dental hygienists can remove any of the plaque and tartar that may still remain.

Gingivitis is usually the first stage in all other periodontal diseases. If it can be prevented or controlled, the more serious forms of the disease are unlikely to occur.

SYMPTOMS

The initial symptoms of periodontal disease are bleeding and inflamed gums and bad breath. Periodontitis follows cases of gingivitis. The key characteristic of periodontitis is a large pocket that forms between the teeth and gums. Pain is often absent until late in the disease. It occurs then when a tooth becomes loose or infected.

The symptoms of trench mouth often appear suddenly. They include pain, fever, fatigue, and foul breath. Trench mouth results in the formation of open sores on the gums and death of tissues surrounding the teeth. The gums may bleed easily, especially when chewing. The pain may become so bad that the patient cannot eat or swallow. The inflammation may spread to nearby tissues of the face and neck.

DIAGNOSIS

Dentists can usually diagnose a periodontal disease quite easily. The most important clues are inflamed gums and the presence of an opening between gums and teeth. The specific form of periodontal disease usually depends on the nature of the opening. In gingivitis, the pocket tends to be small and shallow. As the disease progresses, the pocket becomes larger and deeper. Bone loss can be detected on an x-ray photograph.

TREATMENT

Gingivitis can usually be treated simply. Plaque and tartar are removed from teeth, depriving bacteria of their home. The inflamed tissues around a tooth usually heal quickly and completely.

More serious cases of periodontitis cannot be treated by routine dental procedures. Dental surgery may be necessary to remove plaque, tartar, and infected gum tissue. Treatment with antibiotics may be necessary if infection is present.

Treatment for trench mouth starts with a complete cleaning of the teeth. All plaque, tartar, and dead gum tissue are removed. Regular visits to the dentist and use of mouthwash containing hydrogen peroxide may be needed to ensure that the gums heal completely. Surgery may be needed if damage to the gums is extensive and they do not heal properly.

DAILY BRUSHING AND FLOSSING ARE SUFFICIENT TO PREVENT MOST CASES OF PERIODONTAL DISEASE.

PROGNOSIS

Periodontal disease is easily treated. The gums usually heal quickly and resume their normal shape and function. In more difficult cases, surgery may be necessary. But the surgery is relatively simple and usually successful.

PREVENTION

Most forms of periodontal disease can be prevented with good dental hygiene. Daily brushing and flossing are sufficient to prevent most cases of periodontal disease. Tartar-control toothpastes help prevent the formation of tartar. But they do not remove tartar once it has formed.

FOR MORE INFORMATION

Books

Berns, Joel M. *Understanding Periodontal Diseases,* 2nd edition. Carol Stream, IL: Quintessence Publishing Company, 1993.

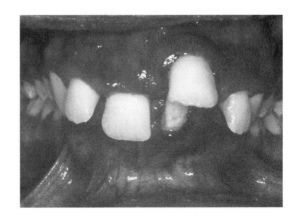

An extreme case of juvenile periodontitis. (Photograph by Edward H. Gill. Reproduced by permission of Custom Medical Stock Photo.)

Sheldon, Sydney. *Ignore Your Teeth and They'll Go Away : The Complete Guide to Gum Disease,* 3rd edition. Pikesville, MD: Devida Publications, 1998.

Organizations

The American Academy of Periodontology. 737 N. Michigan Avenue, Suite 800, Chicago, IL 60611–2690. (312) 787–5518. http://www.perio.org.

Web sites

"Dental Health: Periodontal Disease." *Dental Review Online.* [Online] http://www.dentalreview.com/tooth_periodontitis.htm (accessed on October 28, 1999).

"What Are Periodontal Diseases?" [Online] http://www.perio.org/consumer/2a.html (accessed October 28, 1999).

PNEUMONIA

DEFINITION

Pneumonia (pronounced noo-MOAN-ya) is an infection of the lung. It can be caused by a great many different agents, including bacteria, viruses, fungi, and parasites. In the United States, pneumonia is the sixth most common disease leading to death. It is also the most common fatal infection acquired by patients in hospitals. In developing countries, pneumonia is one of the two most common causes of death. Diarrhea is the other.

DESCRIPTION

The healthy human lung is normally free of disease-causing microorganisms, such as bacteria and viruses. The body has immune system (a complex defense system) is designed to keep it that way. For example, hairs in the nose trap large particles carried along by the air we breathe in. The epiglottis is a kind of trapdoor in the larynx (windpipe; pronounced LAYR-inx) that keeps food and other swallowed substances from entering the lungs. Mucus, a thick liquid, is produced throughout the respiratory (breathing) system to capture dust, bacteria, and other organisms. Cilia (pronounced SIL-ee-uh) are hairlike projections along the lining of the respiratory system that also trap and remove foreign objects from the body. Special types of white blood cells, called macrophages (pronounced MAK-ruh-faj), are also part of this defensive system. They are produced when foreign bodies enter the body to attack and destroy those bodies.

This system of defenses does not work perfectly, however. Sometimes organisms that can cause infection get into the lungs. For example, a person may be exposed to large amounts of smoke. There may be too many smoke particles for the body's defense system to remove. In such a case, the lungs may become infected and pneumonia can develop.

Conditions that Lead to Pneumonia

In many cases, the lungs become infected simply because they are overwhelmed with some foreign agent, such as bacteria or smoke particles. But a variety of conditions can increase the likelihood that a person will contract (catch) pneumonia. In these conditions, the person's lungs may already be weakened or damaged by some other problem. Some of these conditions include the following:

- **Damage to the epiglottis.** Stroke, seizures, alcohol, and various drugs can prevent the epiglottis from functioning normally. When this happens, materials that have been swallowed may get into the lungs, causing an infection there.
- **Viruses.** Viruses can damage the cilia that line the respiratory tract. Foreign bodies may then get into the lungs more easily, causing an infection. One such virus is HIV (the human immunodeficiency virus), which causes AIDS (see AIDS entry). Pneumonia is a major health problem for people with AIDS and those who have HIV in their bodies.
- **Old age.** As people grow older, their immune systems often become weaker. They are less able to fight off infections that once would not have been a problem.
- **Chronic diseases.** A chronic disease lasts for a very long time, usually many years. Examples of such diseases are asthma (see asthma entry), cystic fibrosis (see cystic fibrosis entry), and diseases of the nervous and muscular systems. These diseases often affect the epiglottis. A damaged epiglottis allows food and contaminated objects to get into the lungs, causing infections that can lead to pneumonia.
- **Surgery.** Pneumonia is a common complication of surgery. Some drugs used during surgery affect a person's normal breathing pattern. He or she may not be able to cough or breathe as deeply as usual. Foreign objects are not expelled from the respiratory tract. They may get into the lungs and cause an infection.

WORDS TO KNOW

Cilia: Fine, hair-like projections that line the trachea and bronchi. Cilia wave back and forth, carrying mucus through the airways.

Cyanosis: A condition that develops when the body does not get enough oxygen, causing the skin to turn blue.

Immune system: The organs, tissues, cells, and cell products that work together to protect the body from invasions by bacteria, viruses, and other foreign substances.

Mucus: A mixture of water, salts, sugars, and proteins, which has the job of cleansing, lubricating, and protecting passageways in the body.

Sputum: A thick liquid material consisting of spit and other matter coughed up from the lungs.

pneumonia

The list of organisms that can cause pneumonia is very long. It includes bacteria, viruses, fungi, and parasites. Some examples include:

- Viruses are the most common cause of pneumonia in young children. These viruses also cause other infections of the respiratory system, such as influenza (see influenza entry), tonsillitis (see tonsillitis entry), and the common cold (see common cold entry).
- Bacteria are the primary cause of pneumonia in older children and adults. The most common of these bacteria are *Streptococcus pneumoniae,* (pronounced STREP-tuh-coc-us noo-MOHN-ee-ay) *Haemophilus influenzae,* (pronounced HEE-mof-uh-lus in-floo-EN-zay) and *Staphylococcus aureus* (pronounced STAFF-lo-coc-us or-ee-us).

- An organism called *Mycoplasma pneumoniae* affects older children and adults. The organism is somewhat similar to both bacteria and viruses. It produces a form of pneumonia known as "walking pneumonia."
- A protozoan (one-celled organism) called *Pneumocystis carinii* causes a form of pneumonia in people with weakened immune systems. The condition, pneumocystis carinii pneumonia (PCP), is one of the most serious medical problems for people with HIV or AIDS. It also affects people whose immune systems have been weakened by chemotherapy or cancer.
- An organism known as *Chlamydia psittaci* causes a form of pneumonia sometimes known as "bird pneumonia." The disease is quite rare and was once observed only in humans who came into contact with bird droppings. People infected with HIV are also susceptible to the infection.
- In 1976, a new form of pneumonia was discovered. It broke out among a large group of people attending an American Legion convention. The infection was caused by a previously unknown organism. Subsequently named *Legionella pneumophila,* it causes what is now called Legoinnaire's disease. The organism was eventually traced to the air conditioning units at the hotel where the convention took place.

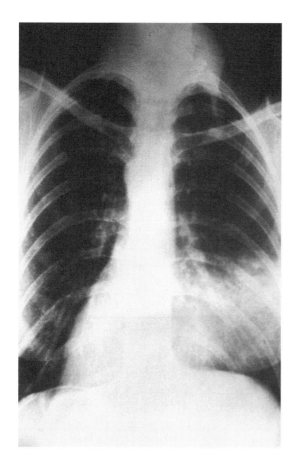

X ray showing pneumonia in the right lung. (Reproduced by permission of the National Audubon Society Collection/Photo Researchers, Inc.)

SYMPTOMS

The primary symptoms of pneumonia are fever, chills, cough, chest pain, and shortness of breath. The patient often coughs up sputum (pronounced SPYOO-tum; usually made up of saliva, mucus, dead cells, and other materials) that may be streaked with pus or blood. In the severest cases, a patient shows signs of cyanosis (pronounced SI-uh-no-sis). Cyanosis is caused when a patient's blood is not getting enough oxygen. It is characterized by a blue tint on the nail beds or lips.

DIAGNOSIS

Pneumonia can usually be diagnosed on the basis of a patient's symptoms. A doctor will also listen to the patient's chest with a stethoscope. If the lungs are infected, they produce an unusual sound when the patient breathes in and out. Tapping on the patient's back is also a test for pneumonia. Normally, the tapping produces a hollow sound because the lungs are filled with air. If pneumonia is present, however, the lungs may contain fluid. In this case, the sound is dull thump.

Some forms of bacterial pneumonia can be diagnosed by laboratory tests. A sample of the patient's sputum is taken. The sample is then stained with dyes and examined under a microscope. The organisms causing the disease can often be seen and identified.

X rays can also be used to diagnose pneumonia. Dark spots on the patient's lungs may indicate the presence of an infection. The appearance of the spots may give a clue to the type of infection that has occurred.

TREATMENT

At one time, many cases of pneumonia were fatal. The discovery of antibiotics changed that. Today, many cases of bacterial pneumonia can be cured. Antibiotics are given as soon as the infection is diagnosed.

Viral pneumonia is more difficult to cure. There are not many drugs that kill viruses. Amantadine (pronounced uh-man-tu-deen, trade name Symmetrel) and acyclovir (pronounced a-SI-kloh-veer) are two exceptions. They are sometimes helpful in treating some forms of viral pneumonia.

PROGNOSIS

The prognosis for pneumonia varies widely depending on the type of infection. The recovery rate is nearly 100 percent, for example, in cases of "walking pneumonia." By contrast, people with pneumonia caused by *Staphylococcus pneumoniae* stand only a 60 percent to 70 percent chance of survival. For the most common form of pneumonia, caused by *Streptococcus pneumoniae,* the survival rate is about 95 percent.

People who are very young or very old are likely to experience complications from pneumonia. Their immune systems may not be completely healthy. Their bodies may find it difficult to fight off infections related to those that cause pneumonia.

Pneumonia can also lead to other complications that are more serious than the original infection. People with chronic illnesses, such as cirrhosis of the liver or congestive heart failure, or who have weakened immune systems are especially at risk for such complications.

PREVENTION

Pneumonia often develops as a complication following an attack of influenza. To protect against this possibility, a person should be vaccinated against influenza each year. This advice is especially important for elderly people and people who live in crowded conditions, such as nursing homes or army camps.

A vaccine has been developed against *Streptococcus pneumoniae.* It works very well and is recommended for patients with chronic illnesses.

One consequence of the AIDS epidemic was the development of a new treatment for PCP. Patients may be put on a regular schedule of the drug trimethoprim sulfate and/or inhaled pentamidine. This treatment has dramatically reduced the rate of deaths from PCP among people with AIDS.

FOR MORE INFORMATION

Books

Stoffman, Phyllis. *The Family Guide to Preventing and Treating 100 Infectious Diseases.* New York: John Wiley & Sons, 1995.

Periodicals

Brody, Jane E. "Pneumonia Is Still a Killer." *New York Times* (January 8, 1997): pp. B10+.

Organizations

American Lung Association. 1740 Broadway, New York, NY 10019. (800) LUNG–USA. http://www.lungusa.org.

Web sites

"Ask NOAH About: Pneumonia." *NOAH: New York Online Access to Health.* [Online] http://www.noah.cuny.edu/respiratory/pneumonia.html (accessed on October 26, 1999).

"Pneumonia." *Yahoo! Health.* [Online] http://health.yahoo.com/health/Diseases_and_Conditions/Disease_Feed_Data/Pneumonia (accessed on October 28, 1999)

"Pneumonia." *American Lung Association.* [Online] http://www.lungusa.org/diseases/lungpneumoni.html (accessed on October 28, 1999).

Pneumonia.Net. [Online] http://www.pneumonia.net/ (accessed on October 28, 1999).

PNEUMOTHORAX

DEFINITION

Pneumothorax (pronounced noo-moh-thor-ax) is a condition in which air or some other gas collects in the chest or the pleural space. The pleural space is the space that surrounds the lungs. When a gas collects in the pleural space, it can cause part or all of a lung to collapse. For that reason, pneumothorax is also called collapsed lung.

DESCRIPTION

Normally, pressure inside the lungs is greater than pressure in the pleural space. This difference in pressure allows the lungs to stay filled with air. But air or some other gas can get into the pleural space. When it does so, the normal condition is reversed. Pressure in the pleural space becomes greater than pressure in the lungs. This extra pressure on the lungs can cause them to collapse partially or completely.

CAUSES

Sometimes pneumothorax occurs for no known reason. In such a case, the process is called spontaneous pneumothorax. This condition occurs most commonly among tall, thin men between the ages of twenty and forty. People with lung disorders are also subject to spontaneous

WORDS TO KNOW

Electrocardiogram (ECG): A test that measures the electrical function of the heart, indicating the presence of any heart problems.

Pleural: Having to do with the membrane that surrounds the lungs.

Thoracentesis: A procedure for removing fluids from the pleural space by inserting a long, thin needle between the ribs.

pneumothorax. Emphysema (see emphysema entry), cystic fibrosis (see cystic fibrosis entry), and tuberculosis (see tuberculosis entry) are examples of such lung disorders.

Pneumothorax can also occur as the result of an accident or injury to the chest cavity. This type of pneumothorax is called traumatic pneumothorax. Certain kinds of medical procedures can cause traumatic pneumothorax. An example is the procedure known as thoracentesis (pronounced thor-uh-sen-tee-sis). In thoracentesis, a large needle is inserted into the chest wall to remove fluids. Sometimes air accidentally enters the chest during this procedure. If so, traumatic pneumothorax can result.

The most serious type of pneumothorax is tension pneumothorax. Tension pneumothorax can be caused by injuries, such as a fractured rib, or by lung disease, such as asthma (see asthma entry), chronic bronchitis (see bronchitis entry), or emphysema. In this form of pneumothorax, a large amount of air gets into the chest cavity and cannot escape. It can cause the lung to collapse quickly. It can also push on the heart and its blood vessels. Without immediate treatment, tension pneumothorax can result in death.

SYMPTOMS

The symptoms of pneumothorax depend on a number of factors. These include the amount of air that enters the chest, the extent to which the lung collapses, and the presence of any kind of lung disease.

Spontaneous pneumothorax can be classified as simple or complex. Simple spontaneous pneumothorax usually occurs with people who are otherwise healthy. It is caused by certain types of activity, such as scuba diving or flying at high altitudes. Complex spontaneous pneumothorax occurs with people who have lung disease. The symptoms of complex spontaneous pneumothorax are more serious than those of simple spontaneous pneumothorax.

The most common symptom of spontaneous pneumothorax is a chest pain that can be dull, sharp, or stabbing. The pain starts suddenly and becomes worse with coughing or deep breathing. Other symptoms include shortness of breath, rapid breathing, and a cough.

Traumatic pneumothorax occurs as a result of medical procedures or of injuries. For example, a stab wound allows air to enter the chest cavity. The air may have no way of escaping from the chest. The wound can result in a collapsed lung. The symptoms of traumatic pneumothorax are similar to those of spontaneous pneumothorax, but they are more severe.

The symptoms of tension pneumothorax tend to be severe with sudden onset (beginning). They include anxiety, swollen neck veins, weak pulse, and decreased breathing sounds from the lung.

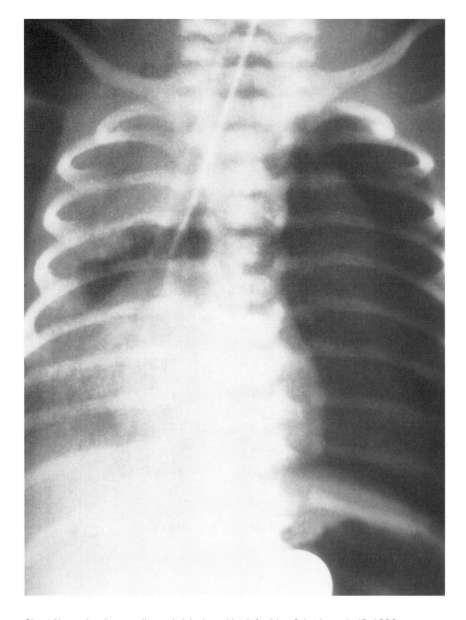

Chest X ray showing a collapsed right lung (the left side of the image). (© 1990. Reproduced by permission of Custom Medical Stock Photo.)

DIAGNOSIS

Pneumothorax is diagnosed by listening to the patient's chest. With a stethoscope, a doctor can tell whether the normal sounds of breathing can be heard in the chest. A chest X ray is often taken to follow up on an initial diagnosis. The chest X ray will show pockets of air and a collapsed lung. An electrocardiogram (ECG; pronounced ih-LEK-tro-KAR-dee-o-gram) can also be taken. The ECG will tell whether the heart is functioning normally. Finally, blood tests can be used to diagnose pneumothorax. They will show the level of gases dissolved in the blood.

TREATMENT

Simple pneumothorax usually gets better on its own, but more complex cases require medical treatment. The object of the treatment is to remove air from the chest or pleural cavity. When the air is gone, the lung can expand to its normal size.

Removal of air is done by inserting a needle into the chest wall. Air is removed through the needle and not allowed to get back in. The lung returns to its normal size on its own within a few days. A person who experiences pneumothorax more than once may require surgery.

PROGNOSIS

Most people recover fully from spontaneous pneumothorax. About half of these people experience spontaneous pneumothorax a second time. Recovery from a collapsed lung generally takes one to two weeks. The prognosis for tension pneumothorax is not as good. In this condition, the patient's heart may fail, causing death in a short period of time. Tension pneumothorax must be treated as a medical emergency.

PREVENTION

Preventative measures for noninjury related pneumothorax include not smoking and having respiratory problems treated whenever they occur. Sometimes pneumothorax occurs in both lungs, or in one lung more than once. In such cases, surgery may be needed to prevent it from occurring again.

FOR MORE INFORMATION

Organizations

American Association for Respiratory Care. 11030 Ables Lane, Dallas, TX 75229. (972) 243–2272. http://www.aarc.org.

American lung Association. 1740 Broadway, New York, NY 10019. (800) LUNG–USA. http://www.lungusa.org.

Web sites

"Collapsed Lung: Non-Injury Related." *InteliHealth*. [Online] http://www. intelihealth.com (accessed on October 28, 1999).

"Pneumothorax." http://www.thriveonline.com/health/Library/sports/sport52. html (accessed on October 25, 1999).

"Spontaneous Pneumothorax." *Healthanswers*. [Online] http://www. healthanswers.com (accessed on October 28, 1999).

POLIO

DEFINITION

Polio (pronounced POH-lee-oh) is a serious disease caused by a virus called the poliovirus. The full medical name for the disease is poliomyelitis (pronounced POH-lee-oh-mi-uh-LI-tis). In its severest form, polio causes paralysis of the muscles of the legs, arms, and respiratory (breathing) system.

DESCRIPTION

The poliovirus causes most of its infections in the summer and fall. At one time, summer epidemics of polio were common and greatly feared.

The poliovirus primarily affects younger children. But it can also infect older children and adults. Poor hygiene and crowded living conditions encourage the spread of the poliovirus.

Paralysis is the most serious symptom of polio. Only about 1 percent to 2 percent of those infected with the virus are paralyzed, however. Risk factors for paralysis include older age, pregnancy, problems with the immune system, a recent tonsillectomy, and a recent episode of very strenuous exercise.

CAUSES

Poliovirus is transmitted through saliva and feces. It is passed on when people do not wash their hands after eating or using the bathroom. Once a person is infected with the virus, it can remain in the mouth and throat for about three

WORDS TO KNOW

Brain stem: A mass of nervous tissue that connects the main part of the brain to the spinal cord.

Epidemic: The widespread occurrence of a disease over a large geographic area for an extended period of time.

Paralysis: The inability to move one's muscles.

weeks. It then travels to the intestine. It can remain in the intestine for up to eight weeks.

Inside the intestine, the virus multiplies rapidly. It may invade the lymphatic (pronounced lim-FAT-ic) system. The lymphatic system consists of organs and tissues that help protect a person against disease. The virus eventually enters the bloodstream. It can then pass to the central nervous system (the brain and spinal cord). The virus can also pass directly into nerves. It can then travel along a nerve to the brain.

SYMPTOMS

About 90 percent of those infected with poliovirus have mild or no symptoms. These symptoms include a low fever, fatigue, headache, sore throat, and nausea and vomiting. These symptoms usually last two or three days. People with these symptoms are still infectious and can pass the disease on to other people.

Another 10 percent of those infected with the virus experience more serious symptoms, including severe headache and pain and stiffness of the neck and back. The stiffness is caused when the tissues around the spinal cord and brain become inflamed. These symptoms usually disappear after several days. The patient usually experiences complete recovery.

About 1 percent of people infected with the poliovirus develop the most serious symptoms of the disease. At first, they experience only mild symptoms. After a few days, however, the symptoms become much worse. They include severe headache and neck and back pain.

THE IRON LUNG

People with polio often lose the ability to move their legs and/or arms. This disability is a terrible disaster. But it does not necessarily cause death. If polio also causes loss of control over the respiratory muscles, however, death can and often does occur. For polio patients, then, a device to help them breathe is an absolute necessity.

In 1982, the American physiologist Philip Drinker (1893–1977) invented the most famous of all devices for helping polio patients to breathe. The device was called the Drinker tank respirator. It is more commonly known as an iron lung.

The iron lung is an airtight cylindrical steel drum. It encloses the entire body with only the patient's head exposed. Pumps connected to the device lower and raise air pressure within the drum. As the drum contracts and expands, it forces the patient's chest to contract and expand also. The iron lung forces the patient's body to continue breathing.

Many polio patients were kept alive by the iron lung. They had to spend many years enclosed in the lung, with only short periods outside it. With the development of the Salk and Sabin vaccines, polio has nearly become extinct. As a result, the iron lung no longer finds much use in today's hospitals.

The worst effects of polio are caused when the virus invades motor nerves. Motor nerves are nerves that control the movement of muscles. The virus can destroy these nerves. As the nerves die, muscles lose their ability to move. They first become floppy and weak. Eventually they become paralyzed and lose the ability to move at all. After a few days, the muscles actually begin to decrease in size. The person does not lose the sense of touch in the affected areas, however.

The virus can also infect the brain stem. The brain stem is located at the base of the brain. It connects the brain to the spinal cord. A person may have trouble breathing and swallowing. In the severest cases, the heart rate and blood pressure may be disturbed. These changes can lead to the patient's death.

THE WORST EFFECTS OF POLIO ARE CAUSED WHEN THE VIRUS INVADES MOTOR NERVES. THE VIRUS CAN DESTROY THESE NERVES. AS THE NERVES DIE, MUSCLES LOSE THEIR ABILITY TO MOVE.

The maximum degree of paralysis usually occurs within a few days. After that time, some healthy nerves may try to take the place of the damaged nerves. This process lasts about six months. After that time, no further improvement is likely.

DIAGNOSIS

Polio is now a rare disease in the United States. Many doctors have never seen a case of polio. A few symptoms are quite distinctive, however. A fever and paralysis without the loss of feeling is one clue to the presence of polio.

If a doctor suspects polio, the usual follow-up test is a lumbar puncture, or "spinal tap." A lumbar puncture is a procedure in which a sample of spinal fluid is removed with a long, thin needle. The spinal fluid can be examined for an elevated level of white blood cells and the absence of bacteria. These two factors taken together are a strong indication of polio.

The spinal fluid can also be tested for the presence of polio antibodies. Antibodies are chemicals produced by the immune system to fight against specific foreign invaders, such as the poliovirus.

TREATMENT

There is no cure for polio. Patients can be treated to make them more comfortable, however. For example, medications can reduce pain. Hot packs help soothe sore muscles. Artificial ventilation (breathing machines) may be necessary if a person's respiratory system is affected. Walking aids, such as crutches and walkers, may be necessary for someone whose leg muscles are damaged by the disease.

Dr. Jonas Salk, developer of the first polio vaccine, 1955. (Reproduced by permission of AP/Wide World Photos)

PROGNOSIS

The prognosis for mild and moderate polio is good. Most patients recover completely within a short period of time. Of those who have the severest form of polio, about half will recover completely. A quarter will experience some disability, and another quarter will have permanent and serious disability. About 1 percent of all those who have the most serious form of polio die of the disease.

In recent years, a new medical problem known as postpolio syndrome has been diagnosed. The condition shows up thirty years or more after a person has had a mild or moderate form of the disease. Postpolio syndrome affects about 25 percent of polio patients. The major symptom of postpolio syndrome is a very slow decrease in muscle strength.

PREVENTION

Polio can now be prevented by immunizations. An immunization is an injection that protects a person against some type of infectious disease. Two kinds of polio immunizations are available in the United States. The Salk vaccine contains dead polioviruses. It is injected just under the skin. The dead viruses cause the immune system to start making antibodies against the poliovirus. If a person is infected with the poliovirus later in life, the immune system can protect the body against the disease.

The Sabin vaccine contains polioviruses that are very weak but not dead. They produce the same effect on the immune system as dead viruses. Both vaccines are highly effective in preventing polio. In fact, some public-health experts think the disease may be completely wiped out in the next decade.

FOR MORE INFORMATION

Books

Daniel, Thomas M., and Frederick C. Robbins, eds. *Polio.* Rochester: University of Rochester Press, 1997.

Gould, Tony. *A Summer Plague: Polio and Its Survivors.* New Haven, CT: Yale University Press, 1997.

Halstead, Lauro S., ed. *Managing Post Polio: A Guide to Living Well with Post Polio.* Arlington, VA: ABI Professional Publications, 1998.

Weaver, Lydia. *Close to Home: A Story of the Polio Epidemic.* New York: Puffin, 1997.

Organizations

International Polio Network. 4207 Lindell Blvd., Suite 110, St. Louis, MO 63108–2915. (314) 534–0475.

March of Dimes Birth Defects Foundation. National Office. 1275 Mamaroneck Ave., White Plains, NY 10605. http://www.modimes.org.

Polio Survivors Association. 12720 Lareina Ave., Downey, CA 90242. (310) 862–4508.

Web sites

"Ask NOAH About: Neurological Problems." *NOAH: New York Online Access to Health.* [Online] http://www.noah.cuny.edu/neuro/neuropg.html# POLIO AND POST-POLIO SYNDROME (accessed on October 28, 1999).

Polio.com. [Online] http://www.polio.com (accessed on October 28, 1999).

"Polio/Post-Polio Information Directory." *Polio Society Home Page.* http://www.polio.org (accessed on October 28, 1999).

POSTTRAUMATIC STRESS DISORDER

DEFINITION

Posttraumatic stress disorder (PTSD) is a condition that affects people who have gone through a major traumatic (shocking) event. PTSD is characterized by repeated thoughts about the ordeal, a dulling of emotions, an increased tendency to become excited and aroused, and, sometimes, dramatic personality changes.

DESCRIPTION

At one time, a condition known as "shell shock" was common among men and women who had been through battle. The condition was also known as battle fatigue. These individuals experienced flashbacks of battle. Memories of the event could totally disrupt their lives. In some cases, they were affected so severely that they were unable to function in everyday life.

Today, we know that this condition is caused by a number of factors, including rape, robbery, a natural disaster, or a serious accident. People who are diagnosed with a serious disease often have the same symptoms. A better name for the condition, then, is posttraumatic stress disorder. That is, a person experiences severe feelings of anxiety following some major disruption in his or her life.

People of all ages can be affected by PTSD. Even children who experience sexual or physical abuse or who lose a parent to death may develop PTSD.

WORDS TO KNOW

Benzodiazepine: A drug used to control the symptoms of anxiety.

Cognitive-behavioral therapy: A form of counseling designed to help patients understand the basic nature of their disorder and to find ways of confronting and dealing with the disorder.

Flashback: A sudden memory of an event that occurred months or years earlier.

Selective serotonin reuptake inhibitors (SSRIs): A class of drugs used to reduce depression.

CAUSES

No one knows what causes PTSD. Two people may go through the same traumatic experience. But only one may experience PTSD. It may be that people differ in their genetic makeup. Or their personalities and upbringing may differ. Or they may experience the same event in two different ways.

SYMPTOMS

The appearance of symptoms varies widely among individuals. In some cases, symptoms appear a few months after the event. In other cases, it may be years before symptoms occur. Sometimes symptoms fade away after a short period of time. In other cases, they last for many years. Some veterans of the Vietnam War, for example, spent decades living alone in rural areas trying to deal with their memories of the horrors of that war.

A FLASHBACK MAY CAUSE A PERSON TO LOSE TOUCH WITH THE REAL WORLD FOR A SHORT TIME. THE PERSON GOES BACK IN HIS OR HER MIND TO THE TRAUMATIC EVENT AND LIVES IT OVER AGAIN.

Among the most troubling symptoms of PTSD are flashbacks. A flashback is a sudden memory of an event that occurred months or years earlier. Flashbacks may be triggered by certain sights, sounds, smells, or feelings. A flashback may cause a person to lose touch with the real world for a short time. The person goes back in his or her mind to the traumatic event and lives it over again.

DIAGNOSIS

Mental-health professionals use a number of standards to diagnose PTSD. These standards fall into three general categories: intrusive symptoms, avoidance symptoms, and arousal symptoms. Intrusive symptoms are experiences that interrupt and interfere with a person's normal life. They include:

• Flashbacks
• Sleep disorders, such as nightmares
• Intense distress when there is mention of the original event

Avoidance symptoms involve attempts by the patient to refrain from dealing with the original event. They include:

• Trying to avoid thinking or feeling anything about the trauma
• Inability to remember the event
• Loss of ability to feel and express emotions
• A sense that the past is approaching very quickly

Arousal symptoms are obvious changes in a person's mental state. They include:

• Problems falling asleep
• Sudden and extreme reactions to unexpected noises
• Memory problems
• Concentration problems
• Moodiness
• Violence

PTSD in children can also be diagnosed based on other symptoms. These include:

• Learning disabilities
• Memory or attention problems
• Increased dependency on other people
• Increased anxiety
• Self-abuse

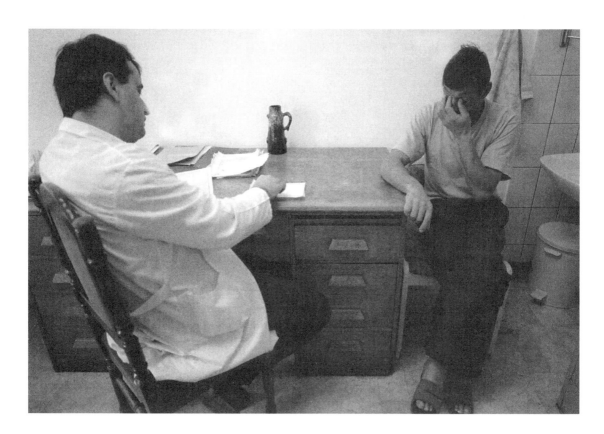

Huseuin Gusic (right), a veteran of the Bosnian war, talking with Dr. Avdo Sakusic (left) about war related nightmares. (Reproduced by permission of AP/Wide World Photos)

TREATMENT

Posttraumatic stress disorder is usually treated with a combination of medications and counseling. The medications are designed to reduce anxiety and to help patients overcome depression. The most common drugs used are the selective serotonin reuptake inhibitors (SSRIs) such as fluoxetine (pronounced floo-OC-suh-teen; trade name Prozac). Sleep problems may be treated with an antianxiety drug such as benzodiazepine (pronounced BEN-zoh-die-AZ-uh-peen). Drugs of this type have serious long-term side effects, however.

A common form of counseling is called cognitive-behavioral therapy. The purpose of cognitive-behavioral therapy is to help patients understand the basic nature of their disorder and to find ways of confronting and dealing with the disorder. Group therapy and family therapy can also be helpful. In group therapy, a number of individuals with similar problems meet and discuss common issues and ways of solving their problems. In family therapy, family members of the patient are helped to understand the nature of his or her disorder and to learn ways in which they can work together to support the patient.

posttraumatic
stress disorder

PROGNOSIS

The prognosis for PTSD differs widely depending on a number of factors. Those factors include:

• Whether the original trauma was expected
• How severe the trauma was
• How long the trauma lasted
• The patient's genetic makeup and personality

When treated, many patients experience significant improvement. However, some individuals never recover fully from a terrible event. Some survivors of the Holocaust, for example, experienced permanent psychological scars as a result of that event.

FOR MORE INFORMATION

Books

Allen, Jon. *Coping with Trauma: A Guide to Self-Understanding.* Washington, DC: American Psychiatric Press, 1995.

Bassett, Lucinda. *From Panic to Power: Proven Techniques to Calm Your Anxieties, Conquer Your Fears and Put You in Control of Your Life.* New York: HarperCollins, 1995.

Bemis, Judith, and Amr Barrada. *Embracing the Fear: Learning to Manage Anxiety and Panic Attacks.* Center City, MN: Hazelden, 1994.

Kulka, Richard A. *Trauma and the Vietnam War Generation: A Report of Findings from the National Vietnam Veterans Readjustment Study.* New York: Brunner/Mazel, 1990.

Matsakis, Aphrodite. *I Can't Get Over It: A Handbook for Trauma Survivors.* Oakland, CA: New Harbinger Publications, 1996.

Shengold, Leonard. *Soul Murder: The Effects of Childhood Abuse and Deprivation.* New Haven, CT: Yale University Press, 1989.

Organizations

American Psychiatric Association. 1400 K St., N.W., Washington, DC 20005. (202) 682–6000; (888) 357–7924.

Anxiety Disorders Association of America. 11900 Parklawn Dr., Suite 100, Rockville, MD 20852. (301) 231–9350.

Freedom from Fear. 308 Seaview Ave., Staten Island, NY 10305. (718) 351–1717.

National Alliance for the Mentally Ill. 2101 Wilson Blvd., #302, Arlington, VA 22201. (703) 524–7600.

National Anxiety Foundation. 3135 Custer Dr., Lexington, KY 40517. (606) 272–7166. http://lexington-on-line.com/nafdefault.html.

National Institute of Mental Health. Panic Campaign. Rm. 15C-05, 5600 Fishers Lane, Rockville, MD 20857. (800) 64–PANIC. http://www.nimh.nih.gov/publicat.index.htm.

National Mental Health Association. 1021 Prince St., Alexandria, VA 22314. (703) 684–7722. http://www.mediconsult.com/noframes/associations/NMHA/content.html.

Society for Traumatic Stress Studies. 60 Revere Dr., Suite 500, Northbrook, IL 60062. (708) 480–9080.

Web sites

Anxiety and Panic International Net Resources. [Online] http://www.algy.com/anxiety/index.shtml (accessed on November 23, 1999).

Anxiety Network Homepage. [Online] http://www.anxietynetwork.com.

"Ask NOAH About: Mental Health." *NOAH: New York Online Access to Health.* [Online] http://www.noah.cuny.edu/mentalhealth/mental.html#PTS (accessed on October 28, 1999).

Ford, Julian. "Managing Stress and Recovering from Trauma: Facts and Resources for Veterans and Families." [Online] http://www.dartmouth.edu/dms/ptsd. (accessed March 19, 1997).

PROSTATE CANCER

DEFINITION

Prostate cancer is a disease in which the cells of the prostate become abnormal. They start to grow uncontrollably, forming tumors. A tumor is a mass or lump of tissue made of abnormal cells. Tumors may be malignant or benign. A malignant tumor can spread to other parts of the body. Malignant tumors are cancerous. Benign tumors cannot spread to other parts of the body.

DESCRIPTION

The prostate is one of the major male sex glands. It is about the size of a walnut and lies just behind the urinary bladder. Together with the testicles and seminal vesicles, the prostate produces the fluid that makes up semen.

Prostate cancer is the most common form of cancer among men in the United States. It is the second-leading cause of cancer deaths. According to the American Cancer Society there were approximately 179,300 new cases of prostate cancer diagnosed in the United States in 1999. About thirty-seven thousand American men died of the disease in 1999.

Prostate cancer affects black men twice as often as it does white men. The mortality rate among blacks is also twice as great. African American men have the highest rate of prostate cancer in the world.

As prostate cancer develops, it may metastasize. Metastasis is the process by which cancer cells travel from one part of the body to another. The most common sites to which it spreads are the lymph nodes, the lungs, and various bones in the hip region.

CAUSES

The cause of prostate cancer is not known. It is found primarily in men over the age of fifty-

WORDS TO KNOW

Benign: A term for a tumor that does not spread and is not life-threatening.

Biopsy: A procedure in which a small sample of tissue is removed so that it can be studied under a microscope.

Chemotherapy: A method of treating cancer using certain chemicals that can kill cancer cells.

Estrogen: A female sex hormone.

Hormone therapy: A method of treating prostate cancer by adjusting the level of testosterone in the patient's body.

Malignant: A tumor that can spread to other parts of the body and that poses a serious threat to a person's life.

Metastasis: The process by which cancer cells travel from one area of the body to another.

Radiation therapy: The use of high-energy radiation to treat cancer.

Seminal vesicles: The organs that produce semen.

Testicles: Two egg-shaped glands that produce sperm and sex hormones.

Testosterone: A male sex hormone.

Tumor: A mass or lump of tissue made of abnormal cells.

five. The average age of diagnosis is seventy-two. As men grow older, their likelihood of getting prostate cancer increases. For men under the age of forty, the chance of getting prostate cancer is about 1 in 100,000. For men seventy to seventy-four years old, the chance rises to 1,326 in 100,000.

Certain factors increase a man's risk for prostate cancer. These factors include:

- A family history of prostate cancer
- A high-fat diet
- Work in the electroplating, welding, and rubber industries
- High blood testosterone (a male sex hormone) levels

SYMPTOMS

In many cases prostate cancer has no symptoms in its early stages. The disease is usually discovered during a routine physical examination. As the

Former U.S. Senator Bob Dole, who was diagnosed with prostate cancer in 1990, helps promote prostate cancer awareness at the National Men's Health and Fitness Conference in Philadelphia, PA in 1999. (Reproduced by permission of AP/Wide World Photos)

disease develops, certain symptoms are more likely to appear. These symptoms include:

- Weak or interrupted flow of urine
- Frequent urination, especially at night
- Difficulty in starting to urinate
- Inability to urinate
- Pain or burning sensation during urination
- Blood in the urine
- Continuous pain in the lower back, hips, or thighs
- Painful ejaculation

DIAGNOSIS

The first step in diagnosing prostate cancer is usually a digital rectal examination. In a digital rectal examination, a doctor places a gloved, lubricated finger into the patient's rectum. The doctor feels for lumps in the prostate.

If the doctor detects a lump, additional tests may be necessary. The first test may be a blood test. The purpose of a blood test is to search for a particular chemical associated with prostate cancer. This chemical is called prostate-specific antigen (PSA). PSA occurs naturally in the blood, but it occurs in much higher amounts if prostate cancer is present.

A second test that may be used is a transrectal (across the rectum) ultrasound. In this test, sound waves are bounced off the prostate gland. The reflected waves form a picture of the prostate. The picture shows the presence of any tumors.

A prostate biopsy may also be necessary. A biopsy is a procedure in which a small sample of tissue is removed. The sample is then studied under the microscope. Cancer cells can be detected under the microscope because of their distinctive appearance.

Other tests may be conducted to see if the cancer has begun to spread. For example, a chest X ray will show if cancer has spread to the lungs. A bone scan may be used to check whether the cancer has spread to the bone.

TREATMENT

A number of treatments are available for prostate cancer. The treatment chosen depends on the patient's age and general health, the stage of the tumor, the presence of other illnesses, and other factors.

The two most common forms of treatment for early prostate cancer are surgery and radiation. Surgery involves the removal of the prostate gland. In addition, a sample of the lymph nodes near the prostate is removed. This sample is then tested to see whether the cancer has spread.

Removal of the prostate also involves removal of the seminal vesicles that lie next to it. The seminal vesicles are the organs that make semen. Since they are usually removed along with the prostate, the patient usually becomes sterile as a result of the operation.

Radiation involves the use of high-energy rays to kill cancer cells. In most cases, the radiation comes from radioactive materials. Radioactive materials are substances that give off high-energy radiation, similar to X rays. The radiation can be given either externally or internally. If it is given externally, the radioactive source is placed above the patient's body in the area of the cancer. Radiation from the source penetrates the body and destroys cancer cells. Radiation can also be given internally by implanting the source in the patient's body.

For more advanced cases of prostate cancer, hormone therapy may be necessary. Prostate cells need the male hormone testosterone to grow. One way to stop the growth of prostate cells, then, is to reduce the amount of testosterone in the body. One way to do that is to surgically remove the patient's testicles. The testicles are the organ that produces testosterone. Another way to achieve the same goal is to give the patient a medication that reacts with testosterone. The medication "cancels out" the testosterone produced by the body.

Finally, the patient may be given a female hormone, such as estrogen. The estrogen makes the body stop producing testosterone. This treatment has some undesirable side effects, however. For example, a man may have "hot flashes," have enlarged and tender breasts, and lose sexual desire.

Chemotherapy may be used if the cancer has metastasized (pronounced muh-TASS-tuh-sized). Chemotherapy involves the use of chemicals that kill cancer cells. These chemicals can be given either orally (by mouth) or intravenously (into the bloodstream). The chemicals spread throughout the patient's body and attack cancer cells wherever they occur. Chemotherapy is sometimes used to treat prostate cancer that has recurred after other treatments.

ACCORDING TO THE AMERICAN CANCER SOCIETY, THE SURVIVAL RATE FOR ALL STAGES OF PROSTATE CANCER COMBINED INCREASED FROM 67 PERCENT IN THE LATE 1970S TO 93 PERCENT IN THE LATE 1990S.

A final form of treatment is no treatment at all. Prostate cancers sometimes develop very slowly. It may take years for them to become a serious threat to the patient's life. That fact is considered in treating older men. In many cases, the man is likely to die of other causes before prostate cancer becomes a serious concern. The approach in such cases is called "watchful waiting." The patient receives regular checkups. If no major change is found, no treatment is offered. If the tumor becomes significantly larger, one of the above forms of treatment is used.

PROGNOSIS

According to the American Cancer Society, the survival rate for all stages of prostate cancer combined increased from 67 percent in the late 1970s to 93 percent in the late 1990s. The main reason for this change is early detection. When tumors are still small, they can be removed successfully in almost all cases.

About 99 percent of all patients diagnosed with prostate cancer now live at least five years. More than 60 percent survive for ten years, and about 50 percent survive for fifteen years after diagnosis.

PREVENTION

There is no way to prevent prostate cancer. However, early detection can dramatically reduce the threat posed by the disease. The American Cancer Society (ACS) recommends that all men over the age of forty have an annual rectal examination. The ACS also recommends an annual PSA test once a year for men over the age of fifty.

A low-fat diet may slow the progress of prostate cancer. The ACS recommends a diet rich in fruits, vegetables, and fiber and low in red meat and saturated fats.

FOR MORE INFORMATION

Books

Bostwick, David G., Gregory T. MacLennan, and Thayne R. Larson. *Prostate Cancer: What Every Man—and His Family—Needs to Know.* New York: Villard Books, 1999.

Dollinger, Malin, Ernest H. Rosenbaum, and Greg Cable. *Everyone's Guide to Cancer Therapy.* Kansas City, MO: Somerville House Books, 1994.

Loo, Marcus, H., and Marian Betancourt. *The Prostate Cancer Sourcebook : How to Make Informed Treatment Choices.* New York: John Wiley & Sons, 1998.

Morra, Marion, and Eve Potts. *Choices.* New York: Avon Books, 1994.

Oesterling, Joseph A. *The ABC's of Prostate Cancer : The Book That Could Save Your Life.* Lanham: Madison Books, 1997.

Wallner, Kent. *Prostate Cancer: A Non-Surgical Perspective.* Seattle: SmartMedicine Press, 1996.

Organizations

American Cancer Society. 1599 Clifton Rd., N.E., Atlanta, GA 30329. (800) 227–2345.

American Urologic Association. 1120 N. Charles St., Baltimore, MD 21201. (410) 223–4310.

Cancer Research Institute. 681 Fifth Ave., New York, NY 10022. (800) 992–2623.

National Cancer Institute. 31 Center Drive, Bethesda, MD 20892–2580. (800) 4–CANCER. http://www.nci.nih.gov.

National Prostate Cancer Coalition. 1300 19th St., NW, Suite 400, Washington, DC 20036. (202) 842–3600.

Web sites

"Ask NOAH About: Prostate Cancer." *NOAH: New York Online Access to Health.* [Online] http://www.noah.cuny.edu/cancer/nci/cancernet/201229.html (accessed on October 28, 1999).

"Prostate Action Network." http://rattler.cameron.edu/pacnet (accessed on October 28, 1999).

"Prostate Cancer." *The Prostate Cancer Resource Center.* [Online] http://www3.cancer.org/cancerinfo/main_cont.asp?st=wi&ct=36 (accessed on October 28, 1999).

The Prostate Cancer Info Link. [Online] http://www.comed.com/Prostate/ (accessed on October 28, 1999).

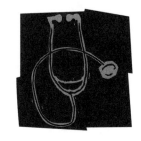

Where to Learn More

BOOKS

Abel, Ernest L. *America's 25 Top Killers*. Hillside, NJ: Enslow, 1991.

American Heart Association. *Living Well, Staying Well*. New York: American Heart Association and American Cancer Association, 1996.

Atkinson, David R., and Debbie Atkinson. *Hope Springs Eternal: Surviving a Chronic Disease*. Virginia Beach, VA: Are Press, 1999.

Bellenir, Karen, and Peter D. Dresser, eds. *Contagious and Non-contagious Infectious Diseases Sourcebook*. Detroit: Omnigraphics, Inc., 1996.

The Burton Goldberg Group. *Alternative Medicine: The Definitive Guide*. Puyallup, WA: Future Medicine Publishing, 1993.

Ciesielski, Paula F. *Major Chronic Diseases*. Guilford, CT: The Dushkin Publishing Group, 1992.

Daly, Stephen, ed. *Everything You Need to Know about Medical Treatments*. Springhouse, PA: Springhouse Corp., 1996.

Darling, David. *The Health Revolution: Surgery and Medicine in the Twenty-first Century*. Parsippany, NJ: Dillon Press, 1996.

Graham, Ian. *Fighting Disease*. Austin, TX: Raintree Steck-Vaughn, 1995.

Horn, Robert, III. *How Will They Know If I'm Dead? Transcending Disability and Terminal Illness*. Boca Raton, FL: Saint Lucie Press, 1996.

Hyde, Margaret O., and Elizabeth H. Forsyth, M.D. *The Disease Book: A Kid's Guide*. New York: Walker and Company, 1997.

Isler, Charlotte, R.N., and Alwyn T. Cohall, M.D. *The Watts Teen Health Dictionary.* New York: Franklin Watts, 1996.

The Johns Hopkins Medical Handbook: The 100 Major Medical Disorders of People over the Age of 50. *New York: Rebus, Inc., 1995.*

Long, James W. *The Essential Guide to Chronic Illness.* New York: Harper Perennial, 1997.

Roman, Peter. *Can You Get Warts from Touching Toads? Ask Dr. Pete.* New York: Julian Messner, 1986.

Shaw, Michael, ed. *Everything You Need to Know about Diseases.* Springhouse, PA: Springhouse Corp., 1996.

Stoffman, Phyllis. *The Family Guide to Preventing and Treating 100 Infectious Illnesses.* New York: John Wiley & Sons, 1995.

Weil, A. *Natural Health, Natural Medicine: A Comprehensive Manual for Wellness and Self-Care.* Boston: Houghton Mifflin, 1995.

WEB SITES

Centers for Disease Control and Prevention. http://www.cdc.gov

The Children's Health Center. http://www.mediconsult.com/mc/mcsite.nsf/conditionnav/kids~sectionintroduction

Healthfinder®. http://www.healthfinder.gov

InteliHealth: Home to Johns Hopkins Health Information. http://www.intelihealth.com

Mayo Clinic Health Oasis. http://mayohealth.org

National Institutes of Health. http://www.nih.gov

NOAH: New York Online Access to Health. http://www.noah.cuny.edu

WHO/OMS: World Health Organization. http://www.who.int

U.S. National Library of Medicine: Health Information. http://nlm.nih.gov/hinfo.html

ORGANIZATIONS

Centers for Disease Control and Prevention. 1600 Clifton Rd., NE, Atlanta, GA 30333. (404)639–3311. http://www.cdc.gov

National Institutes of Health (NIH). Bethesda, MD 20892. (301)496–1776. http:www.nih.gov

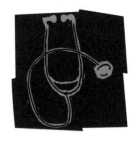

Index

Italic type indictes volume numbers; **boldface** type indicates entries and their page numbers; (ill.) indicates illustrations.